Assessing CEOs and Senior Leaders

Fundamentals of Consulting Psychology Book Series

An Introduction to Consulting Psychology: Working With Individuals, Groups, and Organizations
Rodney L. Lowman

Assessing CEOs and Senior Leaders: A Primer for Consultants
J. Ross Blankenship

Consulting Psychology in National Security Organizations
Laurie B. Moret and Carroll H. Greene III

The Ethical Practice of Consulting Psychology
Rodney L. Lowman and Stewart E. Cooper

Learning Interventions for Consultants: Building the Talent That Drives Business
Manuel London and Thomas Diamante

Transcultural Competence: Navigating Cultural Differences in the Global Community
Jerry Glover and Harris L. Friedman

Using Feedback in Organizational Consulting
Jane Brodie Gregory and Paul E. Levy

APA FUNDAMENTALS OF CONSULTING PSYCHOLOGY

Assessing CEOs and Senior Leaders

A PRIMER FOR CONSULTANTS

J. ROSS BLANKENSHIP

AMERICAN PSYCHOLOGICAL ASSOCIATION

Published by
American Psychological Association
750 First Street, NE
Washington, DC 20002
https://www.apa.org

Order Department
https://www.apa.org/pubs/books
order@apa.org

In the U.K., Europe, Africa, and the Middle East, copies may be ordered from Eurospan
https://www.eurospanbookstore.com/apa
info@eurospangroup.com

Typeset in Minion by Circle Graphics, Inc., Reisterstown, MD

Printer: AGS, White Plains, MD
Cover Designer: Debra Naylor, Naylor Design, Inc., Washington, DC

Library of Congress Cataloging-in-Publication Data

Names: Blankenship, J. Ross, author.
Title: Assessing CEOs and senior leaders : a primer for consultants / by J. Ross Blankenship.
Description: Washington, DC : American Psychological Association, [2022] |
Series: Fundamentals of consulting psychology book series | Includes bibliographical references and index.
Identifiers: LCCN 2021018986 (print) | LCCN 2021018987 (ebook) |
ISBN 9781433837166 (paperback) | ISBN 9781433838118 (ebook)
Subjects: LCSH: Executives—Rating of. | Chief executive officers. | Business consultants. |
BISAC: PSYCHOLOGY / Industrial & Organizational Psychology |
BUSINESS & ECONOMICS / Leadership
Classification: LCC HF5549.5.R3 B55 2022 (print) | LCC HF5549.5.R3 (ebook) |
DDC 658.4/07125—dc23
LC record available at https://lccn.loc.gov/2021018986
LC ebook record available at https://lccn.loc.gov/2021018987

https://doi.org/10.1037/0000264-000

Printed in the United States of America

10 9 8 7 6 5 4 3 2 1

Contents

Series Editor's Foreword

Rodney L. Lowman

The field of consulting psychology has blossomed in recent years. It covers the applications of psychology in consultation to organizations and systems, but also at the individual and team level. Unfortunately, there are few graduate training programs in this field of specialization, so consulting psychology roles are mostly populated by those who came to the field after having trained in other areas of psychology—including industrial and organizational (I/O), clinical/counseling, and school psychology, among others. Such training is rarely focused on consulting psychology and psychologists, and graduate students have to learn through on-the-job training, reading books and articles, attending conferences and workshops, and being mentored in the foundational competencies of the field as they seek to transition into it.

After a number of years of editing *Consulting Psychology Journal: Practice and Research*, the field's flagship journal, I felt that an additional type of educational product was needed to help those transitioning into consulting psychology. The Society of Consulting Psychology therefore partnered with the American Psychological Association to create a new book series. The idea was to create a series of monographs on specific fundamental skill sets needed to practice in this area of specialization. The goal of the editorial advisory board, consisting of Drs. Judith Blanton, Brodie Gregory, Skipton Leonard (and initially Dale Fuqua and the late Edward Pavur, Jr.) and myself, for this book series has been to identify the major competencies needed by consulting psychologists and then to work with expert authors to create short, accessible but evidence-based texts that would be useful both as standalone volumes and in combination with one another. The readers would be graduate students in relevant training programs, psychologists planning a transition into consulting psychology, and practicing professionals who want to add to their areas of expertise.

What constitutes fundamental skills in consulting psychology? The second edition of the *Guidelines for Education and Training at the Doctoral and Postdoctoral Level In Consulting Psychology (CP)/Organizational Consulting Psychology (OCP)*, approved by APA Council of Representatives in 2017, created by the Society of Consulting Psychology, and approved by the American Psychological Association (2017b); the *Handbook of Organizational Consulting Psychology* (Lowman, 2002), and *An Introduction to Consulting Psychology: Working with Individuals, Groups, and Organizations* (Lowman, 2016) provide useful starting points. Each of these contributions was organized around the concept of levels (individual, group, and organizational) as a taxonomy for identifying fundamental skills. Within those categories, two broad skill sets are needed: assessment and intervention.

As with many areas of psychological practice, the foundational skills that apply in one area may overlap into others in the taxonomy. Interventions with individuals, as in executive coaching for instance, usually take place in the context of the focal client's work with a specific team and within a specific organization, which itself may also constitute a client. Understanding the system-wide issues and dynamics at the organizational level usually also involves work with specific executives and teams, and multicultural and international issues suffuse all of our roles. The APA Guidelines and the *Handbook* concluded, properly, that consulting psychologists should be trained in and have, at least, foundational skills and experience at the individual, group, and organizational levels, even if they primarily specialize in one of these areas.

In inviting you to learn more about consulting psychology through this book series, I hope you will come to agree that there is no more exciting or inherently interesting area of study today than consulting psychology. The series aims not just to cover relevant literature on timeless topics in consulting psychology but also to capture the richness of this work by including case material that illustrates its applications. Readers will soon understand that consulting psychologists are real-world activists, unafraid to work in real-world environments.

Finally, as one who trained and practiced in both I/O and clinical psychology, I should note that consulting psychology has been the one area in which I felt that all of my training and skill sets were both welcomed and needed. And in a world where organizations and the individuals and teams within them greatly need help in functioning ethically and effectively, in bridging individual, group, and organization-level needs and constituencies, and in coping with the rapid expansion of knowledge and escalating competition and internationalization, this book series aims to make a difference by helping more psychologists join the ranks of qualified consulting psychologists. Collectively, we can influence not just an area of specialization in psychology, but also the world.

ABOUT THIS BOOK

Assessment of executive and senior leaders is what Dr. Blankenship's book is all about. I realize I have a particular perspective that may exceed what's typical. My next book, titled *Career Assessment: Integrating Interests, Abilities, and Personality,* to be published in 2021 by the American Psychological Association, took many years to write and weighed in at over 900 manuscript pages. The topic seems to be slipping from prominence in many contemporary graduate training programs in areas related to consulting psychology, but it remains important. To take one example, counseling psychology used to be at the forefront of career assessment; now the topic seems to have become an orphan in that home.

I can attest that those who have solid skills in assessing leaders will be advantaged, no matter what the particular specialization they end up emphasizing in their consulting psychology careers. Senior leaders have great influence in organizations, and having the right ones in place, and developing the ones who are in place, is an important value-adding skill.

Dr. Blankenship's book provides thoughtful guidance about the fundamentals of assessing high-level executives and managers. It also tackles the complexity of assessing the particular situations in which prospective leaders will be working. Meta-analytic knowledge matters at the global level, and in choosing what to assess, but, as this book illustrates, so does specificity. Two equally bright (and, among senior leaders, think very bright) and well-experienced executives may succeed brilliantly in one situation and fail miserably in another. The issue is about their fit to a particular set of circumstances and role demands.

The stakes in getting assessment right when working with senior leaders are very high. Imagine, for example, if all candidates for the U.S. presidency had to go through not only a physical exam but also a psychological one evaluating their fitness for the role. If you were to be the assessor, how would you begin? How would you match job duties in the context of their times? And how would you weed out the, as it were, bad apples?

This clearly written, well-illustrated book is an excellent resource for those hoping to master a complicated skill set. It addresses one of the most important skills consulting psychologists have to offer for their organizational clients: evaluating candidates for their potential as leaders.

Assessing CEOs and Senior Leaders

Introduction

Every psychological assessment starts with a question. In executive assessment, the question is usually some variation of "Who should lead?"

Consider the case of Specialist Biopharma (SB).[1] SB was a growing company that had been public for 2 years and was going through a maturation phase as it transitioned from its startup roots into a billion dollar enterprise. The fast-paced entrepreneurial environment was giving way to the systems and processes needed to support a major corporation. This cultural shift, along with a challenging U.S. market characterized by strong competitors and a decline in revenues, led to high turnover in the organization, even among the senior leadership ranks.

These dynamics left the company in a state of vulnerability. Board members worried that continued leadership turnover would drive down

[1] All cases throughout the book are composite representations of actual scenarios. Details have been changed to maintain confidentiality.

https://doi.org/10.1037/0000264-001
Assessing CEOs and Senior Leaders: A Primer for Consultants, by J. R. Blankenship

the stock price and attract an activist investor who might purchase the company's stock in order to pressure management into making specific changes to the business. Additionally, the instability at the top of the organization decreased the engagement and commitment of the workforce at large. When the CEO approached the board with a resignation, the challenge of deciding who should lead became imminent.

Board members agreed that the company was moving in the right direction strategically. They viewed the slowdown in the U.S. market as largely cyclical and agreed that the primary mandate for the next CEO would be to take market share from competitors, optimize the supply chain, and position the company for international growth. However, they also agreed that none of that could be accomplished without first stabilizing the workforce. The next CEO would need to solidify a culture of discipline and execution, without losing the creative energy that made SB a fun and innovative place to work.

Balancing the internal needs of the company with the external demands of the market became a central point of debate among board members. Some believed that an external hire would further damage the organizational culture and raise questions among shareholders, while others questioned whether SB contained the talent for an internal promotion and whether a first-time CEO would be up for the challenge. To help answer these questions, the board hired a consulting psychologist to better understand the requirements of the job, develop a position specification, and assess the top three internal candidates to see whether they might have a successor.

WHY DO COMPANIES PAY FOR ASSESSMENTS?

Assessment provides a systematic way of gathering, organizing, and communicating information about executives and the contexts in which they work. This information is used to help organizational leaders (e.g., CEO, boards of directors) make talent decisions such as whom to hire, whom to promote, and whom to develop (and how). With a well-structured assessment process, consultants advise their clients in navigating challenging situations like the one just described. They do this by helping their clients establish job requirements in a detailed and systematic way, helping them think through how best to prioritize those job requirements to create effective hiring criteria, and by bringing to the surface valuable information about the people and dynamics at play in high-stakes talent decisions. Although those conducting executive assessments do not usually make these decisions, they provide powerful data to the organization and offer suggestions about the best course of action.

WHY ASSESS CEOs AND SENIOR LEADERS?

Although a distinction is made in this book at times between the CEO and other senior leaders, in general the terms *executive* and *senior leader* are used interchangeably throughout. Thornton et al. (2017) provided a succinct definition of executives as "those at the top of the hierarchy in organizations . . . who carry responsibility for major organizational units or who occupy key jobs that are essential to the purpose of the organization" (p. 823). This definition is useful because it is transferrable across different organizational types and sizes; however, it is important to consider that a senior leader in a major corporation may have a dramatically different scope of responsibility than the CEO of a smaller organization.

Because CEOs and senior leaders hold positions that are essential to the purpose and performance of their organizations, understanding their capabilities, motivations, and aptitudes is essential for understanding how they will lead organizations during their tenure. And as the pace of change in the economy increases, the need for executives to be adaptable to changing circumstances increases as well (Bourton et al., 2018). The *digital transformation*, or the incorporation of digital technology into business products and services, continues to reshape the structure of organizations, the competitive landscape, and the traits and competencies needed to lead successfully. Furthermore, the effects of the 2020 COVID-19 pandemic have forced leaders of all kinds to learn how to navigate unprecedented changes in the modern workforce, including the rapid shift to digital teams and working from home, imminent threats to business, and the need in general for leaders to plot a course for others while adjusting to these circumstances themselves (Carnevale & Hatak, 2020). Given this rate of change, CEOs and senior leaders are required to synthesize and interpret what is happening in the environment around them and adjust their strategies in order to stay relevant and competitive, all in real time.

Although much has been made about the cost of making a bad hire (*The Economist*, 2018; Williams & Scott, 2012), it can be even more costly to make an "adequate" hire who causes an organization to miss opportunities for growth and innovation as markets evolve. There are fewer more dramatic examples of this than Kodak missing the shift from print photography to digital photography, even though they invented the technology for digital photography (Anthony, 2016). Kodak's failure to adapt to a changing marketplace occurred over a long period of time and was certainly more complex than just hiring decisions, but the company consistently installed executives who failed to lead the organization through the transformation required, and ultimately the company filed for bankruptcy in 2012 (de la Merced, 2012). A notable example of this was in 1989, fourteen years after the company had invented digital photography, when the board chose to hire Kay R. Whitmore as the successor to Colby Chandler, the retiring CEO (Mui, 2012). Whitmore, a 30-year veteran of the company, was described at the time as a leader who would ensure Kodak stayed focused on core businesses in film and photographic chemicals, where the company had sustained consistent earnings problems (Holusha, 1989). Whitmore chose to double-down on what had worked in the past rather than considering how changing technology might allow Kodak to adapt for the future. He was fired by the board in 1993 and became the first in a series of CEOs at Kodak who failed to effect a digital transformation of the business (Mui, 2012).

INTENDED AUDIENCE FOR THE BOOK

This book is for those who are new to the practice of individual assessment at the top of organizations (e.g., psychologists, human resources professionals, management consultants), or who are interested in learning more about it (e.g., business leaders, executives). Relevant issues and methods in executive assessment are discussed, and some foundation in the research literature is provided, to help frame the evidence and the principles that make this work valid. Given the book's focus on senior leaders, I address the technical and practical differences in assessment that frequently arise at higher levels in organizations. My hope is that this book will help educate and guide graduate students, assessment practitioners, and other professionals who are interested in better understanding, or working with, this population.

Chapter 1 provides a definition of individual psychological assessment and reviews the unique aspects of conducting this work at the senior level in organizations. It touches on the historical context, as well as the research foundations for managerial and executive assessment, and provides some consideration of the "art and science" of this work. Chapter 2 is about context, from the job itself, to the team and organizational culture, to external factors such as economic and political circumstances, all of which can (and should!) impact the nature of an assessment. Chapter 3 provides an overview of the ethical and legal issues at play in assessments. Chapter 4 digs into the details of how to conduct senior level assessments, the types of tools that can be used, and how to pick tools for certain purposes. This chapter also considers the proliferation of tools on the market and provides some strategies for evaluating the validity, reliability, legality, and relevance of a given instrument. Chapter 5 takes a look at current trends in the assessment market and addresses the advantages and limitations of incorporating technology into assessment processes. Chapter 6 looks at how to develop skill as an assessor and provides some thoughts on how the practice of executive assessment may evolve in the future.

1

What Is Executive Assessment?

In the final stages of a CEO search, a public original equipment manufacturer (OEM) had whittled a robust slate of candidates down to the final three. On the basis of multiple rounds of interviews, presentations, and dinners with board members, the selection committee believed it had three credible candidates for the position but was unsure which was best.

The first candidate was a prototypical people leader. She had built a reputation at prior companies for her ability to systematically build the capability of other leaders and coach and develop her direct reports. Though she had held a CEO position before, her prior experience was in an adjacent industry; she thus had only cursory knowledge of, and no existing network within, the organization's industry. The board thought she would make a strong selection but had some concerns about how quickly she could adjust to the learning curve in a new industry, especially with Wall Street analysts keeping a close eye on her every move.

https://doi.org/10.1037/0000264-002
Assessing CEOs and Senior Leaders: A Primer for Consultants, by J. R. Blankenship

The second candidate was a former CEO with a strong commercial sales background. He had served at the helm of two organizations during well-documented public company turnarounds, in which he led failing organizations into recovery and periods of growth. Given his reputation, the board was certain that he could provide firm leadership within an uncertain environment and drive growth; however, he also had a reputation for "clearing house" at the senior leadership level and hiring people he had worked with previously. It was also unclear whether he could develop an industry-leading strategy of his own, or that his *leadership style* would facilitate the long-term success of the organization.

The third candidate had a reputation as an innovator and a visionary. As the CEO of multiple smaller competitors in the OEM space, he had developed a track record of rehabilitating broken research and development (R&D) systems and helping grow organizations through mergers and acquisitions. The board found his ability to envision what the future could hold for the company appealing, but he seemed hard to connect with on a personal level, and members of the selection committee worried about what their working relationship might look like if he was chosen for the job.

With industry leading products and several quarters of demonstrated growth, the board knew the company was in a good position relative to the competition, but was also aware that new entrants into the industry could shake up the competitive landscape overnight (e.g., Amazon). Unable to come to a clear consensus on who would make the best fit for the job, the search firm offered to have the finalists go through their executive assessment process, and the selection committee agreed.

Each candidate participated in an executive assessment process that included an online assessment battery (i.e., a personality questionnaire, a cognitive ability test, and an interest inventory) and a structured behavioral interview. The assessors were able to refer to information collected in the search process, including a job specification based on interviews with the board members about what would make the next CEO successful, and interview notes that provided detailed work histories on each candidate. After gathering all the data, the consulting psychologists who conducted the assessments wrote reports on each candidate and compiled an executive summary report that compared the three candidates on the basis of their strengths and areas for development, considering the job specification.

DEFINITION AND DESCRIPTION OF EXECUTIVE ASSESSMENT

Executive and managerial assessment is a specialized application of individual psychological assessment. As a practice area, individual psychological assessment spans several subfields within psychology and is used to achieve a variety of ends. For example, in a clinical setting, assessment is used for the purpose of diagnosis or classification of categories or degrees of mental health. In this context, the goal of the inquiry is often to understand the nature of the malady and design a plan for treatment. In an organizational setting, assessment is more commonly used to predict how well an individual will perform in a given role. In this context, the goal is to understand an individual's job-related knowledge, skills, abilities, and traits in order to (a) understand how they are likely to perform, and (b) provide guidance on how they may need to develop in order to increase their performance in the future.

At its core, executive assessment is used to help support organizational decision making in circumstances that are often characterized by uncertainty, subjectivity, and high-stakes outcomes. This type of assessment is a process that generates valuable, evidence-based information about individuals in a particular work context that can be used to support selection decisions and/or to provide direction for ongoing development and coaching (Silzer & Jeanneret, 2011; Thornton et al., 2017). Assessment can be designed and used at any level in an organization, but this book focuses on the assessment of those individuals who hold executive and senior leadership positions. This population warrants special consideration because of the distinct elements of higher-level leadership jobs, as described in the following section.

WHAT IS DISTINCTIVE ABOUT SENIOR LEADERS?

The term *senior leader* means different things in different organizations. Organizations differ in size and complexity, so a senior leader in a small business might be more comparable to a middle-level manager in a larger one. In general, a senior leader is an individual in the upper level of an organization who is responsible for managing and leading other people-leaders (Reynolds, McCauley, & Tsacoumis, 2018). In other words, this term typically refers to those who oversee other people who themselves also have the responsibility of leadership. There are four key reasons that this group warrants special consideration when conceiving and designing assessments.

First, senior leaders make up a relatively small portion of organizational leaders, about 5% (Sinar, 2018), and small sample sizes make it harder to calculate statistically significant relationships between assessment results and relevant outcomes (e.g., leadership effectiveness). It is also challenging to collect enough data from senior leaders across enough comparable organizational circumstances to make generalizable claims. Additionally, senior leaders are frequently assessed by consulting firms that use their own proprietary assessment methods and tools, so the resulting data may not be readily accessible to others.

Second, as individuals move up within a company, their span of control increases, their number of direct reports decreases, and their work tends to become more complex. Senior leaders have more latitude to determine organizational strategy and set direction for other employees and have less direct control over the outcomes of their work (Hooijberg et al., 1997; Jaques, 1986; Uhl-Bien & Arena, 2018). This can make assessment challenging, because the criteria of the assessment can become more abstract and less consistent over time. In a traditional assessment paradigm, an assessor determines the specific knowledge, competencies, and traits needed to do a job, and then assesses individual candidates against those criteria. However, part of an executive's job is to determine the direction an organization should take, in part or in whole. This can make it challenging to ascertain the specific types of knowledge that will make an individual successful in an executive role, precisely because the organization's circumstances will likely change as a result of that individual's work. To that end, job descriptions for senior leaders often include forward-looking statements about the strategy or vision of the organization or business unit, which will help shape the requirements of the job.

Consider, for example, the differences in knowledge, skills, and abilities that might be necessary for a leader to take over a failing business and effect a turnaround, compared with those that might be necessary for a leader to step into a healthy, well-functioning business and accelerate growth. Furthermore, in a hyperconnected global economy, a healthy, growing business can swiftly become a business in need of turnaround when markets shift or external circumstances derail business (e.g., the COVID-19 pandemic). Accordingly, traits such as *learning agility*, or the ability to quickly understand and adapt to changing circumstances, are becoming ever more prevalent in the assessment of leaders (De Meuse, 2019; De Meuse et al., 2010) as a way of evaluating those individuals who will be able to apply new learning rapidly as things change.

Third, assessments are frequently used to compare individuals for hiring and promotion decisions, and, at the executive level, this can involve comparing similarly successful individuals who have had alternative career paths in different industries. This makes direct comparisons of experience a challenge; for example, an assessor may need to compare industry-specific achievements at one level versus higher level achievements in a different industry. One way that assessors accomplish this is by evaluating *leadership competencies*, which describe clusters of behavior that relate to leadership effectiveness (Hogan et al., 2011, p. 10), such as "strategic agility," "driving growth," "developing the capability of others," or "leading organizational change." Assessors will create *competency models*, which are frameworks of leadership competencies that characterize the needs of a job role or use existing models that may be in place within client organizations, to define the dimensions that are likely to make a leader successful in a given role. For example, a leader who is being brought in to make an underperforming organization competitive again may need to demonstrate particular capability in competencies such as strategic agility, leading change, and driving growth. Competencies such as strategic agility and driving growth are frequently included in such models, along with behaviorally anchored rating scales (BARS), which are used to define levels of performance for each competency with examples of specific behaviors (Boyatzis, 2008; Stamoulis, 2009). Competency models and

BARS provide assessors with some level of objectivity when comparing the leadership capability of individuals with different career histories and experience.

Finally, in some circumstances, executives may be hesitant to participate in assessments that they perceive to be inappropriate to their experience level or job function. It is well established that cognitive ability demonstrates the strongest validity in predicting job performance at all levels (Schmitt, 2014), but a senior leader may still question what a "math test" has to do with their ability to lead a Fortune 500 organization. Additionally, organizations that are resistant to using cognitive ability measures in an assessment process may pose the argument that executives have already demonstrated their general mental ability by rising to their current level of authority or having attended a well-known and respected university. For example, in a search for the new executive director of a global nonprofit organization, four finalists were invited to be assessed. With extensive funding and a well-known brand, the nonprofit had been able to attract high-profile candidates. One, who had served at a high level within a former presidential administration, refused to participate in the assessment process, saying something to the effect of, "My capability has been proven again and again throughout my leadership career, just look at my resume. And there is no way I can find time in my schedule for this."

These factors create nuanced challenges in conducting assessments at this level, but these challenges can also make assessment work meaningful and enjoyable. Senior leaders have often had quite interesting careers characterized by notable accomplishments both in business and in society. And the positions themselves are generally characterized by a notable amount of influence, which creates opportunities for assessors to consult and advise leaders on decisions that help shape the future of organizations.

A BRIEF HISTORY OF EXECUTIVE ASSESSMENT

As is the case with many aspects of industrial and organizational (I/O) and consulting psychology (CP), individual psychological assessment rose to prominence after its use by military and intelligence services during the 20th century's two World Wars (Schultz & Schultz, 2012). Many applications of assessment in the military are designed to sort thousands of individuals into different types of jobs and leadership positions. However, the use of assessment to evaluate highly competent individuals for complex jobs was largely developed by the Office of Strategic Services (OSS) during World War II. Highhouse (2002) provided a substantive and interesting history of these events; some brief background is offered in this section, as it may be helpful in understanding how the popular methods of executive assessment developed.

The OSS was tasked with helping the military select men and women who could operate behind enemy lines, "conduct destructive operations train resistance groups, and 'disintegrate' the morale of enemy troops" (Highhouse, 2002, p. 369). In addition, the assessors were looking for those who demonstrated an ability to withstand the stress of possible capture and torture by the enemy.

Of particular influence on the program was Henry Murray, a Harvard psychologist well-known for his development of the Thematic Apperception Test (TAT) for assessing unconscious motivation (Morgan, 2002). Murray was not a believer in the psychometric approach to assessment, which involved the statistical combination of results from individual tests to form a predictor variable. Instead, he favored a more holistic approach, in which the assessment of candidates depended largely on the assessor's ability to interpret results from a series of tests and observations (e.g., projective tests, interviews, situational judgment tests, intelligence tests) in order to make a judgement about an individual's likely effectiveness (Highhouse, 2002). Assessors tested, observed, and discussed candidates throughout a 3-day evaluation on a farm outside of Washington, DC. A key component of the assessment, it seemed, was deliberately confusing the candidates and creating stress and anxiety so that assessors could develop some sense of the candidates' personalities and how they would hold up in the stressful situations they would assuredly face once in the field. The validity of the OSS assessment program was mixed. Because validity evidence was not collected for each individual assessment element, it was not possible to calculate incremental validity (the additional validity added by each part of the assessment), and the assessment staff itself concluded that they failed to predict performance overseas (Highhouse,

2002). This task was made more challenging because the team had never established outcome measures to determine successful prediction. However, Super (1949) noted that a sample of 171 men from two of the main assessment locations, who were assessed and later rated for overseas job performance, showed a validity coefficient of .45, suggesting that the assessment accounted for about 20% of the variance in performance.

Ultimately, the methods deployed by the OSS informed those that were later used in organizations to select executives after the war, beginning with such prominent organizations as Standard Oil, Sears, and AT&T, and expanding to other organizations from there (Highhouse, 2002). Notably, consulting firms such as Development Dimensions International (DDI) and McBer and Company (later a division of Hay Group, now a part of Korn Ferry) built on this research to become large executive assessment houses (Highhouse, 2002). These early methods have been used in practice, and the tension between more psychometric approaches and more holistic approaches to assessment has been studied in the literature ever since.

These historical notes inform the challenge of executive assessment in a useful way. It is unlikely anyone reading this book will need to evaluate an individual's ability to withstand the stress of torture by a fascist enemy. However, modern executives do face continuous uncertainty and the need to adapt to and tolerate adverse and uncertain circumstances. In that context, assessors need to be able to provide insight into an individual's ability to navigate and lead others through uncertainty and ambiguity. Additionally, assessors need to be able to assemble multimethod assessment processes that ideally include both quantitative and qualitative elements and are designed to a particular selection task.

Before designing an assessment process, one needs to know how to determine if an assessment method is useful in the first place.

VALIDITY AND RELIABILITY

This section is intended to help refresh or sharpen the critical eye of the assessor who will be deciding what tools to use in an assessment process. For a much more technical and in-depth consideration of this topic,

I recommend reviewing the *Handbook of Employee Selection* (Farr & Tippins, 2017) as well as the *Standards for Educational and Psychological Testing* (American Educational Research Association, American Psychological Association, & National Council on Measurement in Education, 2014).

Before considering some of the methods that are frequently used in this work, it is worth examining the principles underlying assessment: validity and reliability. Essentially, the concepts of validity and reliability represent the following questions:

- Does an assessment method predict what it is supposed to predict?
- Will it measure the same construct consistently?
- Can relevant inferences be made using the assessment's results?

Validity

Validity refers to the compendium of evidence that supports the different types of inferences made based on test scores. That is, does a test measure something useful, and can the results be used to make a prediction about how an individual is likely to behave? Although validity is frequently presented as comprising different dimensions (e.g., construct, content, criterion), it is widely accepted as a single concept aimed at understanding what test scores mean (Kehoe & Murphy, 2010). That said, it can be useful to consider validity by examining the ways in which the meaning of test scores can be evaluated. Thus, different elements of validity are reviewed in the following sections.

Construct Validity

A psychological *construct* is an abstract concept that describes or predicts behavior or an underlying domain of related behaviors. Constructs usually cannot be seen or touched, so they must be measured indirectly. For example, the construct "extraversion" is representative of behaviors such as dominance, assertiveness, warmth, and outspokenness (Hu et al., 2019), which may be measured (e.g., with a personality test) to form an understanding of how extraverted or introverted an individual may be.

When evaluating extraversion/introversion as an overall construct there will be highly extraverted people, highly introverted people, and many in between. The construct itself involves an integration of what differentiates these people, such as why some people tend to seek stimulation internally versus externally. *Construct validity*, then, provides evidence for whether a test measures what it intends to measure; the test itself serving as an operational definition of the construct. This type of evidence essentially answers three questions:

1. Does this construct actually exist?
2. If so, does this test measure it?
3. Is this construct related to the outcome in question? (Putka & Sackett, 2010).

In other words, before testing an individual to understand how extraverted or introverted they are, the assessor must first decide that (a) extraversion/introversion represents a domain of behaviors that can be measured, (b) that it can be measured with an assessment, and (c) that scores on that assessment can differentially predict the success of leaders. So, the inferences made from a measure of extraversion/introversion are thought to be valid to the extent that they represent the individual's actual behavior, and to the extent that those scores can be used to predict job performance.

Content Validity

Content validity refers to the extent to which the items included in a measure adequately represent the domain of knowledge or behavior that they are intended to measure. This is most applicable when the content domain is well-defined, for example, in a job sampling test in which a representative sample of the knowledge and/or managerial judgment required in a role is tested (Kehoe & Murphy, 2010). Consider the role of a chief financial officer (CFO), for example. If a job knowledge test were being developed and the test was intended to measure both job-related vocabulary and managerial judgment about issues related to financial planning and analysis, budget, and taxes, but the test only covered the easier to measure domain of vocabulary, it would not have adequately sampled the full content domain.

Predictive Validity

Predictive validity (also called criterion validity) asks, "Will the results of this measure tell me something of interest about what is likely to happen in the future?" In the context of senior leadership assessment, predictive validity often refers simply to how well a measure will predict an individual's future job performance or ability to lead a group or organization. This type of validity evidence is quite important in supporting the use of an instrument in a high-stakes selection decision. Unfortunately, it is also among the most challenging types of evidence to gather at the senior executive level. The measurement of senior executive performance can be ambiguous, and small sample sizes make it a challenge to collect enough data to directly support predictions in a given situation.

Face Validity

Another consideration is *face validity*, or the degree to which the form of an assessment seems to be measuring its intended content. Face validity is largely irrelevant to the question of whether an assessment is actually measuring what it intends to measure, or whether it is predictive of job performance, but it can be useful to consider when managing the participant experience in an assessment process. For example, managerial populations might prefer an in-basket exercise (described in more detail in the Assessment Centers section in this chapter) to a cognitive ability test because it seems more like what they will be doing on the job, even though the predictive validity of in-basket exercises tends to be lower than measures of cognitive ability. So, assessors need to make sure that assessees understand why they are being assessed by particular measures when the purpose of those measures might not be readily evident to them.

Validity Generalization

Validity generalization refers to the use of previous validation research to inform the design of an assessment protocol (Kehoe & Murphy, 2010), which supports the valid and reliable inferences made from assessment results in a specific assessment situation (Schmidt & Hunter, 1977, 1998; Tett et al., 2017). For example, an assessor might conduct research to understand the personality traits that can predict creative thinking, and then rely on those research findings to support the use of a personality measure within an assessment process at an organization.

Validity generalization is an efficient way to maximize validity evidence by suggesting that research findings can be aggregated across studies to provide general support for inferences made in specific situations (Tett et al., 2017). For example, if cumulative data across studies (i.e., *meta-analysis*) shows that cognitive ability is predictive of job performance across job types and managerial levels, then validity evidence is not necessarily needed to support an inference made in a specific assessment situation.

However, the broader and more general validity evidence becomes (e.g., "Cognitive ability predicts job performance"), as occurs through meta-analysis, the less exact any given inference is in a specific situation (e.g., "What type of cognitive ability predicts performance for this job at this level in this company?"; Tett et al., 2017). Considering only broad summarized relationships between variables suggests that (a) the specifics of a situation do not impact results, and (b) the narrower facets of variables might not have stronger relationships with relevant outcomes; in the case of senior leaders, they might, because broad-based measures may not show enough variability among executives to indicate who may be the most qualified for the job.

To that end, it is helpful for assessors to have a sense of domain-specific information about assessment methods (and related validity evidence) so that they can configure assessment processes to best match the purpose for which they are using assessment. For example, an assessor may use well-validated predictors such as cognitive ability as foundational measures for considering high-level candidates, but the candidates may be comparably intelligent, so other measures may need to be incorporated to account for the specific situation. A careful evaluation of the situation may suggest that the client organization is more in need of an innovator in an executive position who will initiate a large-scale strategic shift versus, say, an incrementalist who will focus on small-scale continuous improvements. Other measures (e.g., personality, interests, values) can help identify the ways in which an individual is likely to approach the job. The assessor then evaluates candidates from a perspective of (a) whether they meet the minimum qualification levels for a position, and (b) whether they meet the situation-specific requirements.

Reliability

Reliability is an estimation of the expected degree of consistency and inconsistency in replicated test scores (Putka & Sackett, 2010, p. 11). Like validity, reliability is frequently represented as comprising different dimensions (e.g., test–retest, interrater) but is also now accepted as a single concept that involves understanding the sources of error that occur in testing, and, indeed, examining what "error" means. Error variance can stem from many sources, including the test items themselves, the raters or test scorers, and changes that occur between test applications (Zickar et al., 2017). As Guion (2010) stated, "at least to some limited extent, unreliability is a function of the test itself" (p. 249). Or, to paraphrase what a mentor once told me, all assessments are wrong, but some are useful. Although that comment was made in jest, it points to the fact that assessors need to understand that no measures are perfectly consistent either in measuring the intended construct, or across multiple measures of the same construct. Even so, it is useful to consider that test scores can vary, especially in the context of executive assessment, as reviewed in the following sections.

Test–Retest Reliability

Test–retest reliability asks the question "If the same assessment is taken twice, how similar will the scores be?" This form of reliability evidence is thought to indicate, to some degree, whether a test is measuring the same construct each time it is taken (Putka & Sackett, 2010). Importantly, however, low test–retest reliability coefficients may be expected when the second measure is conducted after, for example, an individual's participation in coaching or a training program, and scores are not be expected to be consistent in such a scenario. In fact, traits and abilities change over time, and some (e.g., extraversion and openness to experience) predictably decline with age (Donnellan & Lucas, 2008), so low test–retest reliability may not be problematic when there is a clear and sensible explanation for it.

Interrater Reliability

Interrater reliability poses the question "If someone else were to conduct the same evaluation, would they come up with largely similar results?" Assessors differ in their preferences, observations, and interpretations of the same information. These differences can lead to idiosyncratic rater differences that introduce error into the assessment process. For example, if two assessors separately conduct a structured behavioral interview of the same executive using the same method, we might expect the outcomes of their assessments to be similar, but that will depend on how similarly they were trained in the method and how closely each stuck to the structured format, among other factors. To try to limit these sources of error, assessors can take several approaches, when possible, including (a) standardizing the data that assessors observe, (b) training raters in how to interpret common information, and (c) adding assessors to aggregate ratings (when practicable; Zickar et al., 2017). It is worth noting that although adding additional raters can improve reliability, there may be practical limitations to doing so, including increasing the cost to the client and increasing the time frame aligning multiple schedules.

Reliability and validity are closely linked constructs. In fact, reliability is a necessary condition for validity, but just because a measure is reliable does not mean that it is valid (Putka & Sackett, 2010). For example, test takers may obtain consistent scores on a measure of verbal intelligence (demonstrating reliability), but the verbal intelligence score may not accurately evaluate takers' true level of verbal intelligence (demonstrating lack of validity). Evidence of both validity and reliability is critical to an assessor's ability to gather genuine and relevant information in an assessment that can be used to inform a judgment in a specific hiring or development context. To accomplish that goal, most practitioners rely on the extant literature when designing practice approaches and inform the evidence-based application of assessment in applied settings (Reynolds, McCauley, &

Tsacoumis, 2018). Assessors should also obtain and read technical manuals from test publishers. These documents should provide relevant background information about an assessment, statistical evidence of validity and reliability, and information about norm groups that can be useful in understanding how an instrument was designed to be used and with whom.

ASSESSMENT METHODS: THE WHAT AND THE HOW

There are many domains to consider and methods to draw on when designing an assessment process. Every method has advantages and disadvantages, as well as different predictive validities in different circumstances and situations. In this section, I describe the distinction between the traits being assessed (the "what") and the testing approaches used (the "how"), although I do not discuss specific tests and instruments, I do make note of commonly used measures in Chapter 4.[1] Accordingly, I review the domains that should be considered in assessing senior leaders, and then review the methods that are frequently used to measure these dimensions.

The What of Assessments

There are a number of psychological characteristics that can be evaluated within an executive assessment. The domains covered in this section can provide insight into a senior leader's capacity to perform a job, their motivation, and how they might go about getting the job done. Commonly assessed constructs include cognitive ability, personality, values, interests, and emotional intelligence.

Commonly Assessed Traits

Cognitive Ability. Cognitive ability describes an individual's ability to learn, understand, and process information (Van Iddekinge at al., 2018), and has continually been shown to be the most robust predictor of job

[1] The use of specific measures depends on context and should be evaluated for each assessment situation. Inclusion in this book is not intended as an endorsement, but as a way of directing readers to where they can locate and/or purchase tools.

performance across job types, contexts, and organizational levels (Finkelstein et al., 2018; Ryan & Ployhart, 2014). As Ones et al. (2017) stated,

> No other predictor construct in employee selection produces as high validities, as consistently, as does cognitive ability. In addition, no assessment method has so far achieved as reliable assessment of cognitive ability as standardized tests, making such tests the ideal choice for predicting performance in organization settings. (p. 261)

Cognitive ability predicts job performance with validity coefficients ranging from .35 to .55, with a sample size weighted average of .39 (Ones et al., 2017). Additionally, the predictive validity of cognitive ability tends to increase as job complexity increases; Schmidt and Hunter (2004) showed a validity coefficient of .58 for the most complex jobs, such as professional, scientific, and executive level jobs. This suggests that a cognitive ability test can explain as much as 30% of the variance in job performance for complex jobs. Simply put, assessors should use cognitive ability measures whenever possible, and in those situations when it may not be possible, they should explain the limitations of not doing so (i.e., failing to gather important information that generates valid and reliable inferences) to their clients.

Conversely, one important challenge in assessment is that cognitive ability measures can introduce adverse impact into a selection context (Hoffman & Thornton, 1997), meaning that assessment procedures that center on cognitive ability measures tend to overselect members of the privileged group compared to members of underrepresented groups (Sajjadiani et al., 2019). They are also not always viewed positively by candidates. Senior leaders tend to have completed their education some time ago, which can make testing of this sort seem uncomfortable or cause it to be perceived as a threat. The more face valid and job-relevant the cognitive measure, the less pushback one is likely to get from assessees (Partnoy, 2018).

Assessors should be prepared for clients who may downplay a candidate's low score on a cognitive ability test or who may want to simply pick the candidate with highest score. Minimizing a low score can create challenging conversations about the predictive validity of cognitive ability tests. And some research has shown that the positive relationship between cognitive ability and leadership tapers off after a point, suggesting that an individual can be too intelligent to effectively lead a certain group because such leaders use complex language and reasoning that can undermine their influence and communication ability and make them seem socially detached from the group they are intending to lead (Antonakis et al., 2017). Using normative group comparisons (comparing individual scores to the relevant group averages), making use of score ranges (obtained scores plus or minus the confidence intervals), and incorporating cognitive ability tests into a multimethod assessment process tend to be the most effective ways to deploy these powerful tools (Dilchert, 2018; Ones et al., 2005). For example, rather than simply looking at the raw cognitive ability score of a single executive and using that number to make an inference, an assessor might consider how that score compares with executives at a similar level (comparing with a relevant normative group), or whether their score falls within a plausible range of acceptable scores for the job in question (considering confidence intervals).

Again, the assessor is looking for a preponderance of evidence, not just a single test score, to support inferences about an executive's likelihood of performing well. For example, low cognitive ability scores for a senior level leader should cause the assessor to seek to understand why the scores were low. This can include examining a plethora of evidence, including educational background (e.g., what academic level did they achieve?), work experience (e.g., has their work experience, to date, been in complex organizations?), life stage (e.g., could age-related cognitive changes have affected the result more for one assessee than another? [See Chapter 3, this volume, for discussion of ADA and ADEA issues]), scoring (were the norms used age/level/industry specific?), and test setting (e.g., was the test fast-paced, potentially favoring younger respondents? Could the executive have been distracted or unfocused on the material?). Though this list could continue, the point is that low scores and/or scores that seem odd to the assessor should not necessarily be taken at face value but should be interrogated and considered alongside other information to continue building a preponderance of evidence about the assessee.

Personality. Personality traits are consistent patterns of thoughts, behaviors, and feelings that shape how we view ourselves and how others view us (Hogan, 2005; Li et al., 2020). Almost everyone in a work setting has encountered some form of personality or "type" assessment in a selection, coaching, or team building setting. This is in some part because personality testing seems to have crossed over into mainstream consciousness (Chen, 2018; Goldberg, 2019; Menand, 2018; Strauss, 2015), often with a particular focus on popular measures such as the Myers-Briggs Type Indicator (MBTI; Myers-Briggs, 2020). The Myers-Briggs Company refers to the MBTI as "the world's most trusted personality assessment," but the tool has notable psychometric weaknesses that should warrant caution in considering its use, especially in a selection context (Pittenger, 2005).

Not only was the MBTI adapted from Carl Jung's theory of personality type in an uncertain way (Michael, 2003), the measure's psychometric properties make it less than useful in a selection setting. The tool presents personality traits as dichotomous and mutually exclusive, rather than as preferences that exist in individuals across a range of expression (Pittenger, 2005). Further, as Pittenger (2005) noted, because the MBTI uses a dichotomous scale, one that categorizes respondents into one or another category, it reduces the amount of variability that can be measured by a continuous scale—one that places respondents on a scale between two poles—and provides no indication of the magnitude of a given score. For example, two senior leaders may score as Extraverted, but that does not indicate the extent to which one may be more extraverted than the other, which is useful information. This is a particular problem in working with executive populations, where the observed range of traits may be lower than in the general population. For example, Extraverted and Sensing types are more common in managerial roles (Furnham & Crump, 2015), but finer detail is needed to describe differences among executives. Most important, while the MBTI is consistently used in development programs of various kinds, there is limited research on its use with executive populations and sparse support for its ability to predict managerial or leadership effectiveness (Brown & Reilly, 2009; McCaulley, 2000; Pittenger, 2005).

More common in the world of executive assessment, and with more evidence of validity and reliability, are instruments that are based on the

Big Five personality traits (Barrick et al., 2001; Ones et al., 2007; Schmitt, 2014). These traits are:

- Openness to experience, which consists of intellectual curiosity, creativity, unconventionality, and broad-mindedness;
- Conscientiousness, which is defined by dependability, organization, and need for achievement;
- Extraversion, which is associated with sociability, dominance, ambition, and positive emotionality;
- Agreeableness, which consists of cooperation, trustfulness, compliance and affability; and
- Neuroticism, which at low levels is associated with lack of anxiety, hostility, depression, and personal insecurity. (Barrick et al., 2001, p. 11)

The Big Five (or five factor model) first emerged in the 1950s and 1960s from a line of research that aimed to organize the thousands of terms that are used in language to describe individual differences (Digman, 1990). At the time, five independent, respected personality researchers were systematically studying the attributes of personality, and each independently arrived at essentially the same model, which suggested personality could be described by five superordinate constructs (Digman, 1990). Subsequent research over the course of the past half century has supported the robustness of the model across different countries and cultures, different instruments and theoretical frameworks, as observed by different raters (i.e., self-ratings and other-ratings) and over the course of the lifespan (Barrick & Mount, 1991; Barrick et al., 2001; Graham et al., 2020; Matz & Harari, 2020).

A substantial body of research has shown the robustness of the Big Five model as well as its validity in predicting work performance across organizational levels and professions (Barrick & Mount, 1991; Barrick et al., 2001; Ryan & Ployhart, 2014). Meta-analytic results have shown significant multiple correlations (including all five traits as predictors in a regression equation, a way of modeling the relationship between the predictor variables and outcomes) between the Big Five personality traits and outcomes such as leadership emergence, leadership effectiveness, that range between .39 and .53, with specific trait correlations as follows:

- Extraversion showed a correlation with leadership of .31, meaning that factors such as dominance and sociability are positively correlated with the identification of leadership; notably, though the correlation was statistically significant ($p < .05$), a correlation of .31 suggests extraversion only explains about 9% of the variance in leadership;
- Conscientiousness showed a statistically significant correlation of .28 with leadership, suggesting that traits such as need for achievement and organization are positively associated with leaders, accounting for about 8% of the variance in leadership;
- Openness to experience was correlated .24 with leadership, explaining about 5.5% of the variance in leadership, and suggesting broad-mindedness and creativity is associated with leadership;
- Neuroticism, with a correlation of –.24, suggests that factors such as anxiety and depression are negative identifiers of leadership traits and effective leadership, similarly accounting for about 5.5% of the variance in leadership; and
- Agreeableness, though it did display a significant correlation of .08, explained less than 1% of the variance in leadership, suggesting that traits such as compliance and affability are not closely associated with predicting leadership. (Judge et al., 2002, p. 772)

In sum, these results suggest that personality is a useful area to examine in understanding the qualities and dimensions that predict leadership. Though broad traits can clarify general patterns of behavior and individual differences among assessees, the predictive validity of personality tends to be enhanced when the facets of broader personality traits are conceptually aligned with the criterion in question (Hough & Dilchert, 2017; Hough & Johnson, 2012). For example, the personality trait of conscientiousness consists of specific aspects (or facets) such as cautiousness/impulse control, order, dependability, and achievement. Whereas the global conscientiousness trait predicts leadership and leadership effectiveness at .28, the facet of dependability shows a predictive validity of .30, and the facet of achievement shows a predictive validity of .35.

Hough and Dilchert (2017) suggested that the validity of personality facets as predictors can be especially useful when those facets are matched to relevant job duties that call for particular behaviors. This concept is called *synthetic validity*, and it describes the construction of predictive equations that can be used to design assessment protocols for specific situations (Hough & Johnson, 2012). For example, a leadership job description might call for an individual who demonstrates an ability to be innovative and creative. Some studies have shown a correlation of −.25 between sociability (a facet of extraversion) and innovation and creativity, a correlation of .14 with achievement (a facet of conscientiousness), and a correlation of −.29 with the Big Five trait agreeableness. An assessor could use these validity coefficients to create an equation designed to identify those leaders most likely to exhibit a tendency toward innovation and creativity.

Values and Interests. *Values* are the standards or beliefs by which we determine the importance of different aspects of life, including people, activities, behaviors, and work environments (Chan, 2017). Values are often examined in an assessment process to help understand culture and organizational fit. In an assessment, it can be critically important to understand how an individual's values, interests, and motives may be similar to or different from the needs of the position, the team, and the organization. Fit can be conceptualized in several ways. *Supplementary fit* describes when an individual's values and interests are similar to the context for which they are being considered. *Complementary fit* describes when individuals' values are different from the context for which they are being evaluated. For example, a new leader is needed for a sales team that is highly outcome-oriented and focused on individual success. A candidate with a top value of achievement (focused on demonstrating personal success by performing well and gaining social approval; Schwartz, 2012) would demonstrate supplementary fit (having values similar to the context), whereas a candidate with a top value of benevolence (focused on improving the well-being of those around them; Schwartz, 2012) would demonstrate complementary fit (having values that are different from the context). Kristof (1996) further defined *fit* as "the compatibility between people and organizations that occurs when: (a) at least one entity provides what the other needs, or (b) they share similar fundamental characteristics, or (c) both" (p. 4).

Assessors typically evaluate fit in an interview context, and much of the research on fit has been done in that context, as well (Barrick & Parks-Leduc, 2019). Individual values assessments and organizational values surveys can be usefully employed to gain a more data-driven perspective of the most characteristic elements of an organizational culture. To evaluate organizational values, employees may rank order values statements based on prompts such as "the most characteristic aspects of the culture of your organization" (O'Reilly et al., 1991, p. 495). For example, an organization with a culture oriented toward control and efficiency will be primarily concerned with creating stability and predictability within the organization, whereas an organization with a culture oriented toward innovation will be primarily concerned with enhancing adaptability and flexibility to fuel creativity. What is notable about organizational culture is the wide variety of cultures that can facilitate company success in different ways. Consider companies as different as Patagonia, Goldman Sachs, and Pixar. Each is a leader in its category, and yet one imagines their cultures are as dissimilar as their products. Cameron and Quinn (2011) provided an excellent overview and tool kit for understanding and assessing organizational culture in a practical way. However, research has generally lagged behind practice in this area (Barrick & Parks-Leduc, 2019; O'Reilly et al., 2014), so assessors should use surveys thoughtfully as just one part of the compendium of evidence of fit.

Depending on the specific situation, supplementary versus complementary fit may be necessary. For example, if an organization's goal is to drive cultural change, then the type of fit that would describe a good match is more complementary in nature, so the individual who is selected can drive the organization in the direction of the desired change. Consider the previous example of the outcome-oriented sales team. If the goal there was to create a more cohesive team focused on developing more junior salespeople, then a leader whose top value is benevolence may be a good fit for driving the desired culture change. Though this is a simplified example, there are degrees and variations within and between the two basic types of fit.

In practice, hiring a "good fit" tends to refer to an individual who fits the needs of the job *and* who will fit the existing organizational culture—someone who does (or will) behave in a similar manner to those already on the team. In assessment situations, it can be helpful to educate the client on the different types of fit and the multiple levels at which fit must be considered (e.g., job, team, function, organization). Hartnell et al. (2016), for example, showed that differences between a CEO's leadership style and an organizational cultural style can have a positive effect on firm performance. This research suggests that hiring a CEO who fits in with the current culture may prevent the organization from growing as effectively as it could. Additionally, the specific task of a team or the strategy of an organization can influence which type of fit is likely to make a positive or negative impact on performance (Mannix & Neale, 2005).

Interests are stable aspects of people (psychological characteristics) that shape the types of work and leisure activities they find attractive, motivating, and fulfilling (Lowman, 2010; Su, 2018). Interests are most frequently conceptualized using John Holland's RIASEC model (Holland, 1959), which organized clusters of interests and occupations into six types:

- Realistic, which describes individuals who are primarily interested in working with things, their hands, or outside;
- Investigative, which describes individuals who are primarily interested in research and scientific work;
- Artistic, which describes individuals who are primarily interested creativity and self-expression;
- Social, which describes individuals who are primarily interested in helping and working with other people;
- Enterprising, which describes individuals who are primarily interested in leading, influencing, persuading others; and
- Conventional, which describes individuals who are primarily interested in working with data in well-organized and structured environments. (Nye et al., 2017, p. 140)

Meta-analytic results have shown that interests, specifically the alignment between an individual's interests and the characteristics of their work environment, are related to job performance and persistence (Nye et al., 2012, 2017). Though explicit interest inventories are not frequently used in executive assessment, they can provide useful information about the type of work an executive is likely to find motivating. This can be used to help evaluate job and environment fit in the case of selection, or to align development activities with an executive's natural interests in the case of development.

Emotional Intelligence. *Emotional intelligence* refers to an individual's ability to perceive, understand, and regulate their own and others' emotions and feelings (Salovey & Mayer, 1990). There is some debate as to whether emotional intelligence is an ability that describes one's capacity to understand emotion and use that understanding to improve thought (Mayer et al., 2008), or whether it is a combination of traits and skills that shape an individual's ability to cope with the emotional demands of various situations (Bar-On, 1997). Because of this lack of consensus, it is not always clear whether emotional intelligence is a distinct form of intelligence, or whether it is "an umbrella term for a broad array of constructs that are connected only by their nonredundancy with cognitive intelligence" (Joseph & Newman, 2010, p. 55). It is perhaps not surprising then that self-report measures of emotional intelligence tend to show stronger correlations with personality, and ability-based measures of emotional intelligence tend to show stronger correlations with cognitive ability (Joseph & Newman, 2010). Gaining a deeper understanding of an executive's emotional intelligence can provide insight into their ability to manage their own emotions and their ability to relate to others and manage interpersonal relationships. In general, emotional intelligence shows some relationship to job performance (O'Boyle et al., 2011; Pekaar et al., 2017) and leadership effectiveness (Edelman & van Knippenberg, 2018; Kerr et al., 2006), although it is not abundantly clear how much incremental validity is provided by such measures over and above that provided by personality and cognitive ability measures (Boyatzis, 2018). Emotional intelligence is typically evaluated in an executive assessment context by way of the interview, feedback from colleagues (e.g., direct reports, peers, supervisors), and in some cases self-report measures or tests (Mayer et al., 2011), or situational judgment tests (Menkes, 2006).

Assessing Leaders Versus Assessing Leadership

Each of the previously described components can be combined to build an assessment that constructs a useful picture of the individual(s) in question. That said, it is worth taking a brief step back to consider the difference between assessing leaders and assessing individuals for leadership. When considering the assessment of senior leaders, this could seem like the same thing, but each circumstance raises different questions and issues. In the case of assessing leaders, the primary issue is working within a specific population that requires special consideration in terms of how the assessment process is conducted. Many of these issues have been reviewed and will be discussed in more detail in the remainder of this book.

Assessing individuals for leadership, however, raises a different question. Essentially, leadership research focuses on two meta-categories: leader emergence and leader effectiveness. Whereas *leader emergence* is concerned with who is likely to become a leader within a given group, *leader effectiveness* is concerned with an individual's ability to direct and influence a group of people to accomplish a common goal. Leader emergence is a relevant topic because assessors are frequently asked by clients to evaluate whether individuals have what it takes to rise within an organizational hierarchy and continue to be effective. Emergence describes the extent to which an individual is viewed as influential and leaderlike by others (Judge et al., 2002), a perception that may or may not be informed by data or an understanding of an individual's actual performance or ability to lead. This is more commonly a part of the consideration of "high-potential individuals" at the middle- or upper-middle management level (Finkelstein et al., 2018) because senior leaders have, inherently, already emerged as leaders. The variables that predict leader emergence are not always the same variables that predict leader effectiveness (Judge et al., 2002). Leader effectiveness is the extent to which an individual is successful in guiding and influencing a group to achieve a shared objective

(Yukl, 2012). Practically speaking, individuals who may have a propensity to emerge as leaders in an organization are not necessarily those who will make effective leaders. That is, the traits and behaviors that may predict an individual being perceived as "leaderlike" by their peers may not be the same as those traits and behaviors that predict whether an individual can align a team in a common direction and gain their commitment to achieve a common goal. Additionally, in an assessment setting, the primary outcome of interest is leadership effectiveness, or the actual performance of the leader in the job. This distinction matters in evaluating the validity evidence of a given tool or assessment method. For example, conscientiousness is correlated with leader emergence at .33, but only at .16 with leader effectiveness (Judge et al., 2002). Taking time to understand the specific nature of the outcome variable used to calculate validity coefficients could mean the difference between predicting who seems like a leader to others versus who might be able to lead well.

The Specific Case of the CEO

Assessing individuals being considered for the CEO job is a particular challenge because each CEO job is unique. A multitude of factors must be considered together that cannot fully be generalized from any other context including (but not limited to) fit to the job specification, fit to the team and organizational culture, fit to the organizational lifecycle, market dynamics, and board relationships (as relevant). Even still, the most complex element of CEO assessment is the fact that the nature of the job of CEOs is that they shape their role to fit their context. Effective leaders tend to be skilled at observing their environments and adapting their behavior accordingly to accomplish what they need to accomplish (Yukl, 2012). This skill is usually conceptualized as *learning agility*, or the ability to observe and learn from experience and apply new knowledge on an ongoing basis in new situations (De Meuse, 2019; De Meuse et al., 2010; Hoff & Burke, 2017). At the highest level of an organization, individuals are often assessed for fit to future strategy. Job specifications of this nature thus often comprise forward-looking statements that describe the direction in which an organization is likely headed, based on input from board members and other knowledgeable stakeholders. Because job specifications for CEOs can be so conceptual and subject to change based on external circumstances, evaluating constructs such as learning agility can be helpful for evaluating which individuals are likely to be successful in such roles (De Meuse, 2019).

The How of Assessments

There are multiple methods that assessors can use to evaluate the constructs covered in the previous section, and executive assessments often consist of some combination of these methods. Frequently used among senior leaders are interviews, self-report questionnaires, situational judgment tests, and assessment centers.

Interviews

The assessment method that is most used in selection, even for high level positions, is the interview (Levashina et al., 2014). Interviews are used in almost every organization and are frequently the only method used in an assessment process. Fortunately, they can be predictive of future job performance; unfortunately, the predictive validity of an interview is highly contingent on its content and structure. Because they are commonly conducted in an ad hoc and idiosyncratic way, interviews can suffer from weak evidence of validity (Levashina et al., 2014). However, when they are structured properly, and relevant to the job at issue, they can provide useful information and can be an integral part of the data assimilation process in a multimethod assessment (McDaniel et al., 1994).

The advantage of the interview is that it is flexible and can be adapted to the situation at hand, and it can provide information relevant to assessing person–organization fit, job knowledge and experience, personality, situational judgment, social skills, and leadership behaviors (Cable & Judge, 1997; Heimann et al., 2020; Salgado & Moscoso, 2002). All this information is useful input for the assessor who is gathering evidence to deliver to a client in support of the client's decision making.

The disadvantage of the interview is that it is frequently conducted with idiosyncratic questions that are not administered in a standardized way, and responses are not scored in a consistent way. It requires some discipline to stick to an interview structure. Even across interviewers trained to use the same tools and methodologies, the actual structure of the interview can vary quite broadly. Having clearly defined rating dimensions established prior to the assessment process (usually done while creating the job specification) and anchoring those dimensions with specific behavioral scales can help improve the validity of assessor judgments (Reynolds, McCauley, & Tsacoumis, 2018).

The key to making more valid inferences from interviewing revolves around the idea of structure and job relevance (Heimann et al., 2020). Structured interview questions usually focus on how someone behaved in the past or how they would likely behave in hypothetical situations. Questions about past behavior are what make up behavioral interviews, and questions about hypothetical behavior make up situational interviews. Behavioral interview questions ask the interviewee to describe how they behaved in situations similar to those they are likely to encounter on the job. A few examples of behavior interview questions are:

- Tell me about a time you faced a conflict while working on a team. What did you do?
- Describe a situation when you made a challenging decision that others disagreed with.
- Give me an example of a direct report that you have helped to grow and develop. What did you do?

In situational interviews, the interviewer provides a hypothetical situation related to the demands of the job and asks the interviewee to explain how they would likely react to it. Situational interviews are aimed at assessing behavioral intentions as a predictor of future behavior (Levashina et al., 2014), whereas behavioral interviews operate on the theory that past behavior is the best predictor of future behavior. A few examples of behavior interview questions are:

- Say you're leading a team that is experiencing some conflict. How would you go about managing it?
- How do you align others around challenging decisions they may disagree with?
- If hired, how would you grow and develop your direct reports?

Meta-analyses examining the predictive validity of interview methods in a business setting have shown slightly higher average validity for behavioral interviews (.31) than situational interviews (.26; Huffcutt et al., 2004). Importantly, behavioral interviews demonstrate more robust validity in predicting job performance in jobs characterized by high complexity (as is typically the case with senior-level leadership positions) than situational interviews (Krajewski et al., 2006; Taylor & Small, 2002). This effect may be a function of the situational interview method in that it is simply more challenging to design situational interviews that adequately cover the nuances and dynamics of more complex jobs (Huffcutt et al., 2004, pp. 268–269). Additionally, interviewees may be more likely to provide socially desirable answers to situational interview prompts. Unless an assessor has the resources to develop and pretest situational interview questions that provide valid inferences for the job in question, it is best to stick with behavioral interview questions. Furthermore, behavioral interview questions (e.g., "Tell me about a time when you coached a direct report to a higher level of performance") tend to feel more job relevant than situational interview questions (e.g., "Tell me how you would go about coaching a direct report to a higher level of performance").

In an executive assessment, the interview often serves an integrative purpose in which the assessor can look for evidence of patterns of behavior, contextualize data collected from other tools used in the assessment, and delve deeper into the context specific elements of the job. Ideally, assessees will have already completed other tests and measures (e.g., cognitive ability, personality), so assessors can interpret that data prior to meeting their assessees. The interview then provides an opportunity for assessors to continue gathering and structuring evidence in support their inferences.

Self-Report Questionnaires

Self-report questionnaires are a common format of personality assessment. These tools elicit a response from an individual on various items and use these responses to describe the traits of that individual in comparison with a norm group (Hough & Dilchert, 2017, p. 303). Self-report questionnaires demonstrate strong evidence of validity and are easy to administer, making them a go-to tool for assessors. Frequently, an assessment process will include one or more self-report questionnaires, which can provide strong evidence for dimensions such as personality, interests, values, and motives. A persistent concern with self-report questionnaires is "faking" and impression management, which has led to the development of timed assessments, forced-choice formats, and even computer-based adaptive measures that adjust forthcoming questions based on preceding responses. It is important for assessors to note that the question format can impact the inferences that can be made from the resulting data. For example, Likert-type scales (e.g., 1-to-5 scales ranging from *strongly disagree* to *strongly agree*) can produce normative data and can be used to compare individuals to one another. Most forced-choice assessments produce *ipsative data*, which rank orders how traits occur within an individual (e.g., a rank-ordered list of values) rather than providing percentiles, which makes between-person comparisons a challenge.

Situational Judgment Tests

Situational judgment tests (SJTs) are an assessment method in which an assessee is presented with a scenario and must decide on a course of action based on knowledge, skills, abilities, and characteristics that are relevant to the job in question (Christian et al., 2010, p. 84). Depending on how they are designed and how questions are worded, SJTs can measure elements of personality or of cognitive ability (McDaniel et al., 2007). Christian et al. (2010) conducted a meta-analysis reporting relatively strong mean validities for SJTs, including .23 for managerial job knowledge and skills, and .29 for managerial leadership. Like personality measures used in a selection context, SJTs are most valid when the predictor measures are selected for the specific criterion intended to be predicted (Hough & Dilchert, 2017). For example, if a criterion of interest is "working effectively with others," questions may present examples of interpersonal conflict in the workplace with response items that characterize a range of possible responses. Interestingly, although SJTs have demonstrated criterion validity, the constructs that are measured by SJTs tend to be a bit harder to delineate and tend not to fall into specific categories of knowledge, skills, abilities or traits, but instead represent broader categories like "applied social skills," or compound variables comprised of multiple elements of knowledge, skills, abilities, and traits (Ryan & Ployhart, 2014). That said, the incremental validity believed to be added by SJTs is relatively modest (ranging from .03 to .05 over cognitive ability, to .06–.07 over Big Five personality traits; McDaniel et al., 2007), so assessors should be cognizant of the mix of instruments used in a given assessment and balance the likelihood of added validity with the additional time commitment and effort needed to gain additional information.

Assessment Centers

Assessment centers are an assessment method that employ multiple assessment methods and exercises designed to evaluate a range of knowledge, skills, and attributes that are used to make employment decisions. Assessment centers have long been a staple of individual psychological assessment and have maintained their relevance because of the strong evidence of criterion-related validity and their apparent objectivity (Meriac et al., 2008). Overall ratings from assessment centers demonstrate strong criterion validity, accounting for approximately 18% (~.43) of the variance in job performance and adding incremental validity over and above what is predicted by cognitive ability and personality alone (Meriac et al., 2008), likely because of their multimethod nature (Arthur et al., 2003; Hermelin et al., 2007; Woehr & Arthur, 2003). Notable among these methods is the in basket exercise, which provides the assessee with a number of job-related tasks to accomplish and provides some insight into their ability to handle a "day in the life" of someone in role. For example, participants may be presented with a situation that requires them to take certain actions and make decisions based on their interpretation of information presented and various response options. One such situation may present a looming business problem (e.g., data suggesting a factory may soon hit its production capacity) and several pressing issues for the executive to take care of. The participant must then decide what to do first and how to handle each element of the situation. Assessment center participants tend to see these exercises as preferable to cognitive ability tests, because they seem to more closely resemble the job and are thus perceived as fairer (Macan et al., 1994). This is important because the procedural elements of an assessment (e.g., job relatedness of selection methods, explanations about test fairness and the reasons behind certain methods) can affect perceptions of fairness and how feedback is received by the participant (London & McFarland, 2017). Assessment centers are more frequently used among middle to upper middle managers in large organizations that can deploy them with the proper resources.

Returning to the Case of the CEO

When the consulting psychologist presented to the board, the selection committee members were open and receptive to the findings and recommendations. It was noted that each candidate had performed quite well on measures of cognitive ability and that in general each would make a suitable CEO candidate. The scenarios were laid out in which each candidate would be most successful and how each was likely to approach the tasks of the job. The consultant then asked the board to consider what they thought was likely to happen in their industry's market over the next 3 to 5 years and used that input to help the board think through how market conditions and the changing needs of the business might call for a leader with a certain type of leadership style. Ultimately, the board decided that even though the candidate considered to be an innovator might be more challenging to work with from the board's perspective, the business needs demanded a leader who could inspire the workforce to undertake the changes and growth needed to remain competitive in a global marketplace. Additionally, the consultant was able to provide some guidance and strategies for how the board might effectively engage the new CEO based on the results of the assessment.

This case highlights the fact that assessors are advisors in this work and frequently serve as "thought partners" to the business leaders making these complex decisions. To that end, the most effective assessment systems will use various methods fit to the specific situation, so that detailed insights can be provided into how and why a certain individual might perform in a given role. This is especially important in senior leadership positions in which the job requires balance among experience, knowledge, personality, interpersonal competencies, and leadership motivation. The key is to make sure that the multiple methods used are creating incremental validity—that is, are the methods redundant or do they provide new angles and additive information to the overall picture of the executive?

KEY TAKEAWAYS

- Validity and reliability describe the accuracy and precision with which a tool measures what it intends to measure. Diligently evaluate evidence for validity and reliability for tools and methods that you use in the assessment process. Contact assessment providers and ask for technical manuals and review relevant research on instruments.
- Use multiple methods in the assessment process to build a compendium of evidence about job fit. This should include methods that can help you learn what a leader has done in the past (e.g., interviewing) and what they are likely to do in the future (e.g., personality, cognitive ability, values, interests).
- Use structured (rather than unstructured) interviews as a part of the executive assessment process and focus on behavioral questions. Creating behaviorally anchored rating scales can help add objectivity to the collection and analysis of interview data.
- Don't accept isolated test scores by themselves, especially if they seem odd (e.g., an unexpectedly low cognitive ability score for a high-performing senior leader); rather, consider the preponderance of evidence across assessment methods when measuring important variables.
- Consider the balance between the rigor of the assessment and the time commitment required of the executive in deciding which measures to use, and how many.

2

Understanding the Context of Assessment

A 100-year-old nonprofit foundation hired a consultant to help create a succession plan for its executive director (ED) position. The sitting ED was a well-established member of the community, and because of the size of the foundation and the funds that it granted each year, was in a position of notable influence within the city and the state where the foundation was headquartered. Succession was not imminent, but the board had encouraged the ED to take a proactive stance in considering who would lead next.

The size and influence of the foundation made the ED role quite complicated, but the contextual elements of the role were what made it so complex. The executive team consisted of eight individuals, each of whom had been promoted up through the organization over the course of their careers and had an average tenure in the high teens. Each oversaw a

https://doi.org/10.1037/0000264-003
Assessing CEOs and Senior Leaders: A Primer for Consultants, by J. R. Blankenship

large portion of the foundation's operations and had substantial commitment and support from the employees in their divisions. The foundation's board was very hands-on in their governance, and the board members were equally well-established members of the local business community. The culture of the organization was highly relationally oriented, and effective leaders tended to be those who were skilled at building consensus for their ideas and maintaining strong working relationships across boundaries that were not always visible. In some circumstances, those in other departments with long tenure held political sway among decision makers and could derail or stall organizational change programs. Those with the experience and insight to navigate the contours of the culture were the ones who succeeded over the long term.

To begin considering the question of succession, the ED hired a consultant to assess the existing executive team members and help formulate a succession plan that could be executed over the course of the ED's remaining tenure. Prior to conducting any assessments, the consultant had extensive conversations with the ED about the demands of the job but was only allowed to speak to the board as a whole, rather than individually interviewing each board member. As the consultant's understanding of the organization deepened, it became apparent that a formal culture survey would help to gain a broader, more data-driven perspective of the organizational culture, but was not given permission to do so. The consultant then had to reevaluate whether the executive assessments could be conducted effectively without the data requested.

WHAT IS THE CONTEXT OF AN ASSESSMENT?

There are many layers and elements to consider in the context of an assessment. *Context* is multifaceted, and in order to develop a sense of the context of an assessment, consultants should ask themselves questions such as: (a) What is happening? (b) Where is it taking place? (c) When is it occurring? and (d) Who is involved? (Vergauwe et al., 2018). These questions can help shed some light on the many dynamics at play in the assessment context, as well as the many levels involved, including the

- *individual* level, where the assessor may consider the context of the people involved in an assessment, such as the assessee's tenure at the organization, life stage, and racial/ethnic background and gender (as aspects of understanding the assessment context and the need to avoid bias or discriminatory practices);
- *team* level, where the assessor may account for the direct environment in which assessees work, such as the tenure of other team members and team dynamics, such as cohesiveness and quality of interpersonal relationships;
- *organizational* level, where the assessor considers broader contextual dynamics, such as company culture, strategy, and life cycle phase of the organization;
- *market* level, where the assessor may account for industry or economic level conditions, such as whether the market is growing or shrinking and what the competitive landscape looks like for the organization; and
- *regional* level, where the assessor will consider the broader external environment in which all of this work is taking place, such as regional culture, history of diversity, equity, and inclusion efforts, and the current political environment (Vergauwe et al., 2018). Indeed, given the interconnectedness of global financial, political, health, and technological systems (Raddant & Kenett, 2021), the state of the world could be considered context for an assessment (e.g., the COVID-19 pandemic).

The context molds the purpose of the assessment. It helps determine what the assessment ultimately needs to accomplish, how the assessment needs to be conducted, and how the results of the assessment should be presented to best deliver on that purpose.

For example, say a consultant is hired to assess succession candidates and advise a board based on findings as to who would likely make the best CEO and why. How much helpful information can be provided to the board if the consultant is not well-informed about the nature of the business itself or the industry in which it operates? How much does the consultant need to know about the team the next CEO would be leading, or the culture of the organization?

A useful way to understand the contextual elements of an assessment is to think of them as characteristics that are shaped by the assessment, and characteristics that are shaped by the situation in which the assessment takes place. Characteristics of the assessment are those elements that change when the purpose of the assessment changes, such as when assessment is used for selection versus development or coaching. Characteristics of the situation are those elements that will persist to some extent across different assessment purposes but will differ depending on the specific details the assessor will encounter, such as industry specific considerations or concerns that are unique to the organization. The context of a selection assessment will differ from that of a developmental assessment, although both types of assessment require some consideration of the organizational culture in which the assessments are taking place. In the case of an assessment for selection, understanding the organizational culture will help inform elements of job and team fit for the candidates in consideration (van Vianen, 2018). In the case of assessment for development, understanding the culture may shape the type of developmental insight provided by the assessor in the assessment results. For example, if assessment results suggest an executive is a bad *culture fit* for an organization (the executive's behavioral preferences and values do not align with the behavioral norms that exist within an organization; Lu et al., 2019), the assessor may describe what could be challenging or taxing about adapting to the culture and provide recommendations for how to adapt.

CHARACTERISTICS OF THE ASSESSMENT

Assessments can be used in support of a great number of organizational activities, but at the most senior organizational level there are four general purposes that describe the most common uses for assessments: selection, development, succession, and mergers and acquisitions. Though these contexts overlap in certain ways, each involves unique circumstances and challenges that need to be considered in designing and conducting an assessment process.

Assessments for Selection

In selection, the purpose of assessment is to gather information that can be used to help advise organizational decision makers about whom to hire. *Selection assessments* at the executive level have high stakes, and hiring decisions can have major implications for organizations. Senior leaders shape the future of their organizations for a significant period of time, and their impact can be felt across the spectrum of stakeholders (N. Gupta et al., 2019; O'Reilly et al., 2014). These assessments are frequently confidential, so discretion on behalf of the assessor is of the utmost importance. In one case, news of a sitting CEO being considered for a competitor's top job leaked to the business press, causing the stock price of the company where the CEO worked to decline. In response, the board put together an emergency retention package and had the CEO make a public statement about staying at the current company. The stock price rebounded, but the competitor lost their best candidate for the role.

Selection assessments tend to occur in two forms: (a) assessing a slate of candidates, each of whom is a finalist for a job; or (b) assessing a single candidate who is being considered for a job.

When multiple candidates are being considered, the assessment result usually consists of individual reports on each candidate, and an executive summary report that allows for an easy comparison of the most salient differences or similarities among candidates for the organization to use as part of their decision-making process. Individual assessment reports vary based on the design of the assessment process and based on the assessor's and the client organization's preferences and style. A report will generally provide an overview of the individual's experience, competencies, and traits; the dimensions at issue in the assessment and how they performed on each one; as well as an integrative overview of their strengths and areas for development (Reynolds, McCauley, & Tsacoumis, 2018). An executive summary provides a summation of these points across candidates and may include a summary statement of the assessor's overarching recommendation about the candidates and the hiring decision to be made.

Single candidate assessments are somewhat less common, but worth noting. It is rarely the case that a client seeks to conduct a full analysis of a job and then only assesses a single candidate against the job requirements. More frequently, a single candidate assessment occurs when a client organization has already conducted some sort of selection process on its own. Once the organization has identified a finalist for the position, they seek an assessment to help support or confirm their decision. This type of assessment can be somewhat more challenging than the assessment of a slate of candidates. When evaluating a slate of candidates, the assessor advises the client on the relative strengths and weaknesses of each and the comparative issues to be considered among them (Kaiser & Overfield, 2011). In multiple candidate assessments, the assessor's advisory role is primarily to help shape the client's understanding about the finalists they are considering and to assist the client in their decision-making process. In many cases, conversely, when an organization seeks a single candidate assessment, the client has generally implicitly decided that they want to hire a particular individual but wish to have them undergo an assessment before making their final approval. These assessments operate as a sort of "decision-making insurance policy" for hiring managers. This type of client work most frequently occurs between assessors and clients who have worked together for many years (or through many assessments for selection), when the assessor has come to serve as a trusted advisor in hiring decisions (Wasylyshyn, 2019). To that end, the assessment tends to be presented to the assessee as a final step in the hiring process. This can create several challenges for the assessor. Because this type of assessment occurs so late in the recruiting process, clients tend to be looking for support for their decision to hire and may try to discount negative assessment results. As one consultant put it, the client will look at disconfirming evidence and say something like, "Well, can't we coach the candidate out of that?" In this circumstance, the assessor can consult with the client on the implications of making this kind of hiring decision by pointing out that perhaps candidates can be coached out of problematic behaviors. However, making such a decision commits the hiring manager to not only hiring and onboarding a new employee, but also developing that employee to address a preexisting gap in their ability to succeed.

An additional challenge in selection contexts occurs when a finalist slate includes both internal and external candidates (Harrell, 2016). With external candidates, the relationship in an executive assessment is relatively straightforward. They are considered for a job, go through an assessment process as a part of that consideration, and either get the job or do not. Internal candidates, on the other hand, may need to be managed differently throughout the assessment process. They bring to the assessment process a history with the company and pre-existing relationships within it, and their candidacy may involve some internal political issues. If they are not selected for the job, care needs to be taken to ensure that they stay with the company, and that they are not seen as now being less desirable in their current work role because they were passed over for the executive position. In this circumstance, assessment can provide a fair process by which to: (a) evaluate whether internal candidates are well-suited for a senior-level job compared to external candidates; (b) discuss the internal candidates' and the organization's expectations about what is required to take on a senior-level job within that organization; and (c) highlight gaps in knowledge, skills, or experience that can become development opportunities for the candidates' advancement. For internal candidates, establishing development plans after the assessment becomes even more important, so that those who are not selected can address any limiting factors that may have prevented them from getting the job.

Assessments for Development

Development is a rather sweeping term that can describe a host of organizational activities ranging from technical training to behavioral coaching. The purpose of *development assessment* in a leadership context is not only to understand an individual's specific needs relative to their current job but also to help them grow and improve as a leader (Day & Dragoni, 2015). Assessment in this context may be the starting point of a one-to-one coaching engagement or may be part of an extended leadership development program. At times, assessments for development may be simply used to engage certain leaders, or a leadership team, to help communicate that an organization is investing time and resources in helping them grow. Assessments for development may also be conducted to help understand the nature of a leader's struggle to be effective or to try to stem a possible *derailment*, in which a formerly successful leader plateaus below their expected level of achievement or begins to fail (Burrow et al., 2020; Inyang, 2013).

In any case, developmental assessments create opportunities to enhance an executive's self-awareness, and frequently some awareness of how they are perceived by others, to help them become more effective leaders. Because the goal of many development assessments is to help leaders better understand their own leadership strengths (Riggio, 2008), assessors have more leeway in this context to use tools that are not designed or validated for use in a selection context (e.g., Myers-Briggs Type Indicator, CliftonStrengths; Asplund et al., 2014). The assessment market is full of tools like this (e.g., DiSC profiles and other "type" indicators), many of which have limited or nonexistent evidence of validity and reliability. These types of tools should still be used with caution or as a part of an assessment battery, as they may not on their own provide a full view of what an individual's behavior might be (Michael, 2003).

Ultimately, the goal of assessment for development is to establish a starting point for some type of activity that is grounded in a deep understanding of the assessee. The specific purpose of a developmental assessment, however, can depend on the nature of the context. In the case of a high-potential program, in which an organization identifies and aims to develop their top employees (Finkelstein et al., 2018), assessment may be used to understand how leaders with a high potential to advance to a senior leader or CEO role compare with each other, evaluate their relative strengths and weaknesses, and help track how they grow over time (with reassessment in the future). In the case of a leadership development or coaching program, assessment may be used to set a baseline understanding of leaders' strengths and areas for development, or to more deeply understand how the executives are perceived by colleagues.

The results of a developmental assessment are usually presented in a report that describes an individual's strengths and areas for development, which then serves as a starting point for creating a development plan. Although the development context can seem a bit "friendlier" than the selection context, developmental assessments can also be perceived by executives as somewhat punitive. Leaders may express skepticism about such an assessment and ask legitimate questions about the "real" purpose of the assessment, and who will have access to the data derived from it. These types of questions and concerns are best managed when the assessor is obtaining informed consent from the assessee prior to conducting the assessment (see Chapter 3, this volume, for a fuller consideration of informed consent). The clearer the purpose of the assessment, and the communication thereof to the executive, the better the outcome is likely to be.

Assessments for Succession

Succession is a hybrid between the selection and development contexts for assessment. *Succession planning* is a way of evaluating an organization's future leadership needs for a given position (or multiple positions) and then assessing whether the talent already available within the organization can take on those leadership roles when transitions happen (Stamoulis, 2009). Evaluating future leadership needs involves identifying positions that are essential to the long-term health of the organization, and then understanding the talent pipeline available to move into those positions in the event of a transition (Conger & Fulmer, 2003; Schepker et al., 2018).

In smaller organizations, this type of work may only be considered for the CEO role or key C-suite roles (e.g., other chief executive roles such as chief financial officer [CFO] or chief operating officer [COO]). In larger organizations, succession work can include evaluation of many positions as well as the broader issues of creating talent pipelines and considerations of the leadership "bench strength" within different areas of the organization (Conger & Fulmer, 2003).

Many details of a succession assessment will depend on the timing and tenor of the process within the organization. Succession work conducted on a shorter timeline can be like assessing a slate of internal finalist candidates. Depending on how quickly leadership transition is taking place, it may involve an organization accepting an available internal option as satisfactory. Succession planning on a longer timeline may start when an executive decides to retire or, as has become more common, may start the day a new executive takes over their role. The long-term planning context creates time for thoughtful assessment and development planning and allows time for genuine development of the leaders who are assessed. Succession work on a rapid timeline, on the other hand, is usually the result of an unexpected departure or an emergency.

The tenor of the succession process primarily relates to whether the process is being conducted confidentially within the organization or is part of ongoing executive development. In organizations wherein the process is not openly described as succession, it tends to be presented as a part of team development; although it is usually quite apparent to participants that succession planning is the ultimate goal of the process. For this reason, succession can be one of the most politically fraught contexts for assessment (Schepker et al., 2018). At the senior level of organizations, competition for top jobs can be intense, and when executives are openly included in an assessment process, it can increase overt competitiveness among assessment participants for those top jobs. For example, in many of these assessments, *360° feedback* will be collected, in which participants in the succession process will be asked to provide feedback on their peers. In some circumstances, participants may shape their feedback to try to position themselves as the better option or may rely on anonymity in the feedback process to provide feedback that is not accurate or less than accurate. This type of positioning is to be expected to some extent but needs to be carefully weighed and given context when compiling assessment data into a full picture of successor candidates. Assessors can take steps to help ensure more reliable and fair evaluations, such as conducting feedback via interview, framing feedback as a gift to the leader being evaluated, and reminding raters that their feedback is valuable to the individual and to the organization (Bracken et al., 2016).

Succession assessment by trained professionals can lend a sense of procedure and fairness to the succession process and how potential successors are being evaluated; furthermore, it can create an opportunity for those potential successors to develop over time and become more competitive for top jobs (Church et al., 2015; Garman & Glawe, 2004). To that end, the real benefit of assessment in a succession context is that it provides a way for boards and organizational leaders to more deeply understand who may be ready to take over senior leadership positions, and if potential successors are not currently ready, assessment can point to the type of experience, education, and/or development that will be necessary to prepare them. To that end, the comparative element of succession assessments is critical, as is the understanding of how development happens and how long development takes. CEOs and boards engage consultants in succession work to develop a clear picture of the leadership landscape and to understand who might be currently prepared to take over an executive role, who might be capable of taking on such a role with some development, and who is unlikely to be able to successfully step into a CEO or senior leader position on a reasonable timeline (or at all).

Assessments for Mergers and Acquisitions

The combination and subsequent restructuring of organizations lends itself to assessment work because when one company buys or merges with another company, job roles are often made redundant, and the looming question is often "Who will lead?" Assessment is useful in the *merger integration*, the process by which one company incorporates another or two companies combine into one entity, because it provides supportive data and information for decision makers to choose the team that will lead after the merger closes; additionally, it can help to ensure that the best people are selected for the roles that are key to the merged entity's success (Chao et al., 2020). Like assessments in a succession context, assessment in the mergers and acquisitions context can also add a sense of objectivity and procedure to the selection process and can provide a consistent view of executives across companies that may have different cultures, standards, and information on performance (Denison & Ko, 2016). Additionally, assessment in this context can provide a foundational plan that can be used by the organization for ongoing development after selection decisions have been made.

These assessment circumstances have high stakes, often occur on a quick timeline, and can involve a considerable amount of project management. Frequently, when assessment is being used as a part of the merger integration process, it is being used at a fairly large scale, which means that a lot of assessments need to be completed quickly. Essentially, this type of work is a scaled-up version of selection assessments for multiple finalist slates. For example, in a large merger integration, an acquiring company hired a strategy consulting firm to determine the essential leadership roles required to capture the value of the merger. The strategy consultants identified 12 senior level roles across the organization. For each job role, between two and five candidates were considered. Accordingly, the firm hired to conduct the integration assessments was tasked with completing over 40 executive assessments in an 8-week period. The firm was able to accomplish this by assembling a team of assessors and assigning roles to each one. So, for example, one consultant would assess each of the five candidates for the vice president of product development role. Each candidate completed a combination of online measures and a structured interview. After all the assessments were completed, the assessors met to compile results and recommendations for reporting back to the board of the merged companies.

Other Relevant Assessment Contexts

Although selection, development, succession planning, and mergers and acquisitions constitute the main contexts in which assessments tend to occur in organizations, a few other notable situations in which assessments can be used are worth mentioning.

Onboarding Assessments

Onboarding assessments are a type of assessment for development that occur posthire to help executives onboard more quickly and more effectively. *Onboarding* is the process in which new executives are introduced to the organization and begin to socialize and integrate with their team and other colleagues (Allen et al., 2017). Assessments in this context frequently involve some evaluation of the team the individual will be leading to help them understand the team culture and expectations. This can be a useful practice for organizations because it can serve as an opportunity to help an executive begin a new role with a developmental mindset and facilitate their transition, which can be a challenging and stressful time in the life of an executive.

Developmental Assessments for Termination, Derailment, or Vocational/Career Coaching

At times, developmental assessments can be conducted to evaluate an executive for potential termination. Though this explicit situation is not terribly common, clients do seek developmental assessments for individuals they fear may be derailing or failing. In the best circumstances, this is done to help that individual recover and grow, although sometimes the client organization is looking for assessment results to reinforce their existing beliefs and provide support for their desire to terminate an employee. Assessors should be wary of being hired by an organization that has already made its mind up about an individual's prospects. In such instances legal issues may arise around wrongful termination or other selection issues which vary by country and by state in the United States (Sackett et al., 2010). To that end, assessors need to be diligent about determining the true nature of the context in which they are working, and should seek legal advice if they encounter a situation they think may bear some legal liability (Landy, Gutman, & Outtz, 2010).

Developmental assessments can also be conducted with a specific focus on vocational interest or career coaching. Whether a senior leader is considering changing companies, changing industries, moving from a technical career path to a managerial career path, or moving into retirement, vocational/career assessments can help individuals think through their experience, interests, and goals and how those might shape their future career decisions (Lowman, 1991). *Vocational assessments* are somewhat distinctive in that the individual being assessed is frequently the individual who hired the assessor. Additionally, the purpose of a vocational assessment can range from identifying and exploring ideas and themes for career exploration, to making specific job recommendations or even providing connections to potential opportunities, depending on the individuals involved.

When Assessment Contexts Mix

Finally, contexts can and do mix to fit the specific purposes of assessment. Clients may ask to use the data and information from a finalist assessment after a hire is made to help onboard and develop a new leader. Assessments conducted for prior leadership development may provide useful information in a new coaching engagement or succession planning process. The informed consent of the assessee(s) is of utmost importance in these situations (see Chapter 3). Assessment results should not be used for any purpose for which the assessee has not provided prior consent. In situations where historical assessment data may exist, for example as part of an existing human resources file, the assessor may obtain consent to review such information, as it may include evidence of a persistent problem or of an executive's growth and development over time. Communicating with the client organization at the beginning of the assessment process can be a good time to ask whether executives have participated in similar assessment processes in the past, and whether data/information from those assessments might still be relevant. On more than one occasion, I have been in the process of interviewing executive leaders when they have pulled out a stack of reports from prior assessments they have gone through in the past. Understanding how assessment contexts can mix and evolve over time will help an assessor to better understand how an assessment's results may need to be adjusted to fit the context in which they are being used. Assessors also need to be mindful of the ethical issues that can arise in reusing or repurposing assessment results for different situations (see Chapter 3 for further discussion of ethical issues).

CHARACTERISTICS OF THE ASSESSMENT SITUATION

The characteristics of the assessment situation shape how the process is designed and what information will be most relevant to gather. These factors include elements of the job itself, the team, the organization, the strategy, the economy, and the relevant regional cultures. Each of these elements is considered in this section in turn.

Job Requirements

Perhaps the most salient element of assessment context is the job itself. The requirements of the job role shape the criteria of the assessment and help determine which tools should be used to gather information about the assessee(s). *Work analysis* is the process by which an assessor builds an understanding of the knowledge, skills, abilities, and other traits (KSAOs) that would make an individual successful in a given job (Sackett et al., 2011). When conducting assessments for selection, job analyses are a legal requirement in many countries, including the United States, and can be considered relevant for about 5 to 8 years, as long as there is no information that the job has substantially changed (Landy et al., 2010). However, given the rapid pace of change in job requirements at the executive level, it is unlikely that a work analysis for a senior level position would stay relevant for up to 5 years, so an updated job description should likely accompany each new executive selection situation (Brannick et al., 2017).

At the executive level, work analysis is frequently accomplished by conducting structure interviews with board members and other senior leaders to build an understanding of what "success" in a role will look like (Stamoulis, 2009). These interviews allow the assessor to build an understanding across multiple stakeholder perceptions of the key responsibilities and characteristics of the job and what the executive will need to accomplish in the role. In many circumstances, interviewees will offer explicit traits or characteristics that they believe would describe the ideal candidate; however, it is the assessor's job, in conversation with the client, and while applying their professional expertise, to help prioritize job requirements and consult with the client on those lists of characteristics that are so long and internally inconsistent that no candidate is likely to meet all of them. For example, consider a position specification that describes the successful candidate as needing be a visionary leader who can rally the team by casting a compelling vision, while also needing to be a strong operator who can implement the processes needed to maintain efficiency as the organization scales up. The consultant may discuss with the client that those individuals who are process-oriented and skilled at driving efficiency are not always the best at casting a compelling vision for the future, and vice versa. In this way, the most important elements of the job description can be prioritized. Additionally, the team around this individual could be evaluated to determine whether some of these job duties might be delegated to a skilled "number two." That is, if the organization already has a highly effective COO, the operational capabilities may be accounted for on the team, and the visionary capabilities may be prioritized.

The result of a work analysis is usually a job description or position specification (see Table 4.1). This is the document that is used to determine the data that will need to be gathered to evaluate candidates for the job. Work analysis typically includes three types of data: (a) work activities, (b) worker attributes, and (c) work context (Sanchez & Levine, 2012). Whereas the information derived from traditional work analysis tends to be descriptive of the job requirements for a position at a given time, for senior level positions, the output tends to be more predictive about what a leader will need to do in the future to be successful (Sackett et al., 2011).

More recent conceptions of work analysis broaden the purpose of this work as "a systematic effort to identify or define current or anticipated work or worker requirements that are strategically aligned with an organization's mission and goals" (Pearlman & Sanchez, 2010, p. 90). This definition of *strategic work analysis* can also be applied to *senior leader work analysis*, as it captures not only the inherent forward-looking nature of work analysis at this level but also the need to consider the overall trajectory of the organization in considering what will make a candidate successful. To that end, executive level job descriptions usually include a mandate of some sort, or a statement about what a leader would be expected to accomplish in the role. Understanding the mandate of the job is helpful, as it allows the assessor to prioritize material gathered over the course of work analysis interviews and prioritize KSAOs accordingly.

Team Fit

Team fit is a key element of assessment context and refers to the compatibility between individual and team attributes (Hu & Judge, 2017). Those attributes may be similar, as in the case of *supplementary fit*, or they may differ, as in the case of *complementary fit* (van Vianen, 2018). Fit can be assessed in many ways, including in terms of personality, cognitive ability, problem-solving style, motives, values, and competencies (Chan, 2019). In practice, team fit is frequently assessed by comparing data on the personality or values of an individual to other individuals on the existing organizational team or to team averages (Barrick & Parks-Leduc, 2019). This can provide some sense of how similar or different an individual is to a group and can provide context for considering whether they will be a supplemental or complementary fit to that team.

New executives are frequently brought onboard to drive some type of change within the team or in the team's focus and direction. In that regard, supplemental fit may be desirable. That is, organizations may be looking for executives who do not fit in with the existing team characteristics in specific ways. For example, a team that has grown overly process oriented and systematic over time may need a leader who is more open to new ideas and ways of solving problems in order to help drive a change toward greater innovation.

Boards and selection committees may not always agree about the type of CEO the organization needs to hire (Harrell, 2016). In this circumstance, the consultant can help to bring the board to consensus by providing feedback on areas of divergence and encouraging the board members to compromise as needed. This work needs to be undertaken before starting a search or an assessment, and indeed is frequently done by executive search firms, who later bring in a consulting psychologist/assessor to conduct the necessary assessments. Increasingly, search firms may also use proprietary assessment measures and conduct this work themselves or in conjunction with their own internal assessment teams.

In addition to considering an individual's potential fit on the team, understanding the key team members they would be leading can be useful in organizing priorities in a job description. It is also important to know whether the new leader's job will involve training and developing the team or replacing individuals with new hires. These types of job requirements should be incorporated into the job description, and interviews should explore whether specific executive candidates have the experience and ability needed to build a team that can accomplish the needed goals of the organization.

Organizational Culture

As the old saying goes, *organizational culture* is "the way things are done around here." This is simple shorthand, but it does not provide much guidance in evaluating the ways in which an executive may fit with or change the culture of an organization. Edgar Schein provided a useful and dynamic definition of organizational culture as "the accumulated shared learning of a group as it solves its problems of external adaptation and internal integration" (Schein & Schein, 2017, p. 6). As group members learn how to work together to solve problems and achieve goals, they develop common beliefs, assumptions, norms, and values that shape how the individuals in that group relate to each other, and how they respond to threats, opportunities, and changes in their external environment (Cameron & Quinn, 2011). Some recruiting research suggests that up to 68% of senior leaders fail due to lack of culture fit (Groysberg et al., 2018). That said, it is hard to determine what exactly a statistic like this implies because sometimes, if not frequently, a board of directors wishes to hire a leader who explicitly does not fit the culture of the organization in order to drive cultural change. In fact, research on the fit between CEO leadership style and organizational culture suggests that dissimilarity between the two can actually improve firm performance (Hartnell et al., 2016). CEOs who bring differing cultural values to an organization may add to firm effectiveness by providing leadership that does not simply reinforce the social guidance already provided by the existing organizational culture.

Interestingly, there is not much research on how to evaluate "too much" versus "too little" fit in a practical, operational manner (Barrick & Parks-Leduc, 2019). Culture fit is evaluated by comparing the values of the candidate to the values of the individuals on the team they may join, and to the average perception of the values of the organization (van Vianen, 2018). Such values may include a preference for autonomy, independence, and a comfort with risk taking, or perhaps a preference for demonstrating capability and developing mastery in certain areas of expertise. In many circumstances, values are assessed through conversation and interviews, though this can also be accomplished using tools (e.g., the Motives, Values, and Preferences Inventory [Hogan & Hogan, 2010]; the Schwartz Value Survey [Schwartz, 1994, 2012]) that allow for the comparison between individual values and surveyed perceptions of organizational culture values. Cameron and Quinn (2011) provided a highly practical framework for how this can be done using the competing values framework. Models such as this allow assessors to evaluate culture fit by developing an understanding of what the organization is trying to accomplish and what type of cultural values tend to align with those goals and assessing executives accordingly.

Strategy

The strategy and lifecycle of the organization should be considered as an element of the assessment context. Different organizational imperatives, whether issued by the CEO or the board of directors, tend to favor different types of leaders and leadership styles (de Vries et al., 2010; Hartnell et al., 2016; Somech, 2006). Thus, developing an understanding of the organization's strategy will help inform the assessor as to what type of cultural values will best align with the strategic goals of the leadership position. For example, organizations that are developing and bringing new product to market will tend to require CEOs and senior leaders that demonstrate entrepreneurial leadership, a higher tolerance for risk and ambiguity, and more comfort in adapting to rapidly changing circumstances (Uhl-Bien & Arena, 2018). Organizations that are navigating external threats or have recently experienced a dramatic decline in business, on the other hand, will tend to require leadership that is decisive, action oriented, and focused on driving efficiency (Zaccaro et al., 2018). This is not to say that leaders will not adapt as their organizations evolve, and indeed, the ability to adapt to changing market conditions and to navigate external and internal threats is what makes successful senior leaders successful.

The phases of the organizational lifecycle are not necessarily mutually exclusive, and organizations will grow and adapt in different ways. Larry Greiner's classic 1972 *Harvard Business Review* article (republished in 1998), "Evolution and Revolution as Organizations Grow," provided a useful shorthand for understanding organizational growth and change. To summarize, the phases are:

1. *Creativity*: The startup/entrepreneurial phase is characterized by flexibility, informality, and discretion. Effectiveness is driven by innovation and marketplace feedback, and the strategic imperative is making and selling a new product or service. Think of a startup that is developing a product where the team is small and nimble and works closely with early customers to learn how their product can deliver the most value to the client.
2. *Direction*: Once a company or product achieves some level of product–market fit, the strategic imperative shifts toward growth and the need to compete. Competitiveness, customer orientation, and profitability become the focus, and specialization and incentive compensation drive growth. Once that startup finds a strong fit between their product and the clients they are trying to serve, they will begin growing the sales and marketing team in order to generate more market interest and revenue.
3. *Delegation*: If an organization succeeds in scaling up, it tends to become more diverse and complex. Added size and complexity often creates a shift toward decentralization. The strategic imperative will encourage autonomy and authority in responding to local market and customer issues. As the hiring continues at our example company, the headcount grows and eventually becomes too large for the CEO or founders to manage directly, so they begin to delegate roles to create more managerial freedom.
4. *Coordination*: Continued growth then leads to a "crisis of control" (Greiner, 1998, p. 10) in which decentralization makes coordinated action and cost containment challenging. So, the strategic imperative shifts to one of driving efficiency and controlling cost to maximize productivity at scale. This growth and addition of layers at the company makes it harder for senior management to have visibility and control over what is occurring within the company, so they may begin to install processes, procedures, and systems to professionalize operations.

5. *Collaboration*: The addition of process and procedures tends to become burdensome over time and begins to hinder growth and employee engagement. To boost employee engagement and reinvigorate productivity, the strategic imperative shifts to an emphasis on teamwork. Ad hoc teaming and collaboration across a matrix organization become the keys to adapting to market challenges. The centralization driven by the crisis of control at the company eventually makes the company feel like a well-oiled but impersonal machine. So management aims to create more flexibility and shifts into a matrix-type structure where teams have more autonomy to accomplish tasks together, and where individual employees are given opportunities to grow and develop.

Other relevant phases are *turnaround* and *integration* after a merger or acquisition. A turnaround occurs when an organization is failing or has become stagnant, and in many cases new leadership is brought in to drive change and reenergize the workforce. The strategic imperative tends to shift toward consolidation and realignment of the workforce toward a common goal/vision. Merger or acquisition integration may occur at any point in the lifecycle and may catalyze an organization moving into a different stage. The key strategic imperative in an integration is achieving the value of the merger (Rabier, 2017), whether that takes the form of, for example, capturing operational synergies, cutting costs, or expanding and moving into new markets.

Assessors should consider the stages of organizational growth and evolution in which they are consulting and how the related demands may shape the needs of the role. In large complex organizations, multiple lifecycle phases may be occurring on a smaller scale across functions or departments. Assessors should evaluate whether different phases may be occurring simultaneously, and how the competing demands of the function and the organization inform what is needed in the job role.

Economic Conditions

Economic and market conditions play a role in assessment contexts in two ways. First, economic conditions impact organizational growth, which may impact the requirements for CEO and senior leader job roles. For example, if the board of a company is expecting a cyclical slowdown in their business, as they are considering bringing in a new CEO, they may look for a different type of leader than if the same work is being conducted while expecting rapid growth. Second, economic conditions impact the achievements that executives bring into the assessment process. An executive's accomplishments in a given role should be weighed against the economic growth or contraction they may have experienced while in that role. In addition, economic conditions serve as a context for understanding an executive's competencies. The assessor will benefit from having at least a basic understanding of market cycles and general time periods when the economy was expanding or contracting. In some circumstances, an executive's experience in growing a business may seem compelling but may simply be a result of being in a growing industry at the right time. For example, in one assessment, the head of a major business unit touted their ability to drive results by pointing to the growth the group had experienced during their tenure. However, when that growth was compared to growth in the industry during the same time period, it became apparent that the unit had lagged behind competitors, suggesting market share had in fact been lost during an expansion.

Regional Culture

In a hyperconnected global economy, regional culture is just as important a consideration in executive assessment as other elements of context. An assessor may need to evaluate an individual's ability to lead in another culture, or to lead a multicultural workforce that may be based in a number of countries. Though not every leadership position will be characterized by a need for cross-cultural competence, elements of culture are always at play in assessments.

Assessors will benefit from a heightened sense of cultural awareness, both in their own way of doing things, and how that may differ from the conventions of those whom they are assessing. *Cultural relativity* means avoiding being judgmental or viewing any cultural difference as inherently better or worse (Glover & Friedman, 2015). An assessor's ability to incorporate this way of thinking into their practice will be more attuned to interpreting the types of behavior characterizing job-relevant individual differences versus those that are more indicative of cultural differences. For readers interested in a deeper consideration of these important issues, the book *Transcultural Competence: Navigating Cultural Differences in the Global Community* is a good resource (Glover & Friedman, 2015).

Diversity, Equity, and Inclusion

Additionally, assessors must consider the historical context and biases that exist around race/ethnicity, sex, gender identity, and sexual orientation, which will vary by culture. As humans, our general bias toward similarity is at issue in an interview context. This occurs when an assessor consciously or subconsciously "evaluates another person, perceived to be similar to him/herself, in a more favorable light than a less similar person" (de Kock & Hauptfleisch, 2018). Assessors must be cognizant of these tendencies, build an awareness of and examine their own biases, and employ assessment methods that have been shown to reduce their effects (e.g., highly structured interviewing [de Kock & Hauptfleisch, 2018], which is discussed in more detail in Chapter 4, this volume). Although demographic factors should not be incorporated into the assessment in a discriminatory way, the social, political, and historical context that shapes the life and work experience of people of different backgrounds and identities must be a part of the assessor's framework for understanding the assessment context.

The Specific Case of the CEO

At the CEO level, the board members' perspectives on the future of the organization usually constitute multiple elements of the assessment context, which is critical for building an understanding of the specifications for the top job. How the board perceives current firm performance, where the organization is functioning well and where the organization is not functioning well, and their perspectives on economic conditions, as well as the traits and behaviors they expect in the new CEO, all help shape the criteria for the incoming chief executive. In these conversations, it is helpful for the assessor to have an understanding of the general market conditions as well as the specific industry conditions, which can help contextualize board members' perspectives and can also help the assessor in determining the lifecycle of the business.

It would be naive to think that board members share the same perspectives on everything, and indeed, board members are frequently selected to bring a diversity of perspectives and opinions to the board on complex matters. Disagreements are typically highlighted in the work analysis process when the assessor is conducting interviews with relevant board members (i.e., the selection committee). After completing interviews and assimilating information into a position specification, the consultant can report back to the board those areas in which members expressed agreement, and those areas in which there was disagreement. Not only can this be useful information to the board on where their perspectives are more or less aligned, but it also creates an opportunity for the assessor to ask questions and clarify issues that may impact the design of the position specification or the prioritization of elements therein.

KEY TAKEAWAYS

- *Context* describes the circumstances that surround the assessment and can involve factors at multiple levels, such as the requirements of the job, the composition of the team, the distinct elements of the organizational culture, the life cycle of the organizational strategy, the prevailing industry and economic conditions, and relevant aspects of regional culture.
- Take time to fully understand the purpose of the assessment with the client. Whether it is for selection, development, or succession, keep in mind that clients may want to repurpose assessment results (e.g., using selection assessment results for onboarding), and describe the limits and conditions of doing so up front with the client and the assessee.

- Prioritize job requirements with input from the client organization to ensure that the most salient elements of the job can be highlighted and evaluated in the assessment process.
- Don't rely on an overly simplistic or singular description of an organization's culture—get multiple perspectives when you can and use data-driven methods for assessing team and organizational culture when possible.
- Develop an understanding and awareness of issues related to diversity, equity, and inclusion, and work to make your practice as an assessor more equitable and inclusive.

3

Ethical and Legal Considerations in Executive Assessment

A psychologist was hired by a private equity (PE) firm to conduct finalist assessments for the CEO position of a recently acquired company. A full search had been conducted, but the final two candidates were the sitting chief operating officer (COO) of the business and an external candidate, both of whom were being assessed. The psychologist conducted assessments and compiled results into a report to be presented to the private equity partners. Prior to that feedback meeting, the psychologist met with the PE firm's talent director, who managed recruiting, assessment, and development engagements, to discuss the results and prep for feedback to the partners. The psychologist shared that both candidates appeared to be skilled and capable leaders, but that the COO demonstrated a stronger capability and propensity for building the team, and would likely make a stronger CEO, given the criteria for the job. The

https://doi.org/10.1037/0000264-004
Assessing CEOs and Senior Leaders: A Primer for Consultants, by J. R. Blankenship

psychologist's report clearly showed the COO as the frontrunner for the position, based on evidence gathered during the assessment.

However, the talent director disagreed, saying the external candidate had led another company in the portfolio and grown it considerably, and successfully sold it. The talent director was sure bringing in external talent would be better for the company ultimately. After some conversation, and the consultant holding firm in the recommendation, the talent director proposed that the consultant could "soften the report" to make the candidates appear more equal so that the partners of the firm could make their decision by considering the underlying data themselves.

How should the psychologist have responded?

The purpose of this chapter is to identify and discuss some of the central ethical and legal issues that occur in the context of executive assessments, like the case just mentioned, in order to help assessors better recognize and navigate these situations. Several areas of ethical concern are first identified, then a number of legal issues that may arise in the assessment process are discussed. There are many great resources that discuss ethical issues in the practice of consulting psychology and organizational consultation more generally (e.g., Lefkowitz & Lowman, 2017; Lowman, 2006, 2018; Lowman & Cooper, 2018; Newman et al., 2002).

Because these types of ethical issues are relatively common and predictable in this practice area, it is even more important for individuals who conduct executive assessments to have a clear understanding of the elements that define the scope of ethical practice. One way of parsing ethical issues that arise in organizations is to consider the level of consultation, that is, whether the consultant is primarily working at the individual, team, or organizational level (Lowman & Cooper, 2018), although ethical issues that arise frequently overlap multiple levels of consultation. For example, in the case above, the psychologist may have expressed concern that editing the report may constitute an intentional misrepresentation of fact (American Psychological Association [APA], 2017a, Principle C: Integrity), or that it may lead to a misuse of their influence (APA, 2017a, Principle A: Beneficence and Nonmaleficence). The case raises the question of who exactly the client in this situation is (an issue discussed in more detail later in this chapter), among other considerations.

Although licensed psychologists who are APA members, and many who are not members (depending upon state licensing regulation), must comply with the APA *Ethical Principles of Psychologists and Code of Conduct* (APA, 2017a; hereinafter referred to as the Ethics Code), nonpsychologists who may conduct senior executive assessments (e.g., management consultants, former attorneys, former managers/organizational leaders, human resources [HR], and talent managers) do not have such a requirement. However, as an example, practicing attorneys in the United States may be governed by a code of ethics that informs the ethical practice of law under their state bar association or a professional association such as the American Bar Association (ABA; 2020). Although the ABA's *Model Rules of Professional Conduct* certainly speaks to relevant issues such as competence, confidentiality, and conflicts of interest in the practice of law, it does not directly address the specific types of issues that frequently occur in executive assessment and selection (ABA, 2020). That said, ethical dilemmas do occur and must be managed. The more informed and prepared any type of professional is to navigate such issues, the better off they and their clients will be. Accordingly, anyone who is conducting assessments should have an understanding of the nature of ethical issues that are present in this type of work so they recognize them when they occur, can evaluate the potential for harm, and manage through them. The APA Ethics Code is a robust resource for this purpose, even for nonpsychologist assessors.

AREAS OF ETHICAL CONCERN

Ethical dilemmas can take many forms and often represent multiple ethical content areas. Following Lowman and Cooper (2018), I consider the content areas for the majority of ethical concerns a consultant is likely to encounter in this type of work, including:

- who the client is
- informed consent
- confidentiality
- multiple relationships and conflicts of interest

- competence
- evidence-based practice
- multicultural issues

Who Is the Client?

Issues around understanding the client in organizational consulting stem from the fact that there are almost always multiple interested parties in an assessment conducted within an organization. There are the individuals with whom the consultant deals directly, such as the hiring manager who brings in the consultant to conduct the assessment and the assessees themselves. However, the person who hires the consultant is not always the main audience for the assessment debrief. For example, a consultant may be hired by the head of HR, but the main audience for a debrief may be the CEO or the board of directors, depending on who is making the relevant decisions with the assessment data.

In one situation, a consultant was hired by a professional services firm to conduct developmental assessments for senior leaders who were en route to being considered for partner. The managing partner hired the consultant, and they worked together to shape the nature of the engagement, which included an in-depth assessment designed to highlight the leadership potential of each participant, as well as the development of an individualized development plan that each participant could put into action in the months following the assessment. The consultant conducted the assessments, delivered feedback to the managing partner as well as to each individual participant, and worked with each participant to assemble a development plan. Six months after the engagement had concluded, the consultant received an email from one of the participants who, in the interim, had been promoted to partner. The managing partner had asked the new partner to take ownership of the development process for high potential leaders who were being considered for partner. As such, the new partner requested that the consultant share the assessment results and development plans of the other leaders, and that they schedule a phone call to discuss.

This case illustrates the fact that defining the client is not always straightforward, and in fact, there may be many clients with whom a consultant is working, and they may shift over time (Lowman & Cooper, 2018). If the consultant considers the system in which they are operating, and the impact that assessment results and hiring/promotion decisions can have on teams, organizations, and the systems in which they operate, they could feasibly consider the client to be: (a) the team on which the individual(s) being assessed will work if hired; (b) the organization itself; (c) the organization's clients, investors, and suppliers; and (d) the community in which the organization operates. Interestingly, the APA Ethics Code does not directly define the term client, and the definition of the client can differ depending on who is asking the question and what issue is being addressed. Fuqua et al. (2012) identified 11 questions that can assist the assessor in considering the complex nature of determining who the client is and the ethical responsibilities that the assessor may have to various stakeholders:

1. Who is paying for the assessments?
2. What roles do the contracting parties play in the organization?
3. What formal and informal authority do the contracting parties hold?
4. How are the contracting parties related to the assessees?
5. What procedures will be used to ensure that informed consent is established with all those who are being assessed?
6. What consequences exist or may come to exist for parties who decline to be assessed?
7. What are the exceptions to the confidentiality of information produced by the assessment, and how are they communicated in advance?
8. What classes of people may be directly or indirectly affected by the assessment who will not be participating in the consultation process?
9. Will the roles and/or structures of the organization create the perception of coercion for any class of participants and, of course, how do we confront the perceived coercion?
10. What kinds of information are required to meet the terms of the contract and who will be expected to provide the information?
11. What roles will the assessor(s) play in managing information resulting from the assessment? (p. 116)

Taking the aforementioned case as an example, the client could reasonably have been interpreted as the managing partner who initiated the project and contracted with the consultant, the professional services firm itself that paid the fees for the assessments, the assessees who participated in the assessments and received feedback on assessment results and guidance on their professional growth, and indeed the new partner who had been placed in charge of the development of senior leaders in the firm. In this case, rather than simply turning over the assessment data to the new partner, the consultant advised the partner that because the initial engagement had not included consent to share results with others besides the managing partner, that a better course of action may be to work internally with the assessees to gather assessment results and set up development meetings directly. Though the partner was miffed initially, it was ultimately agreed that gaining the other leaders' buy-in by working directly with them would lead to better results in the long run.

Informed Consent

Informed consent refers to an individuals' ability to voluntarily decide to participate in an assessment with an understanding of the parameters, risks, and benefits of participation (Newman et al., 2002). Informed consent is usually obtained at the outset of a consulting engagement, and if this process is conducted properly and thoroughly, can lay the groundwork for fewer ethical issues to arise, and a clear way to manage them when they do. Standard 9.03 of the Ethics Code, Informed Consent in Assessment, provides guidance on informed consent, particularly Section (a), which states,

> Psychologists obtain informed consent for assessments, evaluations, or diagnostic services, as described in Standard 3.10, Informed Consent, except when (1) testing is mandated by law or governmental regulations; (2) informed consent is implied because testing is conducted as a routine educational, institutional, or organizational activity (e.g., when participants voluntarily agree to assessment when applying for a job); or (3) one purpose of the testing is to evaluate decisional

> capacity. Informed consent includes an explanation of the nature and purpose of the assessment, fees, involvement of third parties, and limits of confidentiality and sufficient opportunity for the client/patient to ask questions and receive answers. (APA, 2017a, p. 13)

The most common issues around informed consent in executive assessment involve ensuring that the client and assessment participants understand and agree to the type of information being collected, who will have access to that information, and what will be done with that information after it has been used for its intended purpose. In this case, such information can include psychometric test results, interview notes, 360° feedback, and performance data.

Informed consent may take the form of a conversation that is conducted at the start of an engagement, though in executive assessments an informed consent document is frequently signed by assessment participants that explains the assessment process, the data to be collected, and what will be done with the data afterward. Informed consent can also play a more dynamic role in certain assessment contexts. Consider a case in which a candidate was recruited by an executive search firm to be considered for the CEO position at a medical device company. The candidate made it to the finalist stage and was asked to participate in an assessment process, which included online psychometric tests, a half-day structured behavioral interview, and interviews with references. Prior to beginning the assessment engagement, the candidate signed a consent form that described the type of data that would be collected, how the data will be handled by the search firm, and who would have access to that data. The candidate completed the assessment but was not selected for the CEO position; 18 months later, however, a similar position opened for a different medical device company. When the client organization asked that assessments be conducted on all finalists, the search firm returned to the candidate and provided the option of participating in the assessment process again or agreeing to let prior assessment data be used to compose a report for the position at hand. Uninterested in participating in a half day interview for a second time, the candidate declined and said the firm could just send the old report with an updated title for the new company.

The search firm told the client that the assessment had been conducted in another search process for a similar type of company but did not mention that the assessment results had aged 18 months.

This case highlights a number of ethical issues that may arise in the assessment process besides informed consent, including test results that may become outdated over the course of long-term consulting relationships (see Standard 9.08 of the Ethics Code, Obsolete Tests and Outdated Test Results), and how informed consent may need to be revisited as the circumstances around an assessment change, and whether assessment results gathered in one situation can reasonably be used to make valid inferences in other situations (see the Evidence-Based Practice section later in this chapter). This type of experience, if not this exact experience, is commonly encountered when managing issues related to who can access assessment results and reports. Assessors should be mindful that executive assessments usually occur within hierarchical systems with power dynamics that may shape or alter exactly how "voluntary" participation is. In many circumstances, participation in assessment is required by an individual to be considered for a given job, or as a part of an organizational activity or program instituted by senior leaders or directors. The job candidate still has the option to decline, the consequence of which would be being removed from consideration for the position. Of course, that is a different circumstance from an employee being asked to participate in a developmental assessment by their employer.

For example, imagine a consultant who is coaching a CEO using methods the CEO finds helpful and invigorating. The CEO asks if the consultant would coach the CEO's team at an upcoming team building meeting. The consultant has experience with coaching teams and is looking forward to the prospect of taking on this additional role with this company. Having made the decision, the CEO emails the team introducing the consultant and lets the team know that as a part of the work at the upcoming meeting, each team member will need to complete a number of online personality assessments and will have a feedback call with the consultant prior to the meeting. The CEO closes the email saying that the consultant will contact each employee to follow up.

The consultant emails each team member a brief personal introduction, a description of the online questionnaires they will be taking, and a consent form for them to sign and return prior to receiving the links to the online assessments. The consultant receives a response from one individual on the team who states that they do not want to be "psychoanalyzed" by the consultant and thinks such exercises are a waste of time, but asks the consultant to go ahead and send the links so the process can be completed, if it is required; however, this individual does not return a signed consent form. The consultant replies, reminding the team member that the links cannot be sent until the signed consent form is received. The consultant also asks if the team member has discussed these concerns with the CEO and inquires whether the team member would be comfortable with the consultant having a conversation with the CEO about the issue as well.

Informed consent, as described in this example, is more complicated in this type of development context than it typically is in a selection context, because the implication of not consenting in a development context is less clear. Opting out of a developmental assessment in such a circumstance could lead to missed opportunities for advancement or even termination. In the preceding case, the consultant did (with consent) have a conversation with the CEO about the team member's discomfort. The CEO was genuinely surprised and dismayed, since the CEO's intention had been to leverage the assessment process to develop more awareness of individual differences on the team and improve working relationships. To that end, the consultant suggested that the CEO speak to the team to provide more context for the decision to request assessments and let them know that the assessments would only be used for developmental purposes. It was also suggested that the CEO include the consultant on a follow-up message to the team, so that the consultant could make a personal introduction, describe the background and purpose of this type of assessment work, and help make the process feel more participatory than the original email from the CEO had made it seem. After some conversation, and assurance that each participant would be given a full debrief of any assessment results, and that the purpose of the assessment was genuinely designed for the team's development and growth, the reluctant participant decided to go forward with the assessment.

Confidentiality

In general *confidentiality* refers to the obligation that psychologists have to take reasonable measures to protect confidential information, to discuss the limits of the confidentiality with their clients, and to obtain consent from clients before disclosing confidential information (APA, 2017a). Confidentiality can be a complicated issue in executive assessments because there are usually more than a few people with legitimate access to assessment data. To the extent that it is possible, issues that may arise around confidentiality can best be mitigated up front in the contracting phase of the assessment. That is when the consultant has a clear opportunity and responsibility to communicate with all participants regarding what type of data will be collected, and who will receive what forms of the data. Information about the limits of confidentiality should be included in that communication, and informed consent should be secured from each participant in the evaluation process, including the nature of the data to be collected and the identities of those with whom it will be shared (see Standard 4.01, Maintaining Confidentiality, and Standard 4.02, Discussing the Limits of Confidentiality).

Standard 3.11 of the Ethics Code, Psychological Services Delivered to or Through Organizations, provides additional guidance on how consultants should engage with organizations:

> Psychologists delivering services to or through organizations provide information beforehand to clients and when appropriate those directly affected by the services about (1) the nature and objectives of the services, (2) the intended recipients, (3) which of the individuals are clients, (4) the relationship the psychologist will have with each person and the organization, (5) the probable uses of services provided and information obtained, (6) who will have access to the information, and (7) limits of confidentiality. As soon as feasible, they provide information about the results and conclusions of such services to appropriate persons. (APA, 2017a, p. 7)

In the case of assessment results in particular, external finalist candidates may not receive the results of an assessment if they are not selected for the job, depending on whether the client has agreed to provide unselected candidates feedback, and these details should be clearly stated at the outset of the assessment in the engagement letter with the organizational client, in the informed consent obtained from the assessee, as well as in the description of the assessment process. The consultant should also explain and describe the form the results of the assessment will take to the organizational client. Communicating these details in writing to the client about the form the assessment results will take (e.g., written report, scores, verbal feedback, or some combination) and the type of data to which the organizational client will have access not only helps to manage expectations but also allows the assessor to clearly delineate the bounds of confidentiality.

Similarly, if the assessee will receive feedback on the assessment results, the form that feedback will take should be communicated prior to the assessment. If assessment results will be stored by the consulting company for future reference or for research purposes, that should also be communicated to the assessee up front. In one circumstance, an executive was so concerned about taking an online values survey and the possibility of a data breach exposing the results, that it was agreed the survey could be taken under a pseudonym. This kind of reaction is relatively rare; however, such concerns should be considered and managed. Standard 6.02 of the Ethics Code, Maintenance, Dissemination, and Disposal of Confidential Records of Professional and Scientific Work states, "Psychologists maintain confidentiality in creating, storing, accessing, transferring, and disposing of records under their control, whether these are written, automated, or in any other medium" (APA, 2017a, p. 9). In the context of organizational consulting, the question of who "owns" the assessment results is relevant. A rule of thumb that is generally applied in consulting is that whoever paid for the assessment owns the data, but that does not diminish the need to communicate up front the details of services to be provided as per Standard 3.11. Additionally, in some circumstances, assessors may gather data over time to conduct research or teach. Standards 8.02,

Informed Consent to Research, and 4.07, Use of Confidential Information for Didactic or Other Purposes, should be consulted regarding the use of assessment data for research or teaching purposes, though in general it is the responsibility of the psychologist not to disclose personally identifiable information unless written consent has been provided.

Issues of confidentiality are also quite salient in the context of 360° feedback. Research shows that raters (i.e., those providing 360° feedback to the assessor) are most forthright in their feedback if it is anonymous, and when the feedback is explicitly being used for development, rather than for selection or other administrative decisions (Gregory & Levy, 2015). The best 360° survey publishers have rules that require more than three raters to submit feedback before scores for a certain rater group (e.g., direct reports, peers) will be reported to the individual. At the senior executive level, the number of possible raters decreases due to the nature of high-level positions, which tend to have fewer direct reports, and direct reports may thus be more concerned about the possibility of the CEO identifying comments they have made.

When there are too few individuals to make up rater groups wherein confidentiality can be maintained, interviews may be used instead, in order to collect 360° feedback. The work is far more time-consuming than using online surveys but offers detailed insight into the perspectives of those working with a given individual. When gathering 360° feedback via interviews it is essential to inform the raters up front that their individual comments will be kept confidential, and that rater comments will only be reported back to the executive as themes observed across several raters. This can be a helpful way to build trust and get raters to open up and provide useful information.

The issue of confidentiality can become quite complex in these interviews, especially if illegal or material nonpublic information (i.e., news or information that may affect a company's stock price but has not yet been publicly reported) is disclosed to the assessor. At the senior executive level in public companies, assessors will likely have knowledge of pending management decisions that may constitute material nonpublic information. Not keeping such information confidential (e.g., trading on such information in the stock market, or sharing information with others who trade on it) can have serious legal consequences (e.g., insider trading charges). In such situations, confidentiality and professionalism in the client interaction is not just good business; breaches of confidentiality carry significant legal liability.

Multiple Relationships and Conflicts of Interest

The issue of *multiple relationships*, sometimes called dual relationships, comes up when a consultant is operating in more than one professional capacity with a client or is in potentially conflicting relationships with more than one client. Multiple relationships in organizational consulting are not just common, but are the norm because consultants will tend to be working with those in leadership positions and their team members (Lowman & Cooper, 2018). A developmental assessment is a good example where an individual in a leadership position (e.g., the CEO) may hire a consultant to perform assessments on individuals on the executive team. Standard 3.05, Multiple Relationships, Section (a) states,

> A multiple relationship occurs when a psychologist is in a professional role with a person and (1) at the same time is in another role with the same person, (2) at the same time is in a relationship with a person closely associated with or related to the person with whom the psychologist has the professional relationship, or (3) promises to enter into another relationship in the future with the person or a person closely associated with or related to the person.
>
> A psychologist refrains from entering into a multiple relationship if the multiple relationship could reasonably be expected to impair the psychologist's objectivity, competence, or effectiveness in performing his or her functions as a psychologist, or otherwise risks exploitation or harm to the person with whom the professional relationship exists.
>
> Multiple relationships that would not reasonably be expected to cause impairment or risk exploitation or harm are not unethical. (APA, 2017a, p. 6)

Multiple relationships can shift or diminish a consultant's professional judgment and/or competence and can potentially lead to manipulation or exploitation of the client. In one circumstance, an assessee's flight was delayed en route to an assessment for a CEO position. The delay pushed the assessment to late in the afternoon, ending around 7 p.m. The assessee felt bad for the massive adjustment to the assessor's schedule and offered to buy dinner as a thank-you. The interview had been quite engaging, and the assessor thought it might be interesting to continue the conversation. As the evening wore on, it became clear that the relationship had moved beyond a simple work engagement. When it came time to deliver the feedback to the client, the consultant brought in a colleague to assist and make sure that the feedback was as objective as possible.

This case is a dramatic example of a multiple relationship situation, but the ethical issue itself is almost always present in executive assessment work because the assessor's work will entail obligations to the client (e.g., the board, the CEO), the assessees themselves, and other interested parties (e.g., the chief human resources officer [CHRO], the talent director). Each of these stakeholders in the assessment may have their own agenda, from which may arise conflicts of interests.

Conflicts of interest are addressed in Standard 3.06, Conflict of Interest, in the Ethics Code, which states,

> Psychologists refrain from taking on a professional role when personal, scientific, professional, legal, financial, or other interests or relationships could reasonably be expected to (1) impair their objectivity, competence, or effectiveness in performing their functions as psychologists or (2) expose the person or organization with whom the professional relationship exists to harm or exploitation. (APA, 2017a, p. 6)

In most circumstances, assessors will be able to maintain objectivity, competence, and effectiveness in the conduct of their work, and the stakeholders within the client organization are usually relatively aligned on the goal of the assessment. When assessors move into additional roles with organizational clients (e.g., coaching), however, conflicts of interest can become more problematic. Assessing a former coachee on behalf of the board for succession planning purposes, for example, may limit an assessor's objectivity and may be cause not to take on a given assignment.

For example, a consultant who had been hired to conduct succession assessments for a company in their hometown. The consultant successfully assessed six executives, worked with the executives to create development plans, and then participated in a series of feedback conversations, first with the assessees themselves, and then with each assessee and the CEO to review and commit to the development plan. The CEO was impressed with the work and asked the consultant to stay on as a coach for two of the assessees. The consultant agreed based on past experience and training in coaching, and because this type of engagement had become relatively common practice. At the end of the 3-month coaching engagement, the CEO called the consultant and asked that the engagement be extended further, and that development assessments be conducted at the next level down in the organization. The consultant was thrilled by the prospect of an expanded engagement and ongoing work, but recognized the name of a family friend on the list of assessees. Concerned that the prior relationship may impact an objective assessment, the consultant proposed to the CEO that another assessor be brought in to conduct the next level of assessments but that the consultant would stay on and advise, to which the CEO agreed.

Competence

Standard 2.01, Boundaries of Competence, Section (a), speaks directly to the issue of competence in the practice of assessment:

> Psychologists provide services, teach, and conduct research with populations and in areas only within the boundaries of their competence, based on their education, training, supervised experience, consultation, study, or professional experience. (APA, 2017a, p. 5)

The issue of competence is salient in the practice of assessment precisely because assessment can be conducted at multiple levels in various ways. Executive assessment itself is considered a specialized competency within the domain of assessment. As such, it is critical that consultants be realistic in their judgments about their capability to conduct executive assessments based on their training and experience. For those who trained in health services roles (e.g., clinical or counseling psychology) and are now transitioning into work-related assessment roles, the transition may require some retraining and supervised experience. This may include training and certification in a new set of assessment measures, developing a deeper understanding of how businesses are structured and how they operate, and the specific dynamics at play within such organizations. It may also be beneficial to gain supervised experience to learn on the job the differences in interview techniques and legal boundaries that may differ from a clinical setting.

Limitations of competence in executive assessments can reveal themselves in a number of ways. For example, in my own consulting for a private equity group, I had conducted a number of assessments for executives within portfolio companies. Because of that work and my relationship with the firm, I was asked to conduct an assessment for a finalist candidate for an operating partner position within the firm. Operating partners at this firm functioned as internal consultants and were deployed to portfolio companies to help solve problems specific to their area of expertise. I had conducted several operating partner assessments in the past, but this particular assessment was for an individual with deep expertise in health care technology. The firm was interested not only in better understanding the candidate's leadership capability, but also their knowledge and capability in the health care technology industry in particular. Recognizing that I was at the limit of my knowledge and experience in this area, I was fortunate to be able to partner with a colleague with deep experience in health care technology, and we conducted the assessment together.

Issues of competence can also emerge due to the nature of the business of organizational consulting. Because clients are accustomed to consulting groups frequently offering a host of services, they may expect an individual consultant to be able to deliver all such services with equal competence. Additionally, a common refrain in consulting strategy is "land and expand," or sell an initial consulting engagement and then sell more consulting services once you are working with the client. Because of this strategy, consultants may find themselves at the limit of their competence over the course of a working relationship with a client. For example, a consultant with deep expertise in executive coaching may have the opportunity to offer assessment for selection services to an existing client because of the existing working relationship, but may have far less knowledge and experience in doing assessment for selection at the executive level.

Executive assessment work can pair naturally with closely related organizational consulting domains such as individual coaching and development, team effectiveness consulting, and even team and organization design (Lowman, 2016). Furthermore, when executive assessments are conducted well and provide value for a client, a level of trust is established, and clients will often return to the same consultant for insight and guidance (Wasylyshyn, 2019). It is the consultant's responsibility to know the limits of their ability and pursue appropriate training and experience.

Another critical element of competence concerns the unfair treatment or discrimination of assessees. The Ethics Code addresses this in a broad way in Standard 3.01, Unfair Discrimination:

> In their work-related activities, psychologists do not engage in unfair discrimination based on age, gender, gender identity, race, ethnicity, culture, national origin, religion, sexual orientation, disability, socioeconomic status, or any basis proscribed by law. (APA, 2017a, p. 6)

It is a basic requirement of competent, ethical practice that a psychologist not engage in intentional discriminatory behavior in their assessment work, and they should work to ensure that their assessment methods minimize the potential for adverse impact and differential treatment of protected groups (as defined by the U.S. Equal Employment Opportunity Commission). The deeper challenge for the competent assessor, however, is developing an awareness of one's own implicit biases—the attitudes, stereotypes, and prejudices that one possesses without intention or conscious awareness (Jost et al., 2009, p. 43)—and cultivating an assessment practice that mitigates their impact.

Evidence-Based Practice

The issue of *evidence-based practice* refers to the need for consultants who are conducting executive assessment to use methods that have been shown to make valid and reliable inferences at the executive level. Relevant standards from the APA Ethics Code include Standard 9.01, Bases for Assessment:

> (a) Psychologists base the opinions contained in their recommendations, reports, and diagnostic or evaluative statements, including forensic testimony, on information and techniques sufficient to substantiate their findings. (APA, 2017a, p. 12)

Standard 9.02, Use of Assessments, is also relevant:

> (a) Psychologists administer, adapt, score, interpret, or use assessment techniques, interviews, tests, or instruments in a manner and for purposes that are appropriate in light of the research on or evidence of the usefulness and proper application of the techniques.
>
> (b) Psychologists use assessment instruments whose validity and reliability have been established for use with members of the population tested. When such validity or reliability has not been established, psychologists describe the strengths and limitations of test results and interpretation.
>
> (c) Psychologists use assessment methods that are appropriate to an individual's language preference and competence, unless the use of an alternative language is relevant to the assessment issues. (APA, 2017a, p. 13)

The issue of evidence-based practice relies heavily on an understanding of the validity and reliability of the measures used in executive assessment. A particular challenge in this area is the gap the frequently exists between the science and evidence-based study of individual and executive assessment, and its practice in applied settings (Lowman, 2012). Assessments continue to become more prevalent and easier to access online, and the commoditization of such measures is not always matched by the same advances in evidence and scientific support (Winsborough & Chamorro-Premuzic, 2013). Accordingly, assessors may wind up using methods that have dated validity evidence or evidence gathered under dramatically different economic and social circumstances, which may alter norms or other underlying principles of the assessment. Evaluating the evidence base of their practice on an ongoing basis is thus a key issue for assessing consultants.

For example, consider a psychologist who transitioned from working primarily as a clinician into working primarily as an executive assessor for organizations. The psychologist had a deep base of knowledge and experience in individual assessment and the interpretation of assessment results, and so, not wanting to diminish the insight they could provide their clients, continued using the same assessment tools that had informed their clinical practice. This can be problematic because assessment tools that are designed to be used in a clinical setting have norms that are calculated for clinical populations. Applying those same standards to an executive population may skew scores or lead to an inaccurate interpretation of testing results.

EMERGING ETHICAL ISSUES

Although the ethical considerations that exist within technology and web-based assessments and multicultural and international practice are not new per se, they are certainly evolving and growing in importance as the world becomes more interconnected. Assessors will benefit from building their awareness around these issues and maintaining an ongoing interest in how they develop over time.

Technology and Web-Based Assessment

The world of assessment is currently suffused with technology (see Chapter 5), which carries with it is own ethical and legal issues. Use of internet-based tools, video conferencing, and even internet research all fall under the purview of *telepsychology* (Lowman & Cooper, 2018). The APA (2013) *Guidelines for the Practice of Telepsychology* define *telepractice* as follows:

> Telepsychology is defined, for the purpose of these guidelines, as the provision of psychological services using telecommunication

> technologies. Telecommunications is the preparation, transmission, communication, or related processing of information by electrical, electromagnetic, electromechanical, electro-optical, or electronic means (Committee on National Security Systems, 2010). Telecommunication technologies include but are not limited to telephone, mobile devices, interactive videoconferencing, email, chat, text, and Internet (e.g., self-help websites, blogs, and social media). The information that is transmitted may be in writing, or include images, sounds or other data. These communications may be synchronous with multiple parties communicating in real time (e.g., interactive videoconferencing, telephone) or asynchronous (e.g., email, online bulletin boards, storing and forwarding information). (Definition of Telepsychology section)

Suffice it to say, telepractice is found in almost every part of a modern-day assessment engagement—with good reason, as the use of technology in assessments increases the speed, reach, and convenience of assessment. Telepractice is also a necessity in certain circumstances, for example, restrictions on in-person meetings during the COVID-19 pandemic. It also raises a number of ethical issues around competence, informed consent, data security, and confidentiality (APA, 2013). Many of the standards in the APA (2013) *Guidelines for the Practice of Telepsychology* resemble standards in the Ethics Code but highlight specific issues that telepsychology enables or brings to the foreground. For example, the increased reach enabled by technology allows consultants to conduct assessments across distances and geographic borders with relative ease, but this ease does not diminish the need for maintaining ethical practice, including the need for cultural competence. Guideline 1, Competence of the Psychologist, is relevant to this:

> Psychologists make reasonable effort to understand the manner in which cultural, linguistic, socioeconomic and other individual characteristics (e.g., medical status, psychiatric stability, physical/cognitive disability, personal preferences), in addition to, organizational cultures may impact effective use of telecommunication technologies in service delivery. (APA, 2013)

Additionally, Guideline 8, Interjurisdictional Practice, is relevant:

> . . . psychologists strive to keep abreast of developments and changes in the licensure and other interjurisdictional practice requirements that may be pertinent to their delivery of telepsychology services across jurisdictional boundaries. (APA, 2013)

The implication of these guidelines is that it may now be easier for an assessment practitioner to conduct assessments for clients all over the world, given the advantages of telepsychology, but doing so in a manner uninformed by laws or regulations of clients' native countries may cause unexpected ethical and, perhaps, legal issues to emerge.

Multicultural and International Practice

Understanding cultural differences and how assessors' values and implicit biases shape their perceptions of another individual is critical, especially when assessing individuals who may have a different background, racial or ethnic identity, sex, gender identity, sexual orientation, and/or country of origin than the assessor. The *Multicultural Guidelines: An Ecological Approach to Context, Identity, and Intersectionality* (the Multicultural Guidelines hereinafter; APA, 2017c) provide in-depth consideration and guidance on how mindful assessment practitioners can become more aware of the influence of their own background on themselves and how that shapes their perceptions and understanding of others. This issue is directly addressed in Guideline 2 of the Multicultural Guidelines:

> Psychologists aspire to recognize and understand that as cultural beings, they hold attitudes and beliefs that can influence their perceptions of and interactions with others as well as their clinical and empirical conceptualizations. As such, psychologists strive to move beyond conceptualizations rooted in categorical assumptions, biases, and/or formulations based on limited knowledge about individuals and communities. (APA, 2017c, p. 4)

It is the job of the assessor to develop an awareness of their own social and cultural milieu and the layers of their own identity that shape how they perceive and evaluate others. Social and cognitive psychologists have consistently shown over the past 40 years or so that individuals' perceptions are shaped by implicit biases (Jost et al., 2009; Vuletich & Payne, 2019). Effects of these biases have been across a multitude of environments and circumstances; in hiring situations in particular, studies have shown that applicants with names perceived as African American on their resumes are 50% less likely to get a job interview (Bertrand & Mullainathan, 2004) and female managerial candidates who present themselves as highly qualified, confident, and ambitious are less likely to be recommended for hiring (Eagly & Karau, 2002; Heilman et al., 2004; Rudman & Glick, 2001). Studies show that implicit prejudices are malleable through activities such as education, training, and self-reflection (A. M. Gonzalez et al., 2021; Rudman et al., 2001), and that biases can be heavily informed by an individual's environment (Vuletich & Payne, 2019). The more awareness practitioners can develop about such issues, the better equipped they will be to navigate them thoughtfully and ethically when they come up.

In conducting global assessment work, the reality of cultural differences is frequently brought to bear on issues related to language diversity. Guideline 3 of the Multicultural Guidelines addresses this issue directly:

> Psychologists strive to recognize and understand the role of language and communication through engagement that is sensitive to the lived experience of the individual, couple, family, group, community, and/or organizations with whom they interact. Psychologists also seek to understand how they bring their own language and communication to these interactions. (APA, 2017c, p. 4)

For example, a U.S.-based consultant was engaged to deliver feedback and brief coaching on developmental assessments to three executives as part of an organization's global leadership development program. One participant was from the United States, another was from Italy, and the third was from China. The consultant volunteered to be a part of this coaching team and was eager to work with individuals from across the globe. The consultant was assigned the three participants at random, each of whom had been assessed by a colleague at an earlier stage of the engagement. The assessment report included results that the consultant was adept at interpreting, and the feedback was conducted on the phone prior to the beginning of the development program, which was hosted at a resort in the United States.

The feedback phone calls with the participants from the United States and Italy went smoothly. Although the participant from Italy spoke heavily accented English, they were able to have a conversation largely uninhibited by the language difference. But when the consultant spoke with the participant from China, the participant's English was so heavily accented that the consultant struggled to comprehend much of what was being said. The consultant fumbled through the feedback, wondering how much was being effectively conveyed in their conversation and how much was lost in the language gap between them. However, rather than raise the issue with a colleague or look for a way to mitigate the language barrier, the consultant pressed on through the engagement and conducted three subsequent brief coaching conversations with each participant as a part of the leadership development program, each conversation with the participant from China as halting as the last.

For those working in a multinational context, this type of circumstance may occur with some frequency. When this does happen, an assessor may pair themselves with a colleague who is fluent in the language at issue, may pass the work on to a colleague who is fluent in the language, or may hire an interpreter. Use of an interpreter is addressed in the Ethics Code (Standard 9.03c), and assessors who make use of interpretation services will need to obtain informed consent from the client to do so, and consider how to maintain confidentiality and test security (APA, 2017a).

Equally relevant to the issue of language diversity in this case is Standard 2.01, Boundaries of Competence, Sections (b) and (c):

> (b) Where scientific or professional knowledge in the discipline of psychology establishes that an understanding of factors associated with age, gender, gender identity, race, ethnicity, culture, national origin, religion, sexual orientation, disability, language, or socioeconomic status is essential for effective implementation of their services or research, psychologists have or obtain the training, experience,

> consultation, or supervision necessary to ensure the competence of their services, or they make appropriate referrals, except as provided in Standard 2.02, Providing Services in Emergencies.
>
> (c) Psychologists planning to provide services, teach, or conduct research involving populations, areas, techniques, or technologies new to them undertake relevant education, training, supervised experience, consultation, or study. (APA, 2017a, p. 5)

Although the consultant may have been competent in delivering feedback and coaching, it was inappropriate, given limited language skills, not to seek help from a more qualified colleague.

Being culturally naïve or judgmental about the values and customs of others (Glover & Friedman, 2015, p. 19) can cause an assessor to discount or misperceive both the perceptions and behavior of an assessee (Lowman & Cooper, 2018). For example, individuals may be more relationship oriented and value getting along with others over being more task- and results oriented, or they may be more oriented toward flexibility and openness in the face of change rather than toward stability and planning for the future.

A full exploration of multicultural competence in consulting is beyond the scope of this chapter, but there are many useful resources on the topic, including *Transcultural Competence: Navigating Cultural Differences in the Global Community* (Glover & Friedman, 2015).

Legal Considerations

In this section, my goal is to provide a brief overview of the types of legal issue that can occur in the assessment process. Landy et al. (2010) provided a useful resource that goes into more depth about the legal principles and types of cases that occur in employment selection. I am raising these issues as areas assessors need to be knowledgeable about, but not speaking as a legal expert. Additionally, local and state laws may apply when conducting assessments in particular jurisdictions that may have different or more restrictive legal requirements than in others (e.g., California, the European Union).

Executive assessment is a specialized area of practice within individual assessment, which is covered under laws related to employment testing and evaluation. Primarily, these include the following:

- the Civil Rights Acts of 1866, 1964 (Title VII), and 1991, which include protections for people on the basis of race or color, religion, sex, national origin, and terms and conditions of work;
- the Uniform Guidelines on Employee Selection Procedures, which help employers make hiring and selection decisions that do not exclude people from protected groups disproportionately (unless the test or procedure is justified);
- the Age Discrimination in Employment Act of 1967 (ADEA), which provides protections for people over 40 on the basis of age;
- the Americans With Disabilities Act of 1990 (ADA), which provides protections for people on the basis of disability; and
- other relevant case law (Jeanneret, 1998).

These Equal Employment Opportunity (or EEO) laws and statutes relate to discrimination against protected classes in the workplace (Landy et al., 2010). *Protected classes* include race or color, religion, sex (including pregnancy, sexual orientation, or gender identity), national origin, age, and/or disability and genetic information (including family medical history). Additionally, on June 15, 2020, the U.S. Supreme Court held that "an employer who fires an individual merely for being gay or transgender violates Title VII" of the Civil Rights Act of 1964 (*Bostock v. Clayton County, GA*), which expanded protection under federal law for members of the LGBTQ community.

Broadly speaking, these laws relate to the issues of adverse impact and the job-relatedness of assessment procedures and outcomes. *Adverse impact* refers to the outcomes of assessment procedures that overselect members of privileged groups compared with underrepresented groups (Sajjadiani et al., 2019). Specifically in the United States, "adverse impact occurs when the selection rate for a protected group is less than 4/5th (80%) of the rate for the group with the highest rate (typically the nonprotected group)" (Jeanneret & Zedeck, 2017, p. 611), and it is the employer's burden to supply proof of the validity of an assessment method that has such an effect. That is, in selection assessments where adverse impact is present, the employer must demonstrate the job-relatedness of the selection procedure (Landy et al., 2010). *Job-relatedness* refers to assessment procedures that are accompanied by evidence of validity in predicting outcomes for the job in question. A simple example of this could be a test of physical ability in a firefighter exam that has candidates lift 50 pounds overhead. Such a test may cause adverse impact against some protected groups, but it is demonstrative of an ability that may be highly job-related and necessary to the work of firefighters (Ryan et al., 1996). Of course, if this were a real case, evidence would need to be supplied to support the validity of such inferences. In an executive context, this may typically take the form of requiring a certain level of education. Requirements like this can seem straightforward and appropriate, but even these types of requirements should be questioned and examined in terms of whether they open the door to a discriminatory selection practice, and whether they are genuinely predictive of performance on the job. This can be a challenge to prove at the executive level because numbers are typically too small to do adverse impact analysis, but executive candidates can certainly claim that they received disparate treatment in the assessment process based on their inclusion in a protected class. For example, a frequent travel requirement for a CEO role could potentially be considered discriminatory against a person with a disability for whom travel was challenging or not possible, especially if additional accommodations in terms of physical or financial assistance are not considered by the employer.

Ultimately, these laws and concepts inform the considered approach that assessors must take in constructing and conducting their assessment procedures. Ensuring assessments are predictive of job-related outcomes and are not biased toward one group of people is a key element of sound professional practice in this area. Using unvalidated measures or those that have adverse impact can cause serious trouble for assessors and for their client organizations. This could include sanctions from professional bodies based on their relevant ethics code (e.g., the APA), loss of licensure, and legal liability. All that said, the remainder of this section describes how these issues tend to manifest in the context of executive assessment.

The best way to navigate the complex ethical and legal issues that arise in the course of executive assessment is to have a team or mentor with whom to discuss and process issues. This is a benefit to working in a consulting group that conducts assessments, especially when starting out in this field of practice; participation in such a group allows information to be freely discussed among team members or with a manager, and provides newer assessors with supervisory support. In the absence of a team or other professional to help work through complex issues of this nature, finding a coach or counselor, or other such professional, with whom to process can be helpful. Confidentiality will need to be maintained while seeking counsel, though assessors should remember that the structure and nature of an ethical dilemma can often be discussed without sharing names, details, or other identifying information.

The position of assessor can be quite a powerful and discomforting one at times. Consultants may mentally approach assessment as "people in conversation"; treating participants with this regard can be a useful way to build rapport and lay the groundwork for good practice that will help avoid ethical dilemmas. Consultants should bear in mind, however, that they are also in relationship with the organization as a third party and a client in the assessment conversation (whether figuratively or literally), and that in some circumstances the demands of the organization may conflict with the ethical or legal responsibilities of the assessor. Standard 1.03 in the Ethics Code, Conflicts Between Ethics and Organizational Demands, speaks to this issue:

> If the demands of an organization with which psychologists are affiliated or for whom they are working are in conflict with this Ethics Code, psychologists clarify the nature of the conflict, make known their commitment to the Ethics Code, and take reasonable steps to resolve the conflict consistent with the General Principles and Ethical Standards of the Ethics Code. Under no circumstances may this standard be used to justify or defend violating human rights. (APA, 2017a, p. 16)

It is the goal of the consulting psychologist to work and behave in an ethical manner, even in those situations when organizational work may lead the assessor to ethical gray areas. These dilemmas are often subtle in their presentation, so the consultant must remain aware of important ethical issues. Usually, in the name of pragmatism, a client or colleague will ask a question or float a possibility that should raise a red flag, such as, "It is the same person being considered for basically the same position; can we just send them the report we used last time?" This should raise an assessor's awareness because reusing assessment results may raise issues about the informed consent of the participant, the confidentiality of the assessment results, and evidence-based practice. This is an example of a situation in which the consultant should step back, consider (or review) the ethical standards underlying this work, and take measures to prevent breaches of ethics in practice.

KEY TAKEAWAYS

- Read and apply guidelines related to assessment in organizations, including the *Standards for Educational and Psychological Testing* (American Educational Research Association, APA, & National Council on Measurement in Education, 2014); the current edition of the Ethics Code of the APA (2017); the Society of I-O Psychology's (2018) *Principles for the Validation and Use of Personnel Selection Procedures*; and APA's (2013) relevant guidelines, including the *Guidelines for the Practice of Telepsychology*, and the *Multicultural Guidelines* (APA, 2017c).
- When possible, schedule a short preliminary call with the assessee to introduce yourself, preview the assessment process, set expectations and identify time commitment, and discuss any necessary preparation required on behalf of the assessee, as well as the limits of confidentiality. Invite questions or concerns that the assessee may have. In many circumstances, they have been provided or remember far less about the details and circumstances of an assessment than one might expect; taking time to contextualize the work and answer questions up front can help mitigate issues that may otherwise come up later.
- Obtain (preferably written) informed consent from all people assessed before you start the assessment process. Don't assume informed con-

sent has been obtained by the organizational client. If people do not consent, do not assess them. Decide with the client organization, and communicate to the assessee, who will have access to a copy of the assessment report and recommendations and whether the assessee will have access to feedback from a trained assessor, as well as where raw data and copies of assessment reports will be stored, and for how long.

- Protect the content and copies (physical or electronic) of assessment measures you are using, and the data and information you are collecting. This may include controlling access to, and password protecting, digital folders and files (as well as physical copies), ensuring adequate security standards of cloud databases and other services used, and encrypting files if/as needed. In some circumstances, consultation with an information technology professional may be warranted.
- Except if legally required to do so, do not disclose information agreed to be kept confidential to anyone without the signed authorization of those to whom confidentiality rights have been granted.
- Develop an understanding and awareness of multicultural and intercultural issues and consider not working cross-culturally without first examining the impact of culture on your own judgments and perceptions.
- Familiarize yourself with the testing and employment laws of the jurisdictions where the people being assessed reside, especially when working across international borders.

4

How to Assess Senior Leaders

A consultant was hired to conduct developmental assessments on a cohort of senior vice presidents (SVPs) at a U.S.-based multinational corporation. The executives were being assessed as part of their ongoing evaluation for promotion to the executive vice president (EVP) level. The consultant had worked with the organization before, conducting finalist assessments for new hires and had a good understanding of the competency model they used to evaluate candidates at the SVP level. Additionally, the consultant had an open schedule in the short term and was eager to get started on the work as soon as possible. The consultant emailed the head of human resources (HR), the point of contact at the corporation, with a proposed timeline and an engagement letter that detailed the structure of the engagement and the associated fees. The head of HR signed the engagement letter and agreed to the timeline, so the consultant got to work conducting assessments. The assessment included a series of online tests, a 2-hour structured interview, and a 1-hour feedback conversation

https://doi.org/10.1037/0000264-005
Assessing CEOs and Senior Leaders: A Primer for Consultants, by J. R. Blankenship

in which the consultant and each SVP discussed the assessment results and worked together to assemble a development plan.

After the assessments had been completed, but prior to the feedback conversations, the consultant met with the head of HR to discuss the results. It was in this conversation that the head of HR asked what the consultant thought about each candidate's level of international mobility. The consultant tried to string together a response based on the available results, but ultimately, slightly embarrassed, admitted that the question had not been asked, and that perhaps it could be asked in the feedback conversation.

Because the consultant had sped through the contracting of the consulting engagement, the head of HR never mentioned that there were some concerns about the candidates' willingness to move abroad as part of their development. The CEO had expressed concern to the head of HR that some EVP candidates might be saying they were open to moving to another country but had not actually considered the issue fully or spoken to their families about the possibility. Ultimately, the question was not included in the assessment.

Had the consultant and the head of HR discussed that international mobility was part of the criteria at the EVP level, they might have considered adding an additional personality assessment with robust measures of facets that have been shown to predict cross-cultural adjustment (e.g., achievement, sociability), and perhaps also asked each SVP about their language skills, which have also been shown to predict cross-cultural adjustment and expatriate job performance (Salgado & Bastida, 2017).

Like any good consulting engagement, executive assessment follows a relatively predictable process. It involves a number of activities that include contracting, gathering data, writing and data integration, and delivering feedback. And, as the case illustrates, skipping a step may lead to missing data or other such challenges.

CONTRACTING

Contracting is the process of formally engaging a client to do work. Although contracting frequently involves the signing of actual contracts (e.g., engagement letters, nondisclosure agreements) and agreement on a fee, it is also an opportunity to set and manage expectations. This is the phase of assessment work wherein the consultant begins learning about the context of the assessment, comes to an agreement on the assessment timeline, and defines their own needs in meeting those expectations. Having a clear understanding of the purpose of the assessment will help the assessor build a trusting relationship with the client and enter the assessment situation with an awareness of the organization's goals.

Understanding the Assessment Context in Contracting

Much was said about assessment context in Chapter 2 of this volume that will not be revisited here. Taking the time to understand the assessment context helps the consultant and the client come to a mutual agreement about the purpose of the assessment within the organization, who will need to be involved, and in what form the assessment results will need to be presented to accomplish that purpose. Especially when working with a client for the first time, it is beneficial to share sample (disguised) assessment reports and results to provide a fuller understanding of the process and help the client understand the services for which they are paying.

This early interaction in the assessment process is part of informed consent (discussed in more detail in Chapter 3), and is an opportunity to build a relationship with the client and to provide some clarity around what assessment results can and cannot deliver. It can also help the assessor understand how the client intends to use the information provided by the assessment, insight they hope to gain, and questions they hope to answer. Assessment data is often used for more than one purpose, and early interactions in the assessment process and obtaining informed consent allow the assessor to identify possible mixed motivations on the part of the client organization and clarify the purpose and limits of assessment results.

For example, consider the consultant who is hired to conduct an assessment for purposes of development. The term *development* can have different meanings and perceptions in different organizations (Day & Dragoni, 2015). In one organization it may be perceived by leaders as an opportunity to grow and advance in their career, and in another it may be perceived as a signal that an executive is derailing and is getting remedial assistance to stay on track. Accordingly, executives' view of participation in an assessment process may be perceived as positive or negative, based on how assessment has been used within that organization in the past.

Understanding the Organization's Desired Outcomes

Taking time to understand the ideal outcomes for the client is a good way to set expectations about what can be accomplished with an assessment. It can also help the assessor design the assessment process itself and the final report to fit the purpose (Reynolds, McCauley, & Tsacoumis, 2018). This does not mean changing results to suit what the client wants, per se, but may involve adding additional interpretation or providing a specific framing for results to help the client achieve the goals of the assessment. For example, a client organization may ask for specific commentary, based on assessment results, about how each executive may change a team's culture or how coachable they may be. This may also include the specific form of the results—data, narrative, or a combination of the two. It is not uncommon for clients to ask whether the results of an assessment will take the form of a single score for comparison or a yes/no answer about whether a candidate should be hired or not. Some consulting firms combine assessment results into a single quotient or provide a "grade" based on the assimilation of evidence collected in the assessment process. Other clients will want specific recommendations about candidates assessed. Assessors may provide such recommendations to clients they know well or who explicitly ask, but even then, it is advisable to provide more nuanced feedback than yes/no answers, as it is not the assessor's place to make the decision, but rather to provide interpretations of data that may help the client be more effective in their decision making. For example, based on relevant evidence, an assessor may suggest that "it is possible that this candidate would do well in the job role during routine times, but under stress, they are likely to become overly rigid in their thinking and less open to input from others," or to express a more direct opinion in the form of if/then statements, such as, "if the board is looking for an operationally minded

CEO who may need development and/or support in innovation and creativity, then this candidate could be a good choice."

In general, the more that is understood about the client's concerns and goals going into an assessment process, the better equipped the assessor will be to gather and deliver useful information. This will help the consultant and client organization to clarify and align on common issues and concerns and can help bring to the surface specific questions that should be asked.

Understanding the Assessment Timeline

The timeline of an assessment process is critical to know at the outset of an engagement. Timing is usually driven by the needs of the organization, but the assessor must be upfront about their ability to deliver quality assessment results within realistic timelines. The type of assessment being sought can also affect timing. The timing of succession assessments tends to be driven by the urgency of the succession process within the organization. Longer term succession processes can take months to move from initial contracting with the organization to feedback with the organization and executive participants, while shorter-term or emergency succession processes, on the other hand, can move as quickly as finalist assessments can be conducted. With a slate of finalists, the assessment process is usually conducted after a long list of candidates has been pared down to a short list and the process is leading toward a decision. The hiring manager or committee will likely want assessment results on the final slate of candidates as soon as possible to help make their decision. Assessments conducted in the context of a merger or acquisition tend to be conducted within tight timeframes as well, especially if assessment results are needed prior to the closing of a deal or the formation of a new entity that will need to have leaders in place on day one. Developmental assessments tend to be the most flexible in terms of timing, though that depends on the urgency of the development need and whether assessment results are for only one employee or are being incorporated into a larger development context (e.g., a leadership development retreat).

When conducting assessments at the CEO or senior leader level, results are usually reported to the selection committee at board meetings, so assessors must fit assessment activities around the board meeting schedule. In the grand scheme of immovable dates that consultants must accommodate in their work, board meetings are among the firmest. However, it is just as important to remember the soft deadlines that exist around firmer deadlines. For example, if a board meeting is April 15, the board will likely receive board materials a week or so in advance, and thus the team compiling board documents will likely want supportive materials and information at least two weeks before the meeting. Figure 4.1 shows a sample timeline from a CEO succession project that was scheduled over a 4-month period. Agreeing on the firm deadline for formally presenting assessment results to the client and then working

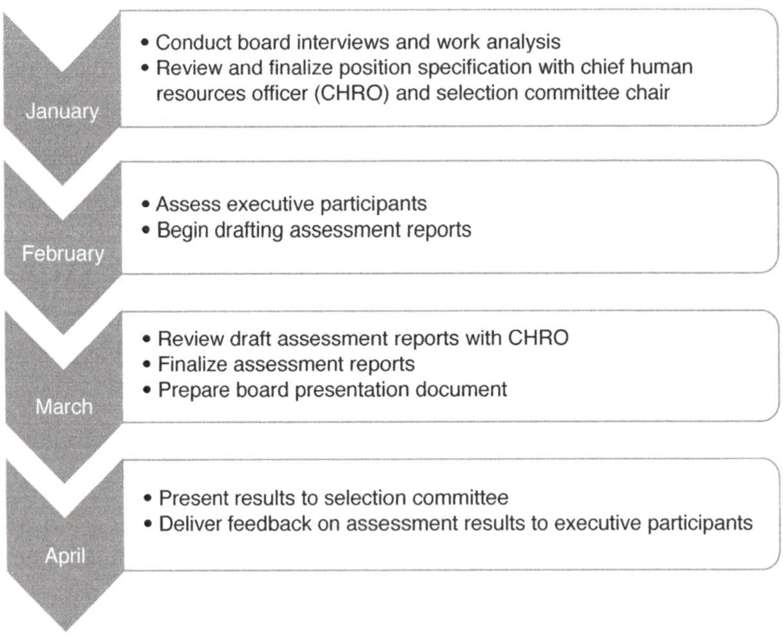

Figure 4.1

Sample timeline of a CEO succession assessment process conducted over the course of 4 months.

backward through the steps of the assessment process that need to take place prior to that point will help delineate the pace at which assessments need to be conducted.

Additionally, assessors need to know when to advocate for their own needs, in order to provide meaningful and effective assessments. Clients will inevitably ask for reports the day after an assessment is conducted or may ask for a phone call to discuss feedback just after the executive job candidate has left the room. Sometimes the client (and the situation) demands immediate feedback, and it may be necessary to provide it in order to meet the organization's goals; however, assessors should be mindful of not committing to unrealistic timelines that will diminish the possibility of delivering effective assessment work. In summary, consultants need to be aware of and realistic about their energy level, workload, work style, and time frames, so that they can proactively manage client expectations and deliver their best work.

Defining Assessment Needs

In addition to understanding and managing the timeline of the assessment, it is helpful at the outset to inform the client of what will be needed for the assessor to best deliver the assessment. That might include a private space to conduct interviews, scheduling support with the assessee and other stakeholders who may be interviewed (e.g., board members, 360° feedback providers), access to the selection committee and committee chair (as well as other relevant board members), and other needs that will be specific to each situation. It is especially important to communicate these types of needs when an assessment is being conducted on a fixed timeline.

GATHERING DATA

This phase of the assessment process includes collecting all the information that one will use in the course of evaluating and providing feedback on an executive candidate's readiness or potential for a given role. Gathering data involves determining the criteria of the assessment and the tools that can be used to predict those criteria, as well as ensuring that the tools one uses are of high quality.

Defining the Assessment Target

Prediction starts with clarifying desired outcomes. At the executive level, this is usually leadership potential or leadership effectiveness, but what that means in a given role needs to be specified. The specific criteria for leadership effectiveness can be defined by creating (and/or editing and reconfiguring preexisting) competency models through high-level work analysis interviews in order to define the behaviors and characteristics of successful leadership within the organization (Reynolds, McCauley, & Tsacoumis, 2018). At their best, competency models form "a set of relatively concrete and meaningful performance standards for often abstract or complex constructs" customized for a given role within an organization (Pearlman & Sanchez, 2010, p. 92).

In general, clusters of leader behaviors (e.g., competencies) can be organized into high-level domains, including task-oriented behaviors (e.g., a competency in this area may be "driving growth"), relationship-oriented behaviors (e.g., "developing capability in direct reports"), and change-oriented behaviors (e.g., "strategic thinking"; Yukl et al., 2019). Although traits such as strategic thinking, driving growth, and developing capability in direct reports are competencies that frequently appear in organizational leadership models, the importance of each will shift depending on the needs of the organization and the associated requirements of the leadership position. For example, if an organization is searching for a new CEO just after completing a robust strategic planning process, the board may be more focused on hiring a candidate who demonstrates a strong ability to drive growth, rather than one who is an exceptional strategic thinker. Competencies, of course, only make up part of the information to be considered, along with the knowledge, experience, abilities, and traits that are incorporated in the target position for which executives are assessed. All of these elements need to be covered in the position specification and be discussed in the work analysis interviews.

These interviews should be structured to ensure information is consistently collected from each source, and should cover areas such as (a) perceptions of the organization, including key opportunities and challenges (e.g., current performance, strategy, market and competitive position, strength of management team); (b) considerations related to the organization's future (e.g., potential strategic shifts); (c) distinctive elements of the organization's culture (e.g., leadership structure, team dynamics, habits and routines); (d) the relationship between management and the board (e.g., communication, relationships, pending changes); (e) job requirements, including needed knowledge and experience; and (f) the most important personal attributes and leadership competencies required for the next CEO (or other senior leadership position). Here is a list (by no means comprehensive) of sample questions an assessor might ask in such an interview:

- How would you describe the current performance of the organization?
- What major developments do you expect to take place within the organization over the next 5 years?
- How do you expect the market to impact organizational growth over the next 3 to 5 years?
- What are the key opportunities and challenges that the next person in this role will face?
- How would you describe the culture of the organization? Of the management team?
- How would you describe the quality of the team the executive will be joining?
- What experience or specific knowledge will make this individual successful in this role?
- What leadership characteristics or traits will make this individual successful in this role? Is there a way you would prioritize those requirements?
- Did the organization gain any useful information from past leaders who were unsuccessful?
- Is there anything that I have not asked that you think is important for me to know or consider in developing this position specification?

The text box below shows a brief transcript that has been edited for confidentiality and brevity that shows a few such questions with responses and follow-up questions to get a sense for how an interview like this might flow:

Assessor: What's your perspective on the current performance of the organization? What opportunities and challenges lie ahead?
Board Director: Our position in the market continues to be strong. Our operations are pretty strong. The company is growing, particularly internationally, but the U.S. market is constrained. We expect that to come back in the next year or two, and as that happens, the company will continue to grow in the 8% to 10% range.

Our biggest challenge, though, is our balance sheet. We've taken on a lot of debt to do acquisitions, and if we keep doing transactions we'll burn through our cash—the next CEO will need to build out our balance sheet to have the flexibility to execute on future opportunities.

Another challenge is culture change. The next CEO will need to find the right blend of entrepreneurship, but also the discipline to execute well on the day-to-day.

How effective is the executive team?
We just brought in a new COO, and other roles will need to be upgraded. The company's growth has outstripped its talent in many circumstances.

And what about the new CEO, what do you think will make them successful?
They must be extroverted, confident, self-assured. They will also need a great degree of humility. The company is very sales driven, and the salesforce likes confident people, but not arrogant people. Confident, smart, articulate.

We need someone who will invest in building relationships. The most critical aspect to this is to do the best we can to maintain a cohesive, continuing, operating organization—and that starts at the top level and filters down.

Other notable elements of the CEO profile to consider?
Strong leadership is a must, but we are also seeking someone who can manage people and not come in and break things unless he or she has to, and even then, do it thoughtfully.

The CEO has to be a strong leader and someone who can start right away—there's not a lot of time to get up to the learning curve, so I suspect they'll need to come from within the industry.

Any other questions or advice and counsel as we go through this process?
Just that this is a key decision that will have a long-term impact on the company. If we make another mistake, that would be very bad. So, we are not telling you anything you don't know . . . we need someone who's capable and who's all in.

In some circumstances, organizational clients may ask assessors whether interviews with the board or other senior leaders need to be done individually or as a group. Although this request makes practical sense given the limited time that executives and board members may have and can certainly be done to accommodate a limited time frame, it is best to conduct these interviews individually. Group interviews tend to decrease the overall amount of information obtained in the work analysis process, and they reduce the possibility of uncovering areas of disagreement about the job specification that may come out in individual interviews. After completing work analysis interviews, the results need to be incorporated and structured into a position specification. To do this, the assessor will review interview notes and begin organizing job demands into relevant categories that typically include knowledge and experience, skills and competencies, traits and abilities, and other variables (e.g., career aspirations, multicultural leadership experience, willingness to relocate internationally). Table 4.1 provides a sample CEO specification.

Once the specification has been created, the assessor should consult with the client liaison (e.g., chief human resources officer [CHRO] or selection committee chair) to ensure that the position is adequately described and to help prioritize those elements of the job that are "must haves"

Table 4.1

Sample CEO Position Specification and Criteria

Dimension	Elements	Definition
Knowledge & Experience	Senior business P&L leadership	Experienced CEO, COO, or business unit president with direct commercial leadership experience and full profit and loss (P&L) accountability for a large, complex, multinational business.
	Credibility and experience working with regulators	Demonstrated track record leading highly regulated business and establishing effective relationships with senior regulators. Ideally, highly regarded by senior regulators and industry peers.
	Leading an organization at scale	Led business unit of $500m in revenue or more. Track record of successfully growing profitable businesses, demonstrating sophisticated financial skills and excellent risk-return judgment. Experience attracting, retaining, developing, and inspiring talented professionals.
Skills & Competencies	"Big picture" thinking	Focuses on larger, longer-term issues, and creates plans and strategies. At higher levels, develops a strategy that conceptualizes and incorporates complex market issues, and provides a clear concept for the future that people can understand and align around.
	Driving results	Drives towards top business performance. Pushes to meet or beat goals. At highest levels, changes what the organization or even the industry can do.
	Enabling organizational change	Aligns people and organizations around change. Challenges the way things are done and expresses the need for change clearly and frequently. At the highest levels, not only acts as change leader, but creates change leaders within the organization to support change efforts.
	Team leadership	Aligns and empowers team members. At the highest levels, creates empowered leaders to execute efficiently through the layers of the organization and across geographies.

Table 4.1

Sample CEO Position Specification and Criteria (*Continued*)

Dimension	Elements	Definition
Traits & Abilities	Critical thinking	Able to accurately draw inferences, identify assumptions, make logical deductions. Facility with data analysis and interpretation.
	Abstract reasoning	Able to think conceptually in order to make sense of complex and uncertain information.
	Growth mindset	Agile learner who is open to different perspectives and adapts to feedback in order to maximize potential.
Other	Multicultural orientation	Brings a global perspective, and ideally direct professional experience not only in the U.S. but also internationally. Can manage competing cross-cultural work styles and effectively lead a diverse workforce.
	Integrity & ethics	Acting in line with stated values and beliefs. At top levels, enabling others or the organization to act in alignment with values.

versus those that are ideal but not essential. Discussing prioritization of these elements with the client before conducting candidate assessments not only helps the assessor determine how different elements in the position specification should be differentially weighted in terms of importance, but also can help orient the client in the feedback process and highlight candidate differences that may be particularly salient given the needs of the job.

Selecting Assessment Tools

The tools used in an assessment process should be selected for their relevance to the situation and their ability to help the assessor make job-related inferences. Each tool will provide some insight, limited by its own advantages and disadvantages. Using multiple methods across a continuum of traits and behavior will describe both what an executive *has done* and what they are *likely to do* in the future. To that end, the assessment should include descriptions of past behavior (i.e., biographical data, career history, etc.) as well as inferences about future behavior (i.e., cognitive ability, personality, interests, etc.; Howard & Thomas, 2010). When possible, assessments should also include work samples requiring demonstrations of behavior (e.g., prioritization and decision making, communication), as in the case of assessment center evaluations.

The specific tools used will vary based on the job dimensions and duties specific to the particular assessment and the assessor's knowledge, training, and comfort interpreting assessment results. In general, an executive assessment should include an evaluation of the following elements:

- biographical data, including work/career history and job knowledge
- work-related personality characteristics
- cognitive and other ability assessments
- values and interests
- emotional intelligence
- 360° feedback and reference checks (when possible)

Biographical Data

Gaining a sense of an executive's experience, job performance, and notable prior achievements can provide information regarding how they are likely to behave in the future. Biographical data are generally gathered through a combination of reviewing resumes or profiles on professional networking websites and in the interview. In the case of internal executive assessments, existing HR data may also be used to help understand an executive's career and past performance. A career history can provide a sense of an executive's life story, their early career origins, how they advanced in their career, and why they made the decisions they made. It can also provide a sense of the job knowledge or expertise that they may bring to the role for which they are being considered. Specific industry and technical knowledge will be important for any senior leadership role, but the degree to which an executive will need to possess and demonstrate deep technical knowledge will vary depending on the expertise represented on the team they will be joining (Reynolds, McCauley, & Tsacoumis, 2018).

Work-Related Personality Characteristics

Understanding an executive's personality in the context of work provides insight into how they are likely to behave, interact with others, and go about doing their job. Insight into leadership style can be gained by evaluating Big Five traits and their facets (e.g., Hogan Personality Inventory [HPI], Workplace Big Five [WPB5]); "red flag" derailing traits, such as narcissism, Machiavellianism, and psychopathy (e.g., Hogan Development Survey [HDS]; Kaiser et al., 2013; Volmer et al., 2016); and compound traits that combine aspects of other traits (e.g., ambition, which is composed of elements of conscientiousness and extraversion; Ones, 2005). For example, those who score high on "learning approach"—a facet of the Big Five trait Openness to experience that describes those who are engaged intellectually and tend to read and seek information—demonstrate stronger task performance in complex jobs (Blickle et al., 2013). However, not all personality traits are equal in their predictive validity of work performance or leadership effectiveness (Hogan & Judge, 2012). Personality has traditionally been evaluated in several ways, including interviews, historical records and reports, observation, and standardized self-report questionnaires (Weiner & Greene, 2017). Personality questionnaires are used frequently within organizations because they provide efficient and systematic measurement and can be easily compared across candidates.

Selecting the right instrument is critical. There are an estimated 2,000+ personality assessments on the market in the United States alone (Ash, 2012; Menand, 2018); not all of them have been validated, and not all of them are relevant for working populations, or for executive populations. There is often a trade-off to be made in selecting these tools between the time needed to measure and validity. Lengthier multi-item measures may demonstrate more reliability and validity (SIOP, 2018), but the assessor will need to consider how much value each additional test truly adds to the comprehensive assessment, and whether it is worth the added time commitment on behalf of the executive.

Self-report personality measures raise some concerns about "faking" or impression management (Mueller-Hanson et al., 2003; Schmitt, 2014). *Impression management* is when an assessee behaves in a certain way or responds to items on a self-report measure in a certain way in an effort to control how others perceive them (Peck & Levashina, 2017). Some tools have impression management scales built into them (e.g., California Psychological Inventory 260 [CPI 260]) which can provide some insight into the degree or severity of impression management tactics. Other survey response methods such as forced-choice items (e.g., Occupational Personality Questionnaire-32r [OPQ-32r]), in which the test taker selects among items of equal social desirability, have been shown to reduce faking (Cao & Drasgow, 2019). To manage the possibility of faking and impression management, one can use multiple personality measures when possible, and to use interviews and 360° feedback to cross-reference results. Additionally, it can be helpful to reiterate to the assessee the importance of representing themselves authentically, and warning test takers that impression management can be detected has been shown to reduce faking (Dwight & Donovan, 2003; Lopez et al., 2019). When results are inconsistent across different methods, the assessor can look for patterns of inconsistency that may provide insight. For example, if an executive scores high on a trait extraversion scale but is described as quiet and retiring by his direct reports, the assessor might look for evidence of extraversion/introversion type behaviors among other rater groups (e.g., peers, superiors) and observe how the executive interacts in the interview process.

Cognitive Ability

Cognitive ability is a valid predictor of work performance at all employment levels, and senior leaders are usually expected to demonstrate strong general intelligence (Reynolds, McCauley, & Tsacoumis, 2018; Schmitt, 2014). Cognitive ability is most frequently measured with tests (e.g., Watson-Glaser Critical Thinking Appraisal, Wonderlic Cognitive Ability, Raven's Advanced Progressive Matrices), which can present a challenge when assessing senior leaders. They may wonder why their performance or career advancement is not perceived as an inherent demonstration of their intelligence, and assessees within an organization who are asked to complete cognitive tests as a part of an assessment process may wonder if their organization is questioning their intelligence. Indeed, sometimes client organizations themselves question the use of cognitive ability measures due to fear of alienating candidates in a search or assessment process. However, cognitive ability remains the best predictor of performance at work (Ones et al., 2017), and not measuring it will result in assessors and their clients failing to gather or consider very important information.

Even in situations where executives have strong educational backgrounds and other markers of general mental ability, cognitive ability tests add value. They can provide insight into problem-solving style and adaptability, both of which can be useful input in evaluating fit for a job and in directing leadership development efforts (Stasielowicz, 2020). Additionally, intelligence can vary or decline over time (Ghisletta et al., 2012), so the argument that an executive has "proven" their intelligence in their career may be misleading. These measures may also provide evidence as to how respondents handle anxiety and frustration, especially when test content exceeds an assessee's abilities.

Values and Interests

Values and interests provide insight into what motivates and energizes a leader. Frequently evaluated in an interview, values and interests are also easily assessed with self-report questionnaires (e.g., Motives, Values, and Preferences Inventory [MVPI]). *Values* are the deeply held beliefs and priorities that shape what individuals view as most important in life (Chan, 2017). Individual values, and values alignment with a group or a team, are frequently referenced to help evaluate a leader's fit to a team's dynamic or an organization's culture and the demands of the job. Leaders who demonstrate strong values around achievement, for example, will tend to focus on demonstrating their capability and accomplishing challenging goals (Schwartz, 2012).

Interests are stable psychological characteristics that determine the types of environments and activities that individuals will find attractive and motivating (Su, 2018). Interest assessments (e.g., Strong Interest Inventory) seem to be used somewhat infrequently in selection (Nye et al., 2017), but interests can provide useful insight into the internal forces that direct an executive's attention and energy. For example, an individual with strong enterprising and social interests will tend to enjoy working with other people and find tasks and environments that involve influence, leadership, and persuasion motivating (Nye et al., 2017). Additionally, interests play a key role in guiding career choice (Wang & Wanberg, 2017), and can provide direction in development or succession contexts.

Emotional Intelligence

Emotional intelligence describes an executive's ability to recognize and understand their own and others' emotions, to manage their emotions, and to use that insight to better direct their behavior (Salovey & Mayer, 1990). Assessments of emotional intelligence (e.g., The Mayer-Salovey-Caruso Emotional Intelligence Test [MSCEIT], The Emotional Quotient Inventory [EQ-i 2.0]) can be quite useful, especially in a development context where an executive may benefit from a deeper awareness of their internal emotional landscape and how better emotion regulation may help them improve their performance (Joseph & Newman, 2010; Kim & Kim, 2017). For example, an executive may let their anger drive overly directive leadership behavior that causes direct reports to burn out. Developing an ability to recognize that emotion as anger and better manage it may allow that executive to become a more self-aware, effective leader (Sadri, 2012). However, research is limited in an executive selection context for these kinds of measures, and results are mixed as to their predictive validity (Boyatzis, 2018; Dabke, 2016; Pekaar et al., 2017), so they should be used advisedly, and likely not independently for the purposes of selection.

360° Feedback

External perspectives on a leader's effectiveness and behavior can provide a point of triangulation for test results and assessor observations. Specifically, the input from those with whom a leader works can serve as another point of reference to strengthen or weaken inferences that the assessor may be making based on assessment and interview data. 360° feedback is also useful because it allows for a comparison between the assessee's self-perceptions and the perceptions of others (Gregory & Levy, 2015). 360° feedback is generally gathered for developmental assessments of internal candidates and can be accomplished via use of online survey tools (e.g., Benchmarks®, Leadership Versatility Index) or through interviews. The survey method can provide an opportunity to gather input from a larger number of people and provide number ratings for relevant behaviors or competencies. Interviews, though more time- and labor-intensive, can be useful because they allow for follow-up questions and clarifications. However, interview 360s are more subject to providing unreliable and unvalidated inferences if they are not properly structured and delivered (Thorsteinson, 2018) than online survey formats. 360° feedback has its advantages and disadvantages (Bracken et al., 2016), but it can provide useful information on an executive's patterns of behavior by looking for themes among observers from specific rater groups (e.g., direct reports, peers).

When assessing external candidates, gathering 360° feedback is not possible, though a third-party perspective may be pursued in the form of reference checks. Reference checks are usually conducted by search consultants or by the client organization's HR team from a list of referees provided by the candidate. Research on the validity and reliability of reference checks is quite sparse and outdated, though studies show that reference checks conducted as structured interviews show the most validity in predicting job performance (Daniel, 1990; Taylor et al., 2004). References are used quite frequently in selection and tend to be structured around gaps or questions that a search consultant or hiring manager may have about a candidate's experience. If the client organization requests reference checks, or the assessor decides reference checks may provide some clarification and insight, it is recommended that they be conducted after the assessment has been completed and the results have been compiled into a provisional report, so that others' perspectives do not bias the assessor's interpretation of the data (Furnham & Boo, 2011).

Determining the Quality of the Tools

There are many instruments and measures available that can predict the abilities and characteristics previously mentioned, and it is up to the assessor to review the purposes of the assessment, the constructs to be measured, and to rigorously review the evidence of validity and reliability for the intended applications. The tasks in which the assessor must be competent include (a) understanding evidence that supports the use of the tool for the intended purpose, (b) gaining facility and comfort interpreting the output of the tool, and (c) being familiar with alternative assessment tools available and how they best relate to the purposes of the assessment in the context at hand. In an assessment market that is ever-growing and evolving, this can be a challenge. The administration and interpretation of many psychological tests requires a certain level of education and experience, and in many circumstances test publishers require certification before being able to use their instruments. Additionally, as assessments are created and marketed to match popular trends in the business press, it can be tempting to use newer approaches that may have poorer reliability and validity. As Reynolds, McCauley, and Tsacoumis (2018) suggested, one should be cautious about using new tools in assessments with high stakes, unless there is significant value to be gained.

Much of the work of determining the quality of a tool depends on the assessor's ability to evaluate the validity, reliability, legality, and relevance of a given instrument. In the case of long-standing psychometric instruments provided by well-respected publishers, the evidence tends to be substantial and forthcoming, usually in the form of a well-maintained technical manual. In many cases, these instruments have been used in studies, as well, which can provide balance to the claims of the publisher. Table 4.2 shows a few examples of tools that are frequently used in executive assessments.

Within the assessment process more generally, taking a multimethod approach that includes several instruments and both qualitative and quantitative methods can help mitigate the limitations of any one measure. For example, using two different personality inventories in an assessment battery may provide some redundant information, but may also provide supporting evidence for the prevalence of an observed trait in the individual. Additionally, within the interview, using clearly defined behaviorally anchored rating scales can improve the consistency of observations and make cross-candidate comparisons simpler.

Table 4.2

Examples of Well-Established and Commonly Used Measures in Executive Assessment

Construct	Measure	Source	Factors assessed
Personality	Hogan Personality Inventory (HPI)	https://www.hoganassessments.com	Measures personality based on the Big 5 model and includes 7 factors such as Sociability and Adjustment, as well as facets
	Hogan Development Survey (HDS)	https://www.hoganassessments.com	Measures personality traits that can emerge under stress, including scales such as Excitable, Cautious, and Skeptical
	Workplace Big Five (WPB5)	https://paradigmpersonality.com	Measure of the Big 5 personality traits as well as 23 facets such as Extraversion, Originality, and Accommodation
	California Psychological Inventory 260 (CPI 260)	https://www.themyersbriggs.com	Evaluates 26 scales related to interpersonal styles, values and motivation, and personal characteristics such as Dominance, Sociability, and Capacity for Status
	Occupational Personality Questionnaire Revised (OPQ-32r)	https://www.shl.com	Measures 32 personality characteristics that map to Relationships with People, Thinking Style, and Feelings and Emotions
Cognitive Ability	Watson-Glaser Critical Thinking Appraisal	https://www.psionline.com	40-item multiple-choice test that measures Recognizing Assumptions, Evaluating Arguments, Drawing Conclusions, and Overall Critical Thinking
	Wonderlic Cognitive Ability	https://wonderlic.com	50-item test that gets progressively harder over time and measures Math, Basic Logic, Language Comprehension, Spatial Reasoning, and Pattern Identification
	Raven's Advanced Progressive Matrices	https://www.talentlens.com/global.html	23-item test that measures an individual's ability to think laterally, learn new concepts quickly, and solve new and complex problems via abstract reasoning testing

(continues)

Table 4.2

Examples of Well-Established and Commonly Used Measures in Executive Assessment (*Continued*)

Construct	Measure	Source	Factors assessed
Interests	Strong Interest Inventory	https://www.themyersbriggs.com	Measures an individual's RIASEC interests and preferences in five areas, including Work Style, Learning Environment, Team Orientation, Leadership Style, and Risk Taking
	Wonderlic Motivation	https://wonderlic.com	Measures individual motivation based on RIASEC model
Values	Motives, Values, and Preferences Inventory (MVPI)	https://www.hoganassessments.com	Measures individual values, drivers and interests on 10 scales such as Recognition, Power, and Affiliation
Emotional Intelligence	Mayer Salovey Caruso Emotional Intelligence Test (MSCEIT)	https://mhs.com	Measures elements of EQ Perceiving Emotions, Using Emotions, Understanding Emotions, and Managing Emotions
	Emotional-Quotient Inventory (EQ-I)	https://mhs.com	Measures elements of emotional and social functioning such as Self-Perception, Self-Expression, Interpersonal, Decision Making, and Stress Management
360° Feedback Surveys	Benchmarks® Assessment Suite	https://www.ccl.org	A group of 360° feedback tools with norm groups for executives, managers, and individual learning agility
	Leadership Versatility Index (LVI)	https://leadershipversatilityindex.com	360° feedback tool with a scale that ranges from "Too Little" to "Too Much" to give insight into strengths and weaknesses.

RECOMMENDATIONS FOR INTERVIEWING

Interviewing is a critical part of senior-level assessment for several reasons. First, it provides the assessor with the opportunity to interact directly with the executive to help confirm or deny theories and hypotheses born out in the previously collected assessment data. Second, the human interaction provides the assessor with a personal point of view in debriefing the client. And third, it provides an important opportunity for the executive to provide context and color on elements of their resume and experience.

Interviewing is a skill that is best learned from a combination of observation, training, and practice. In the sections that follow are a few practical tips that may help fine-tune interviewing skills when working with senior executives.

Be In the Room

"Being in the room" means focusing on the fact that, despite the formal professional setting and context, an executive interview is essentially two (or more) people in a room having a conversation. It can be challenging to take extensive notes and conduct a meaningful conversation simultaneously. If the assessor is taking notes, they should disclose upfront that they are taking notes and explain what will be done with the notes. Recording can be a useful way to allow the assessor to focus on the conversation and the structure of the interview without worrying about missing something important. However, if the interview is being recorded, the assessor must ensure that the executive candidate consents to being recorded and knows what will be done with the recording after the interview. All of these issues are relevant to the topic of informed consent, which is discussed in more detail in Chapter 3. Also, depending on the length of the interview, it is useful to take a break, which can allow the assessor time to collect their thoughts, note impressions and observations, and determine any content areas that need to be covered in more depth.

Assessors should also be mindful of the structure of the room in which the assessment is conducted. If time and circumstances allow, think about who will sit where and arrange the room to ensure that everyone can sit comfortably without being too close or too far away. Where the assessor sits in the room matters, as does body language, both in terms of conducting the assessment and in terms of data to gather as the assessment is conducted. What people do when they are speaking provides information about what they are thinking and how they are feeling. For example, in one interview, a CEO candidate leaned back in his chair and put his arms behind his head. He was so uninterested in engaging in a genuine conversation with the assessors about his career that he basically performed an extended monologue about his life and accomplishments. It was such a challenging interview that the assessors paused and tried to redirect him, reminding him that responding to their questions and engaging in a conversation would help create a better result for both the client organization and him as the job candidate. And yet, still he continued in his monologue.

This type of contextual information can be important. The assessor's perception of the job candidate's behavior within the interview can provide some insight into how an executive may behave while on the job or how their behavior may impact those around them. It is important, however, not to confuse this type of insight with potential biases that may be at play in the assessor's perception. This is where the structured elements of the assessment can help the assessor remain focused on data and information that is job-relevant and not be misled by personal preferences (de Kock & Hauptfleisch, 2018). It is also important for assessors to develop their own self-awareness of the impacts of racial and gender bias in the workplace, so they can incorporate this understanding into how they perceive and understand the context around an executive's behavior.

Stop at the Question Mark

It is best not to ask a question and then continue on about the conditions and circumstances that should inform the answer, or to ask questions in such a way that overly directs the interviewee's answers. For example, a question that might be overly directive would be "Can you tell me about a time when you developed a member of your team by coaching them directly or helping them get training to get to the next level?" when "Tell me about a time when you developed a member of your team" would suffice. Assessors are best served by asking a question and letting the question stand. Stopping at the question mark leaves open-ended questions open-ended and allows the interviewer to see how an executive interprets what has been asked. In the example just provided, by letting the question stand, the interviewer may gain insight into what the executive considers to be development in the first place, which may be as informative as how they go about doing it. Additionally, this practice can help increase the assessor's comfort with silence, which can be a useful tool in an interview. Remaining silent at the right times can create opportunities for executives to share deeper and more personal insights about who they are and what drives them than they might in their typically polished delivery.

In-Person Versus Remote Assessments

Given the state of technology development and the pace at which most executives work, remote assessments are frequently the preferred option. Additionally, cataclysmic events like the COVID-19 pandemic drove almost every business into the virtual realm seemingly overnight, especially those in knowledge work such as professional services and management (Brynjolfsson et al., 2020). Remote work became the norm rather than the exception, and most executive assessments were conducted remotely on video conference. Video interviewing can reduce the cost of an assessment and increase convenience, but it can make it harder for the assessor to read body language, can make conversation more halting, and can make it more challenging to build trust quickly. Some evidence suggests that video interviewing, though not preferable to in-person interviewing, is not perceived as being less fair by managers (Guchait et al., 2014), although video calls can feel less spontaneous and interactive to participants and may cause assessees to perceive the interviewer as less friendly (McColl & Michelotti, 2019). Accordingly, assessors need to be prepared to seek out evidence for vitality and spontaneity in other ways if needed. For example, they might have a follow-up phone call or schedule an in-person meeting if time and conditions allow.

DATA ASSIMILATION AND REPORT WRITING

When data gathering is complete, it is time for the assessor to incorporate information from multiple sources into a report. This can be a daunting task, given the volume of data and information gathered in some assessment scenarios, so having an established process helps. The specifics of that process will manifest somewhat differently for each assessor, but a few basic approaches may be useful starting points in developing a system for integrating large amounts of information into useful and digestible insights for the client. This work begins with reviewing the inferences to be made and the purposes of the assessment, including the job specification and the context. Then the assessor revisits test scores, rereads interview notes, and begins to draw out themes and insights. This work can be accomplished in several ways.

One method is to list the major aspects of the job in two columns labeled "Strengths" and "Development Areas." While reviewing these two categories, the assessor can note thoughts, quotes, and other pieces of data under one heading or the other. Another approach is to list each of the job requirements in a separate column and then list within each column the candidate's strengths and weaknesses on that particular point. Once all the data have been revisited, look through the notes to see how they may coalesce into themes for strengths or development. This approach is particularly useful for drawing out high level insights from a mass of assessment results and can be a good first step in organizing thoughts for a report.

Another method is to create a table that includes a row for each job requirement and competency being assessed. Then, while rereading interview notes and test results, the assessor can add supporting evidence alongside each element. Table 4.3 shows a high-level version of this type of note-taking and organization method. This document can be referred to when writing up specific pieces of evidence that can be included in support of competency ratings or more general perspectives. This slightly more detailed method can result in a slower integration process, but it also provides a helpful reference document when delivering feedback to the client, and detailed support for more general insights that may appear in an assessment report.

Table 4.3

Sample Notes and Summary of Relevant Data on CEO Candidate

Dimension	Elements	Summary of relevant data
Knowledge & Experience	Senior business P&L leadership	▪ Accomplished business unit president with demonstrated track record of advancement through general management positions ▪ Led large organizations through multiple economic cycles, experiencing high growth and scale down mandates ▪ Limited multinational experience
	Credibility and experience working with regulators	▪ Worked in highly regulated industry for many years, though never held a position that required direct or in-depth interaction with regulators ▪ Speaks about regulatory issues with facility and clearly knowledgeable
	Leading an organization at scale	▪ Excellent financial management skills ▪ Has recruited leaders and brought others in to build out the ranks of his organization ▪ Scale does not meet target—largest organization led was ~$250m
Skills & Competencies	Big picture thinking	▪ Continually refers to key strategic initiatives aimed at driving future growth and vitality of the organization. Challenges assumptions about which initiatives are truly most important for future success ▪ Incorporates understanding of external market dynamics with internal performance levers (e.g., reorganizing innovation unit to partner more closely with account lead) to define the evolving future of the organization and better meet customer demands ▪ High scores on openness, information seeking and creativity scales
	Driving results	▪ "Got rid of 10–12 senior people in business unit who were resisting needed change. That was the first thing we had to do. No consistency. So hard to deliver for clients—took about 6 months to do it and to get the operations to come around"

(*continues*)

Table 4.3

Sample Notes and Summary of Relevant Data on CEO Candidate (*Continued*)

Dimension	Elements	Summary of relevant data
		▪ "I've tended to be good at taking something that's not performing well and correcting it. That's what I like. I enjoy getting digging into the business, peeling away the layers"
		▪ High need for achievement
	Enabling organizational change	▪ Reorganized operations group, moving existing director out and conducted national search for replacement—empowered new hire to implement changes in the group and grow staff (team grew from ~6 to ~14)
		▪ Explicitly intolerant toward "we've never done this before" thinking
		▪ "I've pushed for integrated systems and operations across business units. That's what I've been working on. I wanted to make sure we have a critical mass of people at the top who understand our common vision and common goal."
	Team leadership	▪ Delegated leadership of strategic initiatives to team members who are now leading teams to accomplish those goals
		▪ Sets up regular cadence of meetings, in addition to ad hoc meetings—not clear that meetings involve developmental topics or goals.
		▪ Provides open forum for team to come together and discuss issues honestly, though has a bit of a "come to me with solutions" approach that may discourage directs coming to her with problems and/or concerns
Traits & Abilities	Critical thinking	▪ 91st percentile—excellent verbal and numerical reasoning ability under time pressure—likely enhances strategic acumen
	Abstract reasoning	▪ 67th percentile—better than average abstract reasoning—able to absorb and communicate the high concept, but tends to drive the conversation back to tangible examples and concrete details
	Growth mindset	▪ Open to other perspectives, though must be convinced by a strong case with supporting data

Table 4.3

Sample Notes and Summary of Relevant Data on CEO Candidate (*Continued*)

Dimension	Elements	Summary of relevant data
Other	Multicultural orientation	▪ Only worked in the U.S., no non-English language skills ▪ Has led moderately diverse teams
	Integrity & ethics	▪ No apparent cause for concern here

The narrative structure of the assessment report starts with broad-based general insights and recommendations (see Figure 4.2). This represents the culmination of evidence and thought that has gone into considering an executive's development or suitability for a role. After that, the content of the report gets more granular and guides the reader through the details and themes that inform the general perspective. Then, within each theme are specific pieces of data and supporting evidence for the assessor's perspective and recommendations.

In a finalist assessment, a client may expect a direct comparison of the strengths and weaknesses and other relevant factors with which to help the client organization make a decision. In many cases, such as in selection assessments, this may take the form of a summary chart that makes for easier comparison across candidates (see Figure 4.3). In the case of a succession assessment, the client may be focused more on what each

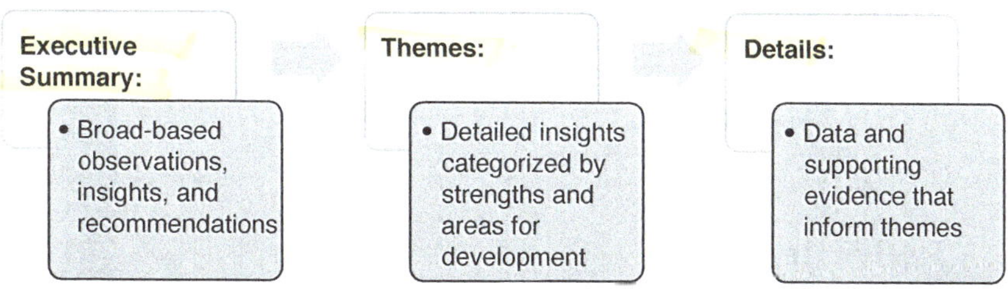

Figure 4.2

Representative content progression of an assessment report moving from broad general comments and recommendations to specific details and data.

Candidate Comparison

	CANDIDATE 1	CANDIDATE 2	CANDIDATE 3
Strengths	• Delivering results by aligning organization • Systematically developing the capability of the team	• Turning around results by empowering sales force • Creating stability in uncertain environments	• Restarting and reenergizing broken innovation systems • Navigating complex regulatory & competitive environments
Development Areas	• Soliciting others' input may slow him down unnecessarily	• Lacks deep industry knowledge • Developing teams	• Clear, concise communications
Leadership Style	• Thoughtful strategist	• Charismatic driver	• Dedicated innovator
Motivation for the Job	• Personal connection to the industry and products	• To deliver a big win for investors	• Opportunity to disrupt an industry with game-changing technology
Best Candidate For	• Aligning strategy and developing internal talent at scale	• Executing a rapid turnaround and driving aggressive sales growth	• Getting ahead of market trends and leading innovation

Figure 4.3

Sample candidate comparison.

candidate will need to do to continue developing as they grow in their career. Understanding the desired outcomes for the client helps the assessor provide the most useful presentation of and feedback on the data gathered.

In my own report writing, I tend to start with the details. After reviewing the position specification, I interpret results from online questionnaires and self-report tools, such as personality scales, values assessments, and cognitive ability test results. Then, I draw out themes from 360° feedback, to build some understanding of how an executive tends to be viewed by those around them. Next, I reread my interview notes and the interview transcript (or listen to the recording, if applicable) as needed, to revisit my thoughts during the interview and to help arrange results into overarching themes about areas in which the executive excels and areas in which they may have opportunities for development. Once I have a clear idea of the overarching themes, I can write a summary paragraph or two that describes my overall perceptions of the executive in the context in which they are being considered, and any relevant recommendations. This is clearly not the only way to approach assessment report writing, but I have found it useful because by the time I am considering themes and crafting a summary paragraph, I have thoroughly reviewed the data.

Another approach that is common among assessors who work in pairs or in teams is to have a dialogue about the executive after all of the information and assessment results have been gathered. This allows each assessor to provide their perception of the different elements of the assessment (e.g., a certain result on a personality measure, or a certain work experience in the executive's career history), and in this way the assessors can build a consensus for where an executive may score on a given competency model or behaviorally anchored rating scale (BARS; see Figure 4.4 for a sample BARS). Detailed competency models and BARS can serve as guidelines for assimilating information on each area of the assessment.

PREPARING THE WRITTEN REPORT

Even with a large amount of data—and perhaps because of the large amount of data that is often involved—writing an assessment report can be a challenge at times. It can be overwhelming to begin integrating so

BARS for "Driving Growth"

Level	Description	Behavioral Anchors
1	Unskilled	• Doesn't achieve goals consistently • Focuses primarily on activity, not on completing assigned tasks • Focuses on others limiting their ability to get things done rather than what they can do to accomplish tasks
2	Progressing	• Looks for ways to improve processes and makes suggestions • Takes action to get things done and demonstrate ownership • Creates tangible goals and plans for how to achieve them
3	Skilled	• Consistently delivers results at a level in line with top performers in the organization • Works hard to meet existing goals, and sets new goals once results are achieved • Can overcome obstacles and deliver even in challenging situations
4	Excels	• Creates better ways of doing things to help drive results for self and others • Considers alternative approaches to accomplishing challenging goals and can pick the best route • Learns from mistakes and adapts to changing circumstances to ensure success

Figure 4.4

Sample behaviorally anchored rating scale (bars) with behavioral anchors.

much information into a coherent report. The best place to start is to revisit the specific purpose of the assessment and the intended audience for the results and feedback. This context can help orient the assessor toward who will be reading the report and what kind of information they will find most relevant to the decision they are making. This distinction will mostly fall along the lines of assessment reports intended for selection decisions and those intended for development purposes. A selection assessment may warrant different elements, a different tone, and specific insights that might be excluded from a development assessment report. For example, whereas a selection report should include a statement that summarizes the assessor's perception of the candidates and reasons they may be good or bad fits for the job (see Figure 4.3), a development report may include the same strengths and areas for development, but should be worded to be more growth oriented, focusing on paths for improvement.

Within the report itself (see Figure 4.5), the assessor may include interpretations of data, quotes from the interview, and expert insights. Quotes from third parties that are attributable or identifiable should not be included in the assessment report unless consent from those parties has been obtained by the assessor. In some developmental contexts, consultants will not report percentile scores for personality traits or cognitive ability test results in developmental reports in an effort to encourage the client to focus on the primary message in the report rather than focusing on individual numbers. That said, perceptions of fairness in the assessment process seem to largely be driven by transparency in the feedback process and clear explanations of the objectivity and job-relatedness of the content included (Gregory & Levy, 2015).

FEEDBACK

Feedback is an essential element of the assessment process. The ultimate goal of an assessment is to gather and process information and communicate it to the client organization and to the executive in a useful manner. Whereas feedback for the client organization is often to help inform decision making in some capacity, for executives, the purpose is to help deepen their insight about themselves and inform their professional development.

Summary

PHOTO

Senior Vice President of Major Business Unit (BU)

International Corporation

2017-Present: SVP of Major BU
2013-2017: VP of Regional BU
2009-2013: VP of Specialized Products
2003-2009: Senior Product Manager
2000-2003: Commercial Manager

MBA: University of Virginia
BS: Engineering, NC State University

Overview

Sam is a confident executive with a composed presence. He drives change and achieves results by building close collaborative relationships with others and redesigning organizational structures. He has a strategic mindset and a clear sense of how to make decisions in order to drive performance. He partners closely with his colleagues and is comfortable delegating and empowering those with expertise beyond his own. He still enjoys working closely with clients and prefers to lead others by example.

Sam has limited experience developing full-scale strategic plans of his own, and more experience implementing strategies that are already given to him. He will benefit by continuing to sharpen his strategic acumen and his ability to communicate a compelling vision of the company to others.

Sam will be able to leverage his relationship building ability to continue to develop his skill as a leader, and as he grows in his ability to coach and develop others, he will become even more effective in leading a large organization.

Recommendation

While Sam could make a solid CEO candidate for International Corporation in the 3-5 years timespan, he does not appear to be ready now. He will benefit from gaining multinational experience and leading a diverse team at scale before.

Overview

	NO EVIDENCE	EMERGING	MEETS	EXCEEDS	BEST-IN-CLASS
Senior P&L Leadership			■		
Credibility w/ Regulators			■		
Leading at Scale		■			
Big Picture Thinking		■			
Driving Results					■
Enabling Change				■	
Team Leadership			■		

Figure 4.5

Sample candidate report.

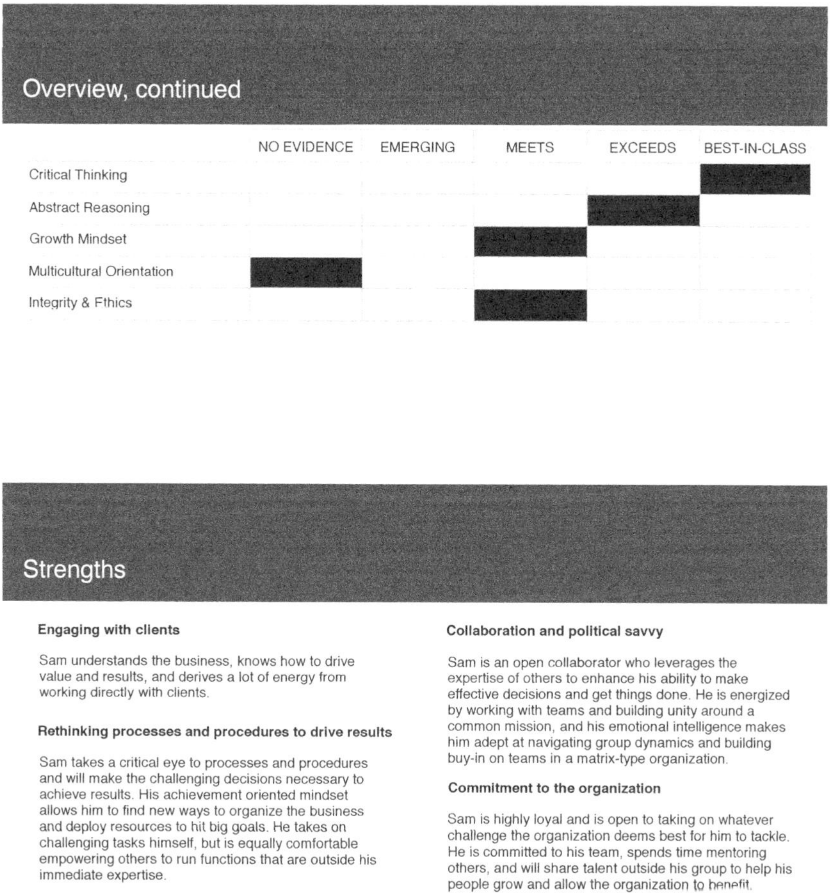

Overview, continued

	NO EVIDENCE	EMERGING	MEETS	EXCEEDS	BEST-IN-CLASS
Critical Thinking					■
Abstract Reasoning				■	
Growth Mindset			■		
Multicultural Orientation	■				
Integrity & Ethics			■		

Strengths

Engaging with clients

Sam understands the business, knows how to drive value and results, and derives a lot of energy from working directly with clients.

Rethinking processes and procedures to drive results

Sam takes a critical eye to processes and procedures and will make the challenging decisions necessary to achieve results. His achievement oriented mindset allows him to find new ways to organize the business and deploy resources to hit big goals. He takes on challenging tasks himself, but is equally comfortable empowering others to run functions that are outside his immediate expertise.

Collaboration and political savvy

Sam is an open collaborator who leverages the expertise of others to enhance his ability to make effective decisions and get things done. He is energized by working with teams and building unity around a common mission, and his emotional intelligence makes him adept at navigating group dynamics and building buy-in on teams in a matrix-type organization.

Commitment to the organization

Sam is highly loyal and is open to taking on whatever challenge the organization deems best for him to tackle. He is committed to his team, spends time mentoring others, and will share talent outside his group to help his people grow and allow the organization to benefit.

Figure 4.5

Sample candidate report. *(Continued)*

Development Opportunities

Delegation

Sam leads by example and enjoys staying close to the client. While this will help him build alignment and followership within the organization, he may benefit from spending more time at a more strategic level and considering how to develop talent and enhance organizational capability at scale. As his span of responsibility grows he'll need to delegate more and let go of the details in many cases in order to be most successful.

Broaden multicultural experience

While Sam is an expert in his area, he does not have experience and knowledge in other parts of the business overall, especially those outside the U.S. Though he likely has the capability to learn, he is effective and highly energized by his current mandate and may not have the motivation to develop the broader skill set.

Increase urgency in driving change

Sam's focus on the long-term health and cultural alignment of the organization make him a skilled influencer, but may cause him to drive change at a slower pace than needed. He will be adept at uniting others around his agenda, but his style may be too conservative in environments characterized by rapid change.

Learning agility

At times, Sam can over-value his ideas. Though he is open to the input of others he trusts and views as experts, he may dismiss insights from those he does not know well, which may be challenging in a much larger organization.

Appendix

- *Data summary*
- *Assessment background & methodology*

Figure 4.5

Sample candidate report. *(Continued)*

Data Summary

Cognitive Ability Results

Critical thinking	Ability to accurately draw inferences, identify assumptions, make logical deductions. Facility with data analysis and interpretation.	91% *(high)*
Abstract reasoning	Ability to think conceptually in order to make sense of complex and uncertain information.	67% *(average)*

Values Questionnaire Results

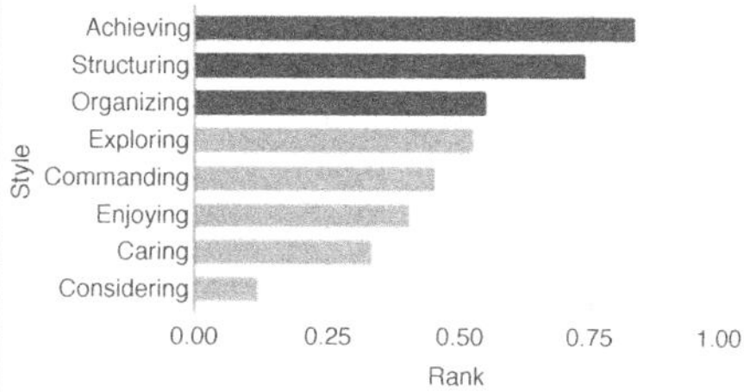

Assessment Background & Methodology

Assessment Background

The purpose of this report is to provide executive assessment and development recommendations to be used for succession planning and for ongoing leadership development.

Methodology

Executives are assessed on both their knowledge and experience, as well as their job-related competencies, traits and abilities. Competencies are rated using behaviorally anchored rating scales that can be viewed upon request.

This report has been written based on data from:

- 2 online psychometric questionnaires
- 1 cognitive ability test
- 2.5 hour structured behavioral interview

Figure 4.5

Sample candidate report. *(Continued)*

Delivering Feedback to the Organizational Client

Delivering feedback to the client can take many forms. In some circumstances, it may mean sharing assessment reports with a hiring manager, discussing candidates, and providing selection advice supported by assessment results. In many cases, especially at the highest levels of organizations, the feedback process will occur multiple times with different stakeholders, such as the CHRO, the CEO, and the board of directors. When feedback will be delivered to the client in multiple stages, it is beneficial to consider who within the organization needs to hear the feedback first so that they can participate in, or at least be aware of, the feedback delivered to other stakeholder groups. This usually means the assessor will deliver feedback to the client liaison with whom they have been working most closely throughout the assessment process, and then determine who else needs to receive the feedback and when. The assessor needs to consider that it is not only the content of their message, but how their message is delivered to the organizational stakeholders, that will affect how feedback is received and incorporated into the decision-making process.

For example, a CHRO was tasked by an organization's CEO with contracting assessment work as part of the process for creating a succession plan to be presented to the company's board. The board was pleased with the performance of the current CEO, but knew that the CEO was approaching retirement, and they wanted to gather some insight into possible successors within the organization.

After conducting work and context analyses, the consultant conducted multiple executive assessments. Having painstakingly completed the assessment work, the consultant felt the evidence did not support consideration of any of the assessees as a viable successor in the short or medium term, based on the organization's identified development needs. For example, one candidate demonstrated skill at building relationships and driving growth based on a strategy provided by the CEO, but was less adept at coming up with creative solutions to problems, especially when faced with technical business challenges. Furthermore, high agreeableness scores on a personality measure raised concerns for the consultant that the candidate might be more effective as a team player, rather than a leader.

As part of development recommendations, the consultant suggested that the CEO let this individual lead the next 5-year strategic planning cycle in order to take on a new challenge and develop. Other candidates had similar deficits that would need to be addressed over time and with consideration in order to expand their leadership capabilities.

The consultant knew that this conclusion might not be received well, especially given the large investment the company had made in having its executives assessed. So, the consultant first had a conversation with the CHRO to deliver the results and discuss the best format for delivering feedback to the CEO. Then, the CHRO and consultant delivered the results to the CEO and discussed the best format for delivering the feedback to the board. By the time the consultant presented the feedback to the board, the CHRO and CEO were well versed in the assessment feedback and had bought in to the value and relevance of the assessment data. After the feedback had been delivered to the board, the consultant set up times to meet with each assessee to provide feedback about their results and help craft development plans based on identified opportunities.

This type of tiered feedback process accomplishes a few things. First, it builds trust between the client and the consultant, and helps the consultant navigate the organizational political environment. In general, executives want to add value to the organization and don't want to be surprised by bad news, so the more a consultant can do to build a sense of control and awareness into the feedback process, the better. Second, a tiered feedback process creates opportunities for the consultant to shape their presentation of feedback so that it will be best received within the organization. The assessment results cannot be arbitrarily changed, of course, but understanding how to structure and position feedback so that it is most relevant to the given context can help make assessment results most useful to the client organization. For example, in one organization it may be preferable for the consultant to simply and directly state that they do not believe there is a viable CEO successor in the group of executives they have been asked to assess. Whereas, in another organization it may be preferable for the consultant to discuss the individual strengths and development areas of each executive prior to arriving at a more definitive conclusion. Finally, a tiered feedback approach helps create buy-in for assessment feedback within the organization. By delivering preliminary feedback to relevant stakeholders, the consultant can help ensure that organizational members understand the core message and the supporting data, so they can address the implications of the assessment within the organization when questions arise.

Both feedback delivery and the quality of the consulting engagement in general are driven by the quality of the client relationship. In the previous example, the consultant had an excellent, trusting relationship with the CHRO and the CEO because they had worked together effectively many times in the past. Even though the feedback raised challenging implications for the organization, it was received in good faith, without the client attempting to discount negative feedback or give greater weight to their own general impressions of the executives in question. It is important to remember that the assessor is an advisor who provides powerful data to help inform the decision-making process, but it is the quality of the relationship that will shape how feedback is received.

Assessors tend to differ somewhat in their thinking and strategies for sharing feedback with the assessed executive. Whether or not to share the results with assessees in a selection context, when to share results with executives, and how to share results are all questions that must be answered in delivering feedback.

Whether to or Not Share Results With Assessees

In general, psychologists are committed to increasing "people's understanding of themselves and others and to the use of such knowledge to improve the condition of individuals, organizations, and society" (American Psychological Association [APA], 2017a, p. 3). To that end, the preference should be to give feedback on assessment results to all participants when practicable. Realistically, this is not always possible when working with organizations. Although assessment results will clearly be shared with executives participating in development efforts, that is not always the case with those who participate in selection assessments. When it is not possible, or it is not the client organization's preference, to have unselected candidates receive feedback on assessment results, that should be included in the informed consent obtained from the participants prior to participating in the assessment (APA, 2017a). Some employers do not want to provide feedback because of fears of lawsuits by those not selected and/or because they do not feel they need to pay for feedback to unsuccessful candidates, especially those from outside the organization. Assessors should consider the jurisdictions in which they are operating and be cognizant of the legal and ethical requirements on the provision of feedback or the explanation of test results to participants. A good starting point for psychologists is to read relevant ethics codes and practice guidelines (e.g., APA, 2017a; British Psychological Society, 2017; Canadian Psychological Association, 2017; European Federation of Psychologists' Associations, 2015).

Assessment can be stressful for participants even though the process generates valuable information that can inform their development. Therefore, I prefer to build participant feedback into the process whenever possible. This warrants a conversation with the client, as there are expenses associated with giving feedback, and it needs to be made clear whether the client is open to feedback being shared with the assessee. Even if the feedback is an attenuated report, it can frequently help create transparency and goodwill among assessment participants, and can increase perceptions of fairness in the selection process (London & McFarland, 2017). In a selection assessment that includes internal candidates, sharing feedback with candidates who are not selected can be a critical piece in maintaining their commitment to the organization (Smith & Robertson, 1993).

Ethical issues are also at play here regarding who exactly the client is in terms of organizational consulting, confidentiality, and informed consent, and who gets to keep the assessment report, all of which also need to be discussed with assessees as a part of their informed consent.

When to Share Assessment Results With Assessees

The feedback process includes sharing the assessment report and reviewing the results. When to share the assessment report with the assessee is also a matter of some difference among assessors. Some will send the report a day or two prior to the feedback meeting with the executive to give them plenty of time to review the results on their own. Others will wait until a few hours prior to a feedback meeting, or even right as the meeting starts, to share the results so the executive does not have a chance to review the report in much depth without the guidance of the assessor. I prefer to send the report about a day in advance of a feedback meeting, so the individual has enough time to familiarize themselves with the report and make note of any questions or concerns, but not enough time to develop unnecessary conjecture about the meaning of the results without some guidance. People tend to have an emotional reaction when receiving negative feedback (Gregory & Levy, 2015), so if the feedback to be delivered is particularly challenging, it may be beneficial to decrease the time between the delivery of the report and the feedback conversation. Ultimately, the assessor will benefit from trying different approaches and evaluating what works best in different situations.

How to Share Assessment Results With Assessees

The purpose of providing feedback to an executive is to discuss the results of an assessment and how the results can be used. The central goal is to ensure that the executive understands the content of the report and how the information ties together to inform overall insights and recommendations. Establishing some structure for the conversation can help to accomplish that. I think about the phases of feedback in terms of (a) purpose, (b) content, and (c) questions.

Start by clarifying that the purpose of the feedback conversation, which is for the executive to have time to talk through results, clarify any questions or concerns, and generally have an open forum to discuss assessment results with the assessor. To that end, it is the assessee's time, and it can be utilized in whatever way they find most productive. After that, it can be useful to ask if they have had time to review the report. This question can shape the structure of the meeting. If they have not, the feedback tends to move into a more explanatory mode, in which the assessment process is reviewed along with the individual elements of the report and how they fit together. Then the specific details of the report can be discussed with more context and clarity.

If the executive has reviewed the report already, assessors can ask if there were any points that stuck out, or if there are any burning questions that should be discussed first. This inquiry is a helpful stopgap, because it can be unproductive to march through a rote explanation of an assessment report, if what the assessee primarily wishes to discuss is a specific development recommendation that they disagree with or find confusing.

Assessors will differ in their approach to debriefing the content of an assessment report. Whereas some may start with high-level insights and move into specifics, others may start with specifics and build to high-level insights. Some assessors may tailor feedback to follow each requirement and/or competency identified in the work analysis (e.g., feedback on strategic thinking, followed by feedback on developing others). When I am delivering feedback, I find it productive to start with data from self-report assessments and objective assessments, discussing why they were measured and how the assessment process related to the job under consideration. Then I move to 360° feedback, and then into broader integrated insights. I take this approach for two reasons. First, insights from self-report questionnaires (e.g., a personality inventory) and objective measures (e.g., a cognitive ability test) tend to be infused throughout an assessment report, so starting with a basic understanding of how that data is interpreted creates a good foundation for understanding other insights in a report. Second, results from measures the candidates complete themselves can generate new insights and self-awareness, which can create interesting conversations with an executive in their own right. In a few instances, I have had an hour-long feedback conversation focused solely on the results from a values questionnaire, because the executive was so interested in that information. After reviewing self-report results, I next discuss 360° feedback, if it was part of the assessment process, then review strengths and areas identified for development, and finally, go through overarching summative comments.

Finally, it is important to make sure that the executive does not have any lingering questions about the report of the specific assessment content. Questions will certainly arise throughout the assessee feedback process, especially if the assessor is treating the feedback as a conversation rather than simply a report. However, I find it useful to pause at the end of the conversation and ask again whether there are any unanswered questions, or anything else we did not discuss that might have been expected. The conversation then usually ends with some discussion of what the executive can anticipate to happen next in the assessment process.

SUMMARY AND CONCLUSION

After the assessment process is complete and feedback has been delivered, the role of the assessor shifts, and the nature of this shift will depend on the assessment context. In a finalist assessment, the work may be finished, and it may then be the job of the client to make a hiring or promotion decision. In succession and developmental assessments, the work will shift into creating plans for how the assessment results will be used to inform the next phase of work, and aligning those plans with the executive's direct manager (e.g., the CEO). This may include creating a plan for the assessed executive to help address development needs that were highlighted in the assessment process. Or it may include pursuing an executive coaching engagement, or seeking specific training and education to expand an executive's managerial capability. Likely at this phase of an engagement, contracting will become necessary again as the assessor and client establish how assessment work can be leveraged and applied, and what role the assessor may play in meeting the future needs of the organization.

KEY TAKEAWAYS

- Make time to contract effectively with client organizations to ensure everyone is in agreement about the goals and purpose of the assessment, how the work will be conducted, and by when. This includes matters of informed consent, such as whether they will receive feedback and when, who will have access to reports, and what will be done with the assessment results afterward.
- Anchor your assessment in a professionally prepared job description/ position specification. This includes the objectives and goals of the assessment and the variables to be measured. Make sure the job

description is accurate, up-to-date, and comprehensive, even if it is the one the company uses or the one developed by a search firm.

- If you write the job description, share a draft with the board and/or hiring manager to confirm all stakeholders agree on selection criteria and the prioritization of criteria.
- Select assessment tools that will allow you to adequately measure/predict the criteria of interest, based on evidence of validity and reliability for doing so.
- Take the time to create a record of your process, including notes on interpretation and data integration, and recommendations—it helps organize thoughts and insights, and can be particularly useful in fielding questions from the client that may require supporting evidence.
- Don't forget that the client is the decision maker and the assessor's job is to provide evidence and advisory support for decision making, not make the decision for them.

5

Technological Developments in Assessment

Imagine an executive candidate sitting down at their computer to complete a group of online tests. This executive is in the final stages of a recruiting process to be the chief product officer (CPO) for a well-funded, midsized software company that is looking to position itself to go public in the next 2 years.

After clicking on the link sent by the assessor, three tests are presented for the executive to complete. The first is similar to what the executive has seen before. It is an assessment with text-based questions and asks the test taker to select one item out of three options that best describes them. After the first item is selected, it disappears, and the test taker is asked which of the remaining two items best describe them. The test is untimed, and the executive proceeds at a pace through this familiar type of questioning and is soon finished with the first of a three-test battery.

The second assessment presents the executive with a set of directions describing a task to be completed. The executive is presented with an

https://doi.org/10.1037/0000264-006
Assessing CEOs and Senior Leaders: A Primer for Consultants, by J. R. Blankenship

image and a text box. After examining the image, they will need to write at least 50 words describing the image and anything that comes to mind based on the image. The images range from abstract items and illustrations, to scenes from an office setting. After the executive has written a number of descriptions, the test ends and thanks them for their time.

The final assessment presents the executive with a screen that is reminiscent of the maze from the arcade game PAC-MAN. The executive is provided with instructions for a task to complete. There is an avatar on the left side of the screen and a finish line on the right side of the screen. The executive's task is to get the avatar from the left side of the screen to the finish line in as few moves and as little time as possible. There is a clock keeping time in the top right side of the screen; once the piece crosses the finish line the time stops, and the executive is presented with a different maze to solve.

Technology, and the internet in particular, has been changing the way assessments are conducted for many years. The internet has allowed for a massive expansion of the number of people who can be assessed and the efficiency with which results can be analyzed and reported, all of which has increased the speed and relevance of assessment results in the modern economy. Additionally, the internet has expanded the types of items that can be used in assessment (as in the first test presented in the preceding case), analytic techniques that can be used to assess individuals (such as in the second test), and delivery formats (such as in the third test). The examples described in the case present some elements of the continuum of the digitalization and gamification that have caused assessment to evolve. Where the first test represents a more traditional assessment that has been modified to a web-based response mechanism, the second test presents an online version of a classic projective test, where results are scored from natural language processing rather than an evaluator. And finally, the last test represents a gamified test where the test taker feels like a game is being played, but behavior within the game and game results provide insight into the individual's cognitive ability and personality.

As one might imagine, these types of technological advancements in the field have created notable benefits for practitioner and user alike, but they are not without their limitations and disadvantages.

INNOVATIONS IN ASSESSMENT TECHNOLOGY

Many of the technological innovations in assessment are the result of putting things online, otherwise known as the *digital transformation* (Chamorro-Premuzic et al., 2016). Early innovations were as simple as the digitalization of paper and pencil tests, which increased scoring speed and reliability (Drasgow & Olson-Buchanan, 2018), and opened new avenues for item construction and scoring (e.g., computer-adaptive testing). Online testing also allowed for the introduction of new types of question prompts, such as audio and video, and expanded the ways in which individuals might respond to assessment items.

More recent developments represent extensions of early innovations, such as the application of tools and techniques to analyze massive amounts of data, higher fidelity and more immersive audio/video question prompts (e.g., virtual reality), and testing methods designed to increase the motivation and interest of test takers (e.g., gamification; Bleidorn et al., 2017; Chamorro-Premuzic et al., 2017, 2016; Drasgow & Olson-Buchanan, 2018). Mobile phones have also introduced the possibility of new response formats (SHL, 2019), and the deluge of data and information about individuals on the internet has created opportunities for unstructured "organic data" analysis (Xu et al., 2019). The effects of the digital transformation of assessments were summarized succinctly by Reynolds, Scott, and Bartram (2018) as:

- broadening the domain of available predictors and perhaps discovering/creating new ones (e.g., building timing protocols into assessments to predict faking or impression management, using online behavior to measure personality and interests);
- changing the measurement of those predictors by creating new response formats and item types (e.g., multidimensional forced-choice items that automatically rerank based on the test taker's first selection), and introducing challenges in maintaining standardized testing conditions (e.g., unproctored internet testing, varying internet speeds);
- better prediction of outcomes and increasing the timeliness/relevance of validity evidence through analytical methods such as machine

learning that automate the building and testing of models (Adler et al., 2018); and
- making assessments more accessible on multiple platforms (e.g., laptop/desktop computers, tablets, and mobile phones).

Research and practice have coalesced around a few specific iterations of these developments that have been most widely applied to date, including online testing, digital interviews (e.g., those conducted over video conference), gamified assessments (e.g., including elements in an assessment to make it more engaging and entertaining to the test taker), and social media analysis (e.g., examining social media posts for evidence of personality traits). Though not all of these developments have been consistently employed at the senior executive level yet, their impact is notable and increasing, so the competent assessor should have a working knowledge of each of these areas.

Online Testing

Online testing refers to the administration of personality measures, cognitive ability tests and the like, in a digital format. Online, or internet-based, testing may be distinguished somewhat from computerized testing in that internet-based tests tend to be accessed remotely and are often unproctored. That is to say, assessees take the test on their own computers or mobile devices and on their own time. In the context of executive assessments, online tests tend to be part of a suite of methods used to evaluate individuals. A candidate for a job or promotion may complete one or more online tests and measures during an assessment process. For example, a senior leader being considered for promotion to the executive team of a major corporation may complete a cognitive ability test, a personality measure, a values survey, and a 360° feedback self-report all on their own computer on their own time in the course of going through an executive assessment.

Some of the benefits of online testing in an executive assessment context are that it is fast, efficient, and provides reliably scored data. At the executive level, free time tends to be scarce, and the easier one can make it to gather assessment data, the better. Additionally, online measures produce reliably scored data that can be incorporated into individual reports and used to help make direct comparisons between candidates or team members in a comparative context.

Though online testing is highly prevalent and largely accepted as the norm today, it can present psychometric and other practical challenges (Adler et al., 2018). Research on the potential challenges with online testing tends to focus on two main areas of concern: measurement equivalence and test security (Woods et al., 2020).

Test security involves maintaining the integrity of test content as well ensuring the test taker's identity. Test security is a particular concern with online testing because in an unproctored environment, it can be harder to determine who has actually completed a test, it can be easier for a test taker to cheat on a test, and it can be easier for test material to be stolen.

Measurement equivalence in this context refers to two essential questions about the validity and reliability of online testing: (a) Is the same construct being measured in the online format as would be measured in a paper-and-pencil format? and (b) Are results the same in proctored versus unproctored situations? These questions also apply to different online testing formats, such as PC versus mobile phone versus tablet. Studies of measurement equivalence show mixed results, but general findings support equivalence across different types of measures (e.g., personality, cognitive ability, situational judgment tests [SJTs]) and across different testing formats (e.g., computer vs. mobile phone; Le Corff et al., 2017; Morelli et al., 2014). Although, findings also suggest that test scores are lower on average when cognitive ability and SJT measures are taken on mobile devices compared to personal computers (Drasgow & Olson-Buchanan, 2018; Morelli et al., 2014). Smaller screen sizes and the increased possibility of distraction may increase the cognitive load required to take these tests on mobile devices, which may account for some of these differences.

Digital Interviewing

Digital interviews include those conducted live over video conference and asynchronous interviews in which interviewees record video of themselves responding to a structured set of questions. Video conference interviewing is quite common, and as of this writing, is becoming more common given the increasing prevalence of video conference technology and remote work (Brynjolfsson et al., 2020). This has been challenging for interviewers and interviewees for many reasons. Interviewees, especially those in senior level positions, tend to view video interviews as colder and less personal than in-person interviews (Guchait et al., 2014). Interviewers may struggle to make a personal connection with the interviewee, which can make it harder to establish rapport quickly (Guchait et al., 2014; McColl & Michelotti, 2019).

Asynchronous digitally recorded interviews are perceived as less personal than video conference interviews; studies have shown that raters tend to rate performance higher for those in digital interviews compared with video conference interviews (Langer et al., 2017). More common as an entry level stage gate, asynchronous digital interviews are a hot area of technological development. Videos are analyzed by machine learning algorithms to rate interview performance (Langer et al., 2017), and interview responses can be analyzed by natural language processing systems to evaluate personality traits (Harwell, 2019).

At the executive level, video conference interviews are frequently used, and becoming more so. Face-to-face interviewing is generally preferred because it is more engaging, makes it easier to build trust and a relationship more quickly, and preserves a more natural opportunity to observe and respond to body language and other nonverbal cues in conversation. Asynchronous recorded interviews tend to be only used for a specific purpose, such as evaluating an executive's media presence, if the position has a significant public relation or speaking requirement. As technology progresses and our comfort interacting with and participating in digital media increases, this could be a technological innovation that is applied at the senior level more frequently.

Additionally, in some situations, in-person interviews may simply not be an option, so assessors may need to become comfortable with digital interviews to be prepared for such situations. This was a notable occurrence during the COVID-19 pandemic, but digital interviews can also occur for more mundane reasons, such as limited schedules and the feasibility of travel between the assessor and assessee.

Gamified Assessments

Gamification refers to the incorporation of gaming elements (e.g., competition, badges, level advancement) into nongaming activities (Georgiou et al., 2019). Game-based assessments are a type of "serious game," in which the purpose of the game being played is not just the entertainment of the gamer; the game also serves the purpose of measuring traits or abilities in the gamer (Georgiou et al., 2019). Hawkes et al. (2018) provided an in-depth treatment on the gamification of selection tools, considering what they measure, how they measure it, and what their utility is in a selection environment compared with more traditional assessment methods.

The aim of gamification is to make assessments more engaging, competitive, and visually appealing, with the goal of increasing the motivation and interest of the test taker (Chamorro-Premuzic et al., 2017). They can also simulate real working environments and provide opportunities for test takers to solve job-relevant challenges. Gamification can also reduce the test taker's feeling of being assessed within the testing environment, which may allow individuals to provide a more honest representation of themselves (Hawkes et al., 2018).

Though gamification is a promising area of innovation in assessment, much of the value is still theoretical, as studies on construct and outcome validity are sparse in the literature (Chamorro-Premuzic et al., 2017). Additionally, in high-stakes environments, game-based assessments lack face validity and raise questions about the fairness and seriousness of the testing program (Gibby et al., 2019). Gibby et al. (2019) suggested that even at lower levels in organizations, test takers in high stakes environments want to feel that they are being tested in a way that gives them the opportunity to perform at their best. Eliminating the feeling of being tested is a feature of gamified assessments, which may make them more challenging to use in high-stakes environments. Especially at the seniormost levels, assessors might expect even more pushback on a gamified assessment than a traditional cognitive ability test. Assessees may ask, "What does this have to do with leading a team/organization?" In that regard, gamified assessments may be more of a threat to a candidate in an executive selection context.

However, gamification elements such as points, leaderboards, and learning badges have shown to increase engagement and participation in training and development contexts (Armstrong & Landers, 2018). Indeed, business schools have begun developing gamified simulations that help students experience and learn from the leadership and decision-making challenges that occur in competitive and ambiguous circumstances (Mollick, n.d.; Sterman, n.d.). Findings like these show promise for the use of gamification in assessments, but assessors working at the executive level will tend to be better served using assessment formats with demonstrated validity and reliability, and that can be clearly shown to be job relevant.

For example, one such gamified assessment presents the test taker with a pattern and two or more building blocks that must be arranged to fit into the pattern (Criteria Corp., n.d.). It plays a bit like a more static version of the game Tetris. Arranging the blocks into the pattern is a timed activity, and once the task is completed, the test taker is presented with another pattern to fill with different blocks. Multiple minigames like this are played in sequence, and the results provide insight into the test taker's critical thinking, problem-solving skills, verbal knowledge, and ability to learn new information, and the results are highly correlated with more traditional cognitive ability assessments (Gibby et al., 2019). Although results like this are encouraging for the innovation of testing systems, executive assessors should consider the face validity of such measures and evaluate whether they are appropriate for a given executive assessment context.

Social Media Analysis

The massive increase in internet usage over the past 10 years has seen a similarly massive increase in the size and reach of online social media and social networking websites. These websites (e.g., LinkedIn, Glassdoor) have expanded usage across the globe, creating a massive store of unstructured data and information about potential job candidates. Social media behavior does have modest correlations to more established personality assessment methods (Zickar, 2018), but research has shown low or no correlation with job performance (Woods et al., 2020). The link between social media and job performance is tenuous and in need of much more research to establish validity evidence (Chamorro-Premuzic et al., 2016). Though social media analysis has the promise to deliver an "outside-in" perspective on an individual's personality, or other traits and abilities, faking and impression management on social media is not well-understood (Zickar, 2018). Outside-in assessments raise serious ethical concerns about informed consent and use of data for those who are being assessed. The public was made particularly aware of these concerns in the Cambridge Analytica scandal revealed in the spring of 2018, in which the firm exploited Facebook data in order to profile millions of individuals and target them with political advertising (Cadwalladr & Graham-Harrison, 2018).

Most employers check social media and/or conduct a web search on job applicants before making hiring decisions. So-called *cybervetting* includes examining any and all information that can be found about an individual on the internet. At the executive level, social media profiles (especially LinkedIn) are almost always examined, though frequently this analysis is conducted by executive search firms or by human resources (HR) at the hiring organization. As an assessor, cybervetting in general should be conducted with caution to avoid adding unnecessary noise to a candidate evaluation. There seems to be now some implicit mutual understanding between employees and employers that some amount of online or social media screening will be conducted (Berkelaar, 2014). Accordingly, there is some evidence that candidates may engage in some level of impression management to make sure their online appearance is acceptable (Cook et al., 2020). This should add to the caution that assessors use in relying on such information for their analysis. If cybervetting is requested by a client, I recommend outsourcing it to a firm that conducts background checks, or conducting the full assessment, analyzing and preparing the results, and only then doing an internet check so that the information does not bias the interpretation of assessment data.

THE SPECIFIC CASE OF THE CEO

At the executive level, many of these innovations are applied more cautiously because of the high-stakes nature of the work, the limited sample sizes, and the perceptions of the executives participating in the assessments. This will certainly evolve as the evidence for and acceptance of new methods increase. Additionally, younger professionals will likely favor internet-based testing and mobile-first delivery (Anderson, 2019; Perrin & Kumar, 2019), suggesting that both methods will become more relevant as these individuals move into more senior positions over time. However, ethical guidance around evidence-based practice and competence (see Chapter 3, this volume) suggests that practitioners should exercise caution when adopting new technologies into their assessment of senior leaders.

For example, a consultant was hired to conduct selection assessments on a tight deadline with a 2-week turnaround, since the client wanted assessment results for a pending board meeting. There were three finalist candidates: one internal candidate (the chief operating officer), and two external candidates, both sitting CEOs of other businesses. The internal candidate was able to create time, on short notice, for an in-person interview, but the external candidates were not. However, the external candidates both agreed to have their assessments conducted via video conference. Unfortunately, at the time of the assessment, one of the external candidates had a slow internet connection that made videoconferencing impractical. In the process of troubleshooting, the candidate and the consultant decided they should use the time they had allotted, given the tight deadline, and so proceeded with conducting the assessment on the phone. Thus, of the three finalist candidates, one was assessed in person, one on video, and one on the phone. In delivering feedback to the board, the consultant had mixed evidence with which to respond to questions about the interpersonal and emotional intelligence of the candidates assessed and later wondered if the candidates who had been interviewed on video and on the phone had been inadvertently disadvantaged.

This case provides an example of how the practical matters that can arise in the course of conducting assessments (e.g., aligning schedules and timing) can have downstream implications for the validity of the assessment. Essentially, each candidate in this scenario received a different assessment, which raises the question of whether the different interview methods used yielded comparable validity for evaluating candidates for the job. After learning about the scheduling limitations, the consultant could have pushed back on the timeline with the client, describing the potential limitations of test results and interpretation that could emerge given the constraints. Alternatively, when it became clear that not every candidate could meet in person, the consultant could have requested that all of the interviews be conducted via video, to ensure the common method was used with each participant. Finally, the consultant might have proposed that the chief operating officer's assessment (the internal candidate) proceed as planned, but that the external candidate's results be reviewed at a later board meeting, so that there would be adequate time to conduct a full in-person interview.

RISKS OF USING TECHNOLOGY IN ASSESSMENT

Advancement in these tools and technology, along with their growing use, promises a major revolution in assessment methods. But technological advancement does not come without its challenges. As new methods of assessment are incorporated into the practice of executive assessment, care must be taken to account for their risks and limitations.

Reynolds, Scott, and Bartram (2018) noted that innovation and technological advancement must be balanced with the fundamental attributes of measurement in assessment. Internet-based testing raises several concerns of this nature, including (a) reduced test security, (b) lack of standardization in the testing environment, (c) measurement equivalence across administrative formats (i.e., is evidence of validity and reliability equivalent when using different testing formats such as PC vs. mobile phone?), (d) construct irrelevant variance (i.e., factors that may affect test results but are not measured or accounted for in the test), (e) reduced reliability, and (f) commercialization at the expense of sound psychometric principles (e.g., validity, reliability—see Chapter 1).

For example, newer companies that are more focused on user experience, or the quality of the test taker's interaction with the test, may prioritize speed and efficiency over validity. Sometimes this is done to enhance marketing (e.g., "short test with incredible insights!") or to avoid survey fatigue, in which test takers become distracted or uninterested in completing a test after a certain period of time (Davies, 2019). Shortening tests, however, can limit test validity and make test results less reliable.

As software and internet-based solutions expand in this area of practice, professionals from many other disciplines are focused on assessment and the prediction of behavior, not just professionals from adjacent fields of psychology (e.g., clinical, counseling) or business, but also from data and computer science, statistics, marketing, and communications. Individuals from different professions hold various perspectives on the ethics of the work being done, as well as the duties and responsibilities of those conducting the work. For example, a data scientist's primary professional duty may be to train machine learning algorithms to predict outcomes (e.g., job performance) as accurately as possible from large data sets. They may succeed, but not be able to explain how or why the algorithm works. This type of atheoretical prediction can be intriguing, but also quite limiting in an organizational setting where theory should orient assessment methods and inform feedback, coaching, and other aspects of development (M. Gonzalez et al., 2019). It may not be the purview of a data or computer scientist to worry about such issues if their primary professional objective is the innovation of software systems.

For example, some companies use data about employees that is publicly available on the internet (e.g., LinkedIn profile information) in order to predict probability of turnover at the individual level over a given period of time (e.g., 3 months, 6 months, 1 year). These companies claim that the predictive validity is quite strong, but the use of such tools raises legal and ethical concerns. Employees may not know their employer is evaluating their turnover intentions using artificial intelligence and machine learning, and so cannot provide informed consent. The data used in these algorithms—essentially set processes that are followed in order to calculate results—may not be job relevant, or may even use data that can be found on social media platforms (e.g., age, race) that falls under the protections of hiring and discrimination laws (see Chapter 3).

For example, a company worked with a consultant to develop a hiring algorithm that could predict with a high degree of accuracy those candidates who were likely to leave after a few months and those who were likely to stay at the company for at least a year. The algorithm used a sophisticated data analytic technique that incorporated any information that could be found about a candidate on the internet, as well as cognitive ability and personality test results. After a year of testing, the company had a data set that seemed to show exactly whom to hire to avoid short-term turnover. The company implemented the program into their hiring process and saw an almost immediate drop in turnover and in the cost of hiring. Management was thrilled.

Not long after the implementation of this tool, a class action lawsuit was filed alleging discriminatory hiring practices at the company. A look at hiring numbers showed a clear pattern of adverse impact, particularly against Black individuals. The management of the company felt their position was defensible because they had a sophisticated machine learning algorithm helping them predict who was likely to work well at the company. However, an investigation was conducted into the components of the hiring algorithm, and it was learned that a key feature that drove the prediction was the candidate's zip-code, which was incorporated from online information. Essentially what they learned was that applicants who lived closer to the company were less likely to turnover. Not only was the predictor not job relevant, but local neighborhoods were disproportionately white, so the method had introduced a discriminatory hiring practice within its complex machine learning features.

ADVANCED COMPUTING TECHNIQUES

Artificial intelligence and machine learning (AI/ML) have become increasingly prevalent in the world of organizational psychology and individual assessment because of the promise of increased predictive validity

(Chamorro-Premuzic et al., 2017). AI/ML are complex statistical methods that can allow a computer to mimic human-like intelligence (e.g., object recognition, problem solving, decision making; West, 2018). This is potentially valuable in assessment because AI/ML algorithms can process vast amounts of data and can open up new sources of information (e.g., social media activity, unstructured text data, biometric sensors) for describing and predicting human behavior (M. Gonzalez et al., 2019). For example, studies have shown that work history questionnaires can be analyzed by machine learning algorithms to predict turnover and on-the-job performance ratings (Sajjadiani et al., 2019).

What is important to know about AI/ML in the context of executive assessment mostly has to do with limitations. AI/ML are big data methods, which means they require a large volume of data that comes from a variety of sources that accrues with some velocity (Guzzo, 2015). This type of data is almost never available in executive assessment. Executive assessments are characterized by small sample sizes, and in many cases executives are assessed by private companies that use proprietary methods, so data sharing and aggregation is limited even further. M. Gonzalez et al. (2019) provided an excellent overview of the potential limitations of AI/ML, including:

- Quality data: AI/ML algorithms require good data to make good predictions, and that data must meet the same professional, legal, and psychometric standards as required in any selection system. For example, if an AI/ML algorithm is "trained" (or validated) with data that overrepresents a certain gender, race, or ethnicity, that bias may be baked into the patterns in the data that it ultimately identifies. Additionally, if the data set is not substantial enough, then predictive models may not be able to achieve any more predictive insight than traditional assessment methods (as may be the case with executives).
- The "black box" problem: AI/ML algorithms work by identifying complex patterns in large data sets that may not be fully explainable to users. So, an algorithm may produce a strong predictive validity, but users may not be able to identify exactly how or why a certain outcome is obtained. Additionally, as suggested in the prior case about

overselecting candidates from certain zip-codes, the driver of the prediction may be data that causes discriminatory treatment.

- Ethical and legal concerns: All of the relevant ethical and legal concerns involved in individual and executive assessment are relevant in the use of AI/ML methods. Informed consent, confidentiality, adverse impact and differential treatment of underrepresented groups are all still at issue in the use of new computing techniques in assessment (M. Gonzalez et al., 2019).

Although it may be some time before these kinds of methods are applied at the executive level with any scale, it is important for assessors to understand the issues at play in these emerging techniques and to be able to evaluate the risks and opportunities of using new methods in their practice.

EVALUATING NEW TECHNOLOGY

Coyne and Bartram (2018) proposed a method they called the "Prime-3" questions for evaluating new assessment systems and technology. It is a simple framework to use as one considers incorporating new tools into practice. The three key questions are: "Is it fair?" "Is it psychometrically sound?" and "Is it secure?"

Is It Fair?

The question of fairness has to do with whether the playing field is level for all test takers. This includes accessibility, elements of design, informed consent, job-relatedness, and equitable treatment. Issues of design and accessibility can range from fast internet access to color-blindness. For example, assessments that have items or result in reports that rely heavily on color may limit access for individuals who are color-blind. Cognitive ability assessments with a timed component may disadvantage those with slower internet connections and upload speeds. Informed consent and job relatedness ensure that testing is appropriate to the assessment context and that test takers have agreed to the terms and conditions of participation, which may include not just consent to take a test, but how the results will be used, who will have access to the results, and what and how data will be stored. Additionally, assessors should consider how best to reduce opportunities for cheating and other construct irrelevant variance.

Fairness also concerns equitable treatment on the basis of race, ethnicity, sex, gender identity, sexual orientation, disability, age, socioeconomic status, and culture; and indeed equitable treatment may factor into other elements of fairness and accessibility. Consider, for example, the issue of mobile phone testing. Evidence suggests there are differences among races and ethnicities in terms of access to digital technology and how they use that technology (Anderson, 2015; Perrin & Turner, 2019). Evidence suggests certain protected groups may make up a larger proportion of mobile test takers, and research on cognitive ability tests has shown that individuals score lower on average on mobile testing formats than on the same test taken on a laptop or desktop computer (Drasgow & Olson-Buchanan, 2018). Furthermore, slower internet speeds may give test takers less time to complete items on timed assessments, which may artificially depress their scores. These are the kinds of downstream implications that assessors should evaluate when considering using new assessments and new technology.

Essentially, the question of fairness encourages the practitioner to evaluate how to best ensure that those participating in an assessment, or a specific element of an assessment, each access the assessment on an equal level so that observed construct-related variance can be reliably and validly interpreted as such.

Is It Psychometrically Sound?

The question of *psychometric soundness* has to do with determining the reliability and validity of new assessment instruments. This question encourages the practitioner to consider that online assessment, and AI/ML-based methods should be held to the same psychometric standards as traditional assessment methods. The practitioner should be wary of mistaking abundant data and strong predictive validities for good data and should look for validity evidence that is job related within the given context (Guzzo, 2015). Large samples do not necessarily mean representative samples, and senior executive ranks are notoriously lacking in diversity (e.g., Larcker & Tayan, 2020). That is why it is important to consider more than just evidence of predictive validity when evaluating new tools. One needs to consider how the tool was made, the samples that make up the evidence of validity and reliability, the job relatedness of the content, and the appropriateness for the assessment context. For example, consider an AI/ML tool that has been trained to predict job performance and shows strong evidence of validity. Given the small numbers problem that exists in senior leadership levels (i.e., it is a challenge to assemble large samples of data on executives), one should investigate the nature of the job performance that is being predicted and the population for whom it is relevant. A tool that works well at the entry or middle management level may not produce reliable information at the executive level.

Is It Secure?

Test security relates to the test itself and protecting the intellectual property (IP) of the assessment. Assessors have a responsibility to ensure IP is not compromised. The second key element of test security is data privacy. Maintaining the confidentiality and authenticity of data, as well as protecting personally identifiable information collected during the assessment process, is of utmost importance. Executives express varying levels of sensitivity to the question of data privacy in an assessment context, but rest assured, nobody wants their cognitive ability assessment scores leaked, stolen, or shared without their consent. And the question of security is relevant at every part of the data transmission chain, from test provider to the assessor to the client.

The idea of a security breach may conjure images of burglars searching file cabinets with flashlights, but in the realm of executive assessment, it is usually not so dramatic. For example, in one circumstance, after assessing a slate of finalist candidates for a public company CFO role, an assessor compiled all the reports and an executive summary into a cloud-based data storage system. Because the file was too large to email to the client, the assessor went to the sharing settings and added the client contact's email address and pressed "send." The assessor then emailed the client contact separately to let them know that a link should have been received to the shared folder with each executive's assessment report. Shortly thereafter, a message was received from the client that the link never came through. The assessor returned to the folder to check the sharing settings and learned that the link had been mistakenly sent to a candidate from a recently completed assessment who shared a similar name to the client. When the assessor was typing in the name, the file sharing software had auto-completed the email address and the assessor had simply jumped to the "send" button without confirming the details.

The consultant had accidentally shared highly confidential assessment information from an ongoing CFO finalist assessment process with an unaffiliated third party. After learning about the error, the assessor changed the sharing settings, emailed the candidate who received the information in error, explained what happened, and asked that the information be disregarded and not viewed. The assessor then called the client to let them know what had occurred and to see if further action was warranted.

Other Considerations

As technological advancements continue to shape and evolve the way assessments are delivered, it is the ultimate responsibility of the assessor (i.e., the test user) to decide the appropriateness of a given method or technology for a given situation, based on a careful review of the evidence. For example, a consultant was working with a creative, energetic, and high-growth software company to create a succession and development plan for top management. The chief human resources officer (CHRO) and CEO, who had hired the consultant, had said they wanted the assessment process to give them insight into who could be a potential successor to the CEO, but that they also wanted the process to be enjoyable for the executives. With that in mind, the consultant decided that it might be interesting to use an innovative online simulation-based personality test as part of the assessment process. The assessor went to incorporate the results of the test into the assessment report and learned that the assessment company only had a general population norm group that was based on a few hundred responses, none of whom were senior leaders or executives. This caused the consultant some concern about the validity of the results of the test, decided not to use the results, and instead asked the CHRO and CEO if another personality measure could be added to the assessment process to ensure useful data were obtained.

Test providers, especially as software companies develop more tests themselves, will likely always produce new instruments more quickly than robust scientific evidence has accumulated to support their use, so it is up to the test user to seek out available evidence to support test use and to make the decision for when and how to apply new testing methods. It is the job of assessors to stay informed and ensure that they have enough information to use assessment methods in a valid way for a given assessment situation. That said, those working for large assessment and consulting firms will often have little choice about what tools to use. In those circumstances, assessors will still benefit from staying up-to-date on new assessment developments and validity evidence. It is not uncommon for assessment consultants to field questions about new assessment technologies and/or how their tools compare to others on the market. Having an informed opinion not only allows an assessor to contextualize the tools they may be using within the broader sphere of assessments, but can also help them learn if and when it may make sense to add new tools (or retire old ones) based on new evidence for validity.

ETHICAL AND LEGAL CONSIDERATIONS

Ethical and legal considerations are discussed in detail in Chapter 3, but the unique issues that arise from technological applications of assessment and telepsychology warrant additional discussion here. The American Psychological Association (APA; 2013) *Guidelines for the Practice of Telepsychology* (hereinafter referred to as the Telepsychology Guidelines) are a key resource and cover these issues in detail. Guzzo et al. (2015) also provided a detailed review of ethical and legal issues that arise in the use of big data and advanced computing techniques in particular, including (a) privacy and personal information, (b) informed consent, and (c) integrity of data and data analysis. Much of the ethical guidance around these issues concerns the need for the practitioner to be competent and knowledgeable about the technologies being used, and to be mindful of the implications and impact that technology can have on an assessment practice.

For example, cloud storage and cloud-based collaboration tools have created massive efficiencies in the way that files can be organized and shared. These same efficiencies, however, introduce vulnerabilities for privacy and data security, including increased possibilities for breaches and mismanagement of data. The complexity of these of these issues can range from simple password protections and limited access to certain folders, to what to do if files are hacked or leaked. The Telepsychology Guidelines provide some insight into these issues, such as the need for psychologists for inform clients of "the potentially increased risks to loss of confidentiality inherent in the use of the telecommunication technologies, if any" (Guideline 4, Confidentiality of Data and Information), to taking "reasonable steps to ensure that security measures are in place to protect data and information related to their clients/patients from unintended access or disclosure" (Guideline 5, Security and Transmission of Data and Information; APA, 2013). These guidelines are relatively straightforward and easy to implement as a part of informed consent and maintaining protocols around access to client files and data security. However, this all becomes a lot more complicated when one considers the fact that data have no borders, but states, and certainly countries, do; and different countries likely have different data privacy standards and laws.

Guideline 8, Interjurisdictional Practice states, "Psychologists are encouraged to be familiar with and comply with all relevant laws and regulations when providing telepsychology services to clients/patients across jurisdictional and international borders" (APA, 2013). The adoption of the General Data Protection Regulation (2016) in the European Union (EU) provides a good case in point of the challenges inherent here. When the laws went into place in the EU, compliance was required by organizations that gather, process, and store information about individuals in the EU

(Harris, 2018). So, for example, if a U.S.-based assessor sends links to an executive in the EU and conducts a video conference interview as part of an assessment, they are operating across jurisdictions and will need to take steps to comply with laws and regulations accordingly. The United Nations Conference on Trade and Development (UNCTAD; n.d.) has a website that provides useful guidance on which countries have data protection and privacy laws, what the legislation is called, and where to find it, although assessors should certainly consult an attorney as needed.

Technological developments in assessment are certainly an exciting frontier in psychology. It is an area in which practice will almost certainly outpace scientific research, and it will benefit executive assessors to stay informed of innovations in the field, even if they may have only limited applicability in common executive assessment contexts.

KEY TAKEAWAYS

- Stay informed about developments in assessment technology and associated research by reading relevant journal articles, attending workshops and webinars on the topic, and reading news in the business press about new developments in HR technology. Additionally, checking updates at professional associations, such as the Association for Computing Machinery (https://www.acm.org/), can provide helpful insight into innovations and developments in advanced computing that may have an impact for consulting psychology in the future.
- Consider the distinctive elements of the executive population (e.g., the high-stakes nature of the work, limited sample sizes) when introducing new assessment methods and technology. Additionally, consider the perceptions of the executives participating in the assessments, and whether they will view tools or methods as face valid. Though face validity does not necessarily impact the quality of the assessment, it can impact the executive's buy-in and engagement in the process.
- Have a carefully developed and continuously updated protocol for managing data privacy and security.

- Evaluate the validity and reliability evidence of new assessment methods and tools with the same rigor that you would a more traditional measure. Is it fair? Is it psychometrically sound? Is it secure?
- Consider the downstream implications of new technological developments in assessment and how they might introduce bias or create risks to validity and reliability (e.g., using timed tests when assessing people whose scores are likely to be lowered by poor internet interconnectivity).

6

Professional Development and Future Directions in Executive Assessment

I did my training in executive assessments when I was in graduate school studying to get my PhD in consulting psychology. I had gone to graduate school having worked briefly in the insurance industry and then in the finance industry, so I had some basic understanding of how businesses were structured and how they operated. During an executive coaching internship at the Center for Creative Leadership, I had helped a mentor gather and synthesize 360° feedback interview data for senior leaders who were going through coaching programs. I had also assessed and coached a number of senior level leaders in small organizations under supervision through the school's organizational consulting center. After I finished my master's, and while I was writing my dissertation, I was hired by a boutique executive search firm to start their leadership assessment practice. I had been invited to the firm to teach the founder and

https://doi.org/10.1037/0000264-007
Assessing CEOs and Senior Leaders: A Primer for Consultants, by J. R. Blankenship

the partners about assessments and how they might be incorporated into the search process to enhance candidate evaluations. I ended the presentation with a few recommendations on where the firm might find candidates to lead such a group. However, the founder asked if I would consider doing it.

At that point in my career, I had limited executive assessment experience, and almost no experience in structured interviewing. I was very cognizant of not wanting to make a mistake or do something unethical, so formed a sort of advisory board for myself. I recruited three consulting psychologists, each of whom had extensive assessment and coaching experience, who could advise me on the development of the assessment process I was creating and provide a form of supervision and mentorship as I worked.

Because I lacked interviewing experience, I designed the assessment process to be as data driven as possible. The plan was to work alongside my search consultant colleagues as they evaluated candidates. Once a slate of finalist candidates had been identified, my colleagues in the search, who had extensive interviewing experience, would conduct the structured interviews and I would collect psychometric information in the form of personality and cognitive ability tests. Then we would collectively give feedback to clients about job, team, and culture fit. The combination made for an effective advisory partnership, and I gained an immense amount of on-the-job training, mentorship from my advisory board, and general business experience.

As my interest in executive assessments grew, I knew I would need to find a job wherein I could gain experience working with more seasoned assessors and learn how to conduct a structured interview. I was also interested in being able to work across a broader array of companies and industries, so that I could gain a better sense for what executive assessment work looked like in different contexts. With two options to choose from, I decided to join an advisory group that was made up of a mix of management consultants and psychologists. I figured that working among former management consultants would provide a unique opportunity to expand my perspective on how to think about assessment and how to work with organizations. Additionally, the group I joined used an assessment process that included a half-day (4-hour) structured interview, so I knew I would get extensive training on that front.

Looking back on that process of my development, I can see how much of the practice of executive assessment I needed to learn. I had business experience, but I certainly had more to learn about how businesses operated, especially at the Fortune 500 level. Additionally, while I had highly practical assessment experience and deep content knowledge in the area, I needed to learn how to conduct interviews, and I wanted more experience integrating insights into a comprehensive report. I was fortunate to join a company that was committed to training new assessors extensively in the classroom and through an apprenticeship-based model where at least two assessors conducted each assessment, generally one more senior and one more junior. Because of that, I began working on high-level executive assessments immediately, sitting in the "second chair," and assisting more senior consultants by taking notes and collaborating on report writing. This progressed to conducting portions of assessments, to conducting full assessments under supervision, to running full assessment processes with a broad swath of clients.

I learned that executive assessment can be a critical component of the talent decisions made at the higher levels of organizations and that it can be equally impactful to the executives being assessed. Assessments can help people build self-awareness, provide a framework and language for them to understand and describe their strengths and development areas, and serve as a starting point for ongoing growth and improvement (Silzer & Jeanneret, 2011). These important outcomes, however, rely on the assumption that the assessment is conducted effectively, and central to effective assessment is the competent practitioner. Ultimately, the competent practitioner of executive assessment needs the knowledge, confidence, experience, and mentorship to deliver impactful results. Accordingly, this chapter provides information on the skills that are required to conduct effective executive assessments, training, education, and development paths for professionals from different backgrounds, and some thoughts on potential future directions in executive assessment.

WHAT DO SKILLED ASSESSORS DO?

At a conceptual level, what skilled assessors do is listen to and observe others, organize and integrate information into useful frameworks, and communicate with and advise others on how to use that information to make decisions and take action. They talk to other people and they listen. They notice details and remember key phrases and insights. They can effectively collect, sort, and interpret data, observations, and insights about others' thoughts, feelings, and behavior. They recognize patterns and can develop hypotheses about an individual and, by probing and looking for more information, can confirm or disconfirm their hypotheses (Silzer & Jeanneret, 2011). They can structure questions to elicit the insights and information that generate useful data and in a way that is not necessarily unenjoyable for the executives involved. They draw on information and data from various sources and integrate them into coherent thoughts and recommendations based on evidence. They engage in metacognition, or examining their own thought processes, and can evaluate how their thoughts and feelings may improve or diminish their judgment about others. Importantly, they investigate their own biases and limitations and understand how their own cultural background, with its attendant norms and assumptions, shapes their perceptions. They consider how race, ethnicity, and gender influence their perceptions of others, and they work to build self-awareness around their own cultural relativity, which helps them to understand that their own culture is simply one among many and not better or worse than others (Glover & Friedman, 2015). They deliver feedback to clients and assessees with credibility (Gregory & Levy, 2015). They use their expertise to help shape others' thinking, and they help organizational leaders weigh the relative costs and benefits of different courses of action, helping them think through complex decisions that are made under uncertain conditions.

For example, a CEO was considering two chief financial officer (CFO) candidates who had been recruited by an executive search firm. The company had just taken a $40 million investment from a private equity firm to fuel their growth for the next 18 months, but as part of the investment, they required the CEO to hire a new CFO who could help professionalize the finance function. Both candidates looked equally qualified on paper in terms of their expertise and their past experience. The CFO was a critical hire. This would be a key member of the executive team, and would ideally be the CEO's right-hand person over time. Unsure what information would tip the scales, the CEO brought in a trusted consultant who had conducted assessments for the executive team in the past. The mandate of the engagement was essentially: "Help me figure out whom to hire, and why." Both candidates participated in an assessment process that included an in-depth personality measure, a personal values measure, and a structured interview.

When the results came in, the consultant agreed with the CEO that the two candidates were similarly qualified for the position. The consultant went on to describe each candidate. The first scored considerably higher on personality traits related to openness to experience and information seeking, and demonstrated values oriented toward exploring new ideas and achieving challenging goals. The second candidate scored high on the same information-seeking measure, but far lower on the openness to experience measure, and demonstrated values oriented more toward creating stability and efficiency to maximize productivity. As the CEO put it, "That's interesting, but what do I do with that information?" The consultant responded, "Think about it this way—both candidates can do this job, no question—but what you need to consider is how you want this job to be done. Based on the assessment results, I expect candidate one will take a more strategic approach to the CFO role, investigating opportunities, considering different paths to the future, and pulling back to help you think about the big picture. I expect candidate two will take a more data-driven approach and will turn the finance function into a smooth-running machine. It might help to consider the type of thought partnership you think you need to be successful and let that help you make the decision." The CEO said that was just the kind of clarity the situation demanded, and that the job would be offered to the second candidate the following week.

KNOWLEDGE, SKILLS, AND COMPETENCIES OF ASSESSORS

The expertise required to conduct executive assessment effectively is multiform. At a basic level, the assessor must be knowledgeable about individual assessment itself, the job, the organization, the industry (to a certain extent), and the assessor's own biases and tendencies in evaluating other individuals' behavior (Thomas, 2010). Though a consultant does not necessarily need to be a trained psychologist to conduct executive assessments, psychological training does provide much of the background knowledge and expertise needed to conduct these assessments effectively. The Guidelines for Education and Training at the Doctoral and Postdoctoral Levels in Consulting Psychology (CP)/Organizational Consulting Psychology (American Psychological Association [APA], 2017b), as well as the *Guidelines for Education and Training in Industrial–Organizational Psychology* (Society for Industrial and Organization Psychology, 2016) provide extensive, detailed, and helpful overviews of the competencies and content areas that are relevant to this type of work. Some of those content areas include

- *professional skills*: including general communication skill, the knowledge and ability to develop and assemble a business proposal, consulting and facilitation skills, and project management skills;
- *individual assessment*: including many of the topics covered in prior chapters in this book including testing, structured interviewing, data interpretation, data integration, writing, and delivering feedback;
- *job/task/work analysis*: classifying the knowledge, skills, and abilities required for a job, developing (and/or interpreting) competency models, and writing behaviorally anchored rating scales;
- *individual differences*: including relevant content areas such as personality, cognitive abilities, interests, values, and emotional intelligence;
- *career development*: including theories of vocational interests, career decision making, as well as some lifespan psychology;
- *core talent functions*: including personnel recruitment, hiring, selection, onboarding, and development;

- *talent management*: including performance appraisal, criterion theory, and motivation theory;
- *judgment and decision making*: including areas such as biases, heuristics, and information processing;
- *work motivation*: including motivation theory, goal setting, and incentives;
- *groups and teams*: including elements of leadership, motivation, team effectiveness, and conflict management; and
- *leadership and management*: including leadership effectiveness, leadership development, leadership behavior, organizational behavior, change management, strategy, and influence.

This list is not exhaustive but represents much of the knowledge and skills that are relevant to effectively conducting executive assessments. Other content areas include general business acumen (e.g., finance, operations, marketing), theories of power, and organizational politics (Ferris et al., 2018). Although it may seem obvious, it is helpful when an assessor has an ongoing interest in and facility discussing business issues and current events. Although it is certainly not required than an assessor be expert in every area, and guidelines such as these serve as more of an aspiration for continued development, a working knowledge in many of these areas is useful because it provides the assessor with a broad context for understanding and evaluating what happens in an organizational context, how decisions get made, and the impact those decisions can have on business operations.

Individual development and self-reflection is a useful competency as well. Whether that takes the form of supervision or mentorship, coaching or counseling, it is helpful for the assessor to reflect on their own behavior and to build a deeper awareness of their personality, values, and ways of thinking, so they can better understand their own personal agendas, tendencies, priorities, and biases (Knapp et al., 2017). This should include knowledge of multicultural issues, diversity, equity and inclusion, and understanding "historical and contemporary experiences with power, privilege, and oppression" (APA, 2017a).

In one circumstance, a relatively inexperienced junior assessor had participated in the assessment of two senior executive candidates, each of whom was being considered for the role of chancellor of a major public university. One candidate was a man, and one was a woman, both of whom were quite confident and direct in their communication and executive presence. The inexperienced assessor sat second chair to a senior assessor who conducted each interview, and mostly observed and took notes for the senior assessor. Once the assessments were completed, the junior assessor was tasked with writing the first draft of each assessment report. A few days later, after having integrated the results of self-report measures, competency ratings, and interview notes into reports, the junior assessor sent drafts to the senior assessor and asked for feedback. The senior assessor met with the junior assessor and pointed out an important discrepancy between the reports. Each report contained key strengths and areas for development for each candidate. In the male candidate's report, the junior assessor had described his directness as indicative of his confidence, and in the female candidate's report, he had described her directness as lacking political savvy. The senior assessor brought up the discrepancy so that the junior assessor would have the opportunity to consider the difference of interpretation, and whether the difference was grounded in job relevant observations or was perhaps more indicative of a latent bias.

DEVELOPMENTAL PATHS FOR ASSESSORS FROM DIFFERENT PROFESSIONAL BACKGROUNDS

Based on my own observation and experience, the professional development for those practicing executive assessment tends to start with some relevant background knowledge and/or experience, usually explicit training in psychology or a background in business with a specific focus in management consulting, organizational behavior, human resources (HR) and/or talent issues. These experiences lead to an interest in working with executive populations in particular. From there, individuals ideally receive specific training and opportunities to observe and apprentice under more experienced assessors. This type of progression is helpful because executive assessment often appears similar in form to simple interviews or to individual psychological assessment in general. However, what makes assessors great at this work is not just a keen ability to assess individuals but also an ability to navigate the consultative and decision-making environment among senior organizational leadership (Jeanneret & Silzer, 2011), a skill that is best learned through applied experience and mentorship. That is why those who come to executive assessment from a background that is not psychology-specific frequently have management consulting experience, or have worked in HR in large organizations, and thus bring some foreknowledge of how to navigate those complex environments. Although it may be slightly reductive, it is useful to consider the most common professional backgrounds that lead to this work in the following categories: (a) psychologists, (b) management consultants, (c) HR professionals, and (d) professionals from other backgrounds.

Psychologists

Industrial and organizational (I/O) and consulting psychologists tend to be well educated to pursue executive assessment work. They bring extensive content knowledge in various areas of psychology and organizational behavior, and they tend to bring an explicit interest in organizational issues and the business context. Individual assessment is viewed as a core content area of I/O and consulting psychology training, so graduates will likely come with a technical level of understanding and awareness about the practice area, that will then need to be deepened and applied through experience. Because many I/O and consulting psychologists come to the field from a background in psychology (N. Gupta & Beehr, 2014), they may need to broaden and deepen their understanding of macro-level business domains such as strategy, marketing, and finance in order to better understand the structure and operations of businesses.

For clinical and counseling psychologists, individual psychological assessment is not only a core competency but also tends to include extensive supervised training in conducting such assessments (Krishnamurthy et al., 2004). Professionals with clinical and counseling backgrounds will bring deep knowledge and theory in psychology to their work, but they may need to broaden the domain of their focus to include issues, research, and theories that are specific to organizational settings. They may also need to learn how to shape their assessment skill to fit the organizational context in terms of tone and demeanor and to develop general business acumen.

Although trained psychologists bring much to the table in the development journey to becoming competent executive assessors, as Kurpius et al. (1995) said,

> Being an effective psychologist is not enough to be an effective consultant. There is a body of knowledge and skills unique to this particular application of psychology, and just graduating from a doctoral program in psychology does not adequately prepare one to provide consultees with the best possible consulting services. (p. 88)

Management Consultants

Management consultants bring a unique skill set to executive assessment work. Many consultants have a background in business training (e.g., master's of business administration [MBA]), and likely bring a strong skill set in consultation in high-stakes business environments. They frequently interact with managers and executives in their work and tend to know how to manage a consulting engagement, communicate with organizational decision makers effectively, and drive results on behalf of organizations. Although some may have a background in organizational behavior, it is less likely that they have training or background knowledge in the various areas of psychology that are brought to bear in executive assessment. Accordingly, professionals from this background will need to learn about relevant organizational psychology research and theories, individual assessment, and structured interviewing practices.

Human Resources Professionals

HR professionals who come to executive assessment will tend to bring a knowledge and understanding of internal operations, HR practices, and how HR interacts with the business to create value. Professionals with this background may need to build knowledge regarding talent development and assessment in particular, depending on their specialty, and may also need to develop their understanding of macro-level business domains. Additionally, if an HR professional moves into an external consulting position, they may need to develop their skills in elements of consultation.

Professionals From Other Backgrounds

Other professionals who get into executive assessment with some frequency include former business leaders and managers, executive search professionals, and attorneys. Those coming from dissimilar professional backgrounds will bring different advantages and gaps within their expertise, though in general, they will ultimately need some psychological insight, business expertise, and consulting savvy in order to develop competence in executive assessment.

The challenge for all is not overvaluing the knowledge they bring or undervaluing the knowledge they lack, and finding opportunities to learn through training, experience, and guidance. In general, those who are more curious in their observation of human behavior demonstrate better short- and long-term memory for psychological information, and can retain a deeper theoretical and conceptual understanding of the patterns and constructs that tend to provide more valid assessments of behavior (Silzer & Jeanneret, 2011).

EDUCATION AND TRAINING

Consultants can take a number of practical steps to develop their skills in executive assessment. The first is to make an honest evaluation of areas of knowledge and experience that they may be lacking and seek to fill in those gaps. Consultants who bring a strong foundation in understanding and analyzing human behavior may have more to learn about business and consulting, while those who bring a strong foundation in business and consulting may have more to learn about the psychological foundations of assessment. All will need training or experience using assessment tools that are appropriate in a work context. And those who only have experience working with a limited number of tools may benefit from expanding their knowledge base so that they can better consider the strengths and limitations of different measures and appropriately select measures to fit the situations in which they are working.

The *Guidelines for Education and Training at the Doctoral and Postdoctoral Levels in Consulting Psychology (CP)/Organizational Consulting Psychology* (APA, 2017b) provide recommended ways one can learn and develop skills in consulting psychology, which have relevance for an executive assessment context in particular. Some of those methods include

- *informational interviewing*: Finding an expert in executive assessment and seeking their advice and direction on how to go about getting into the field and what to learn can help orient oneself to existing opportunities.
- *independent reading/study*: Broadening and deepening one's knowledge and understanding of relevant content areas and staying current in the field is a necessary habit, though it will need to be paired with experience and training.
- *formal course work*: Whether as part of a degree program, or in an ad hoc manner, courses can provide systematic way of learning new topics. Useful degrees include master's (MA/MS) and doctoral (PsyD, PhD) level training in consulting, organizational, or I/O psychology. An MBA degree with a concentration in organizational behavior could be helpful. Some programs focus on business psychology or pair an MBA degree with doctoral level training in psychology, a combination that would likely cover many of the topics and content areas needed to come to the field. Those looking to pursue formal education in this area are advised to look closely at coursework to ensure applied assessment training is part of the curriculum and to research where recent graduates have gone on to work.
- *observation and job shadowing*: Being in the presence of other professionals doing this work can provide a real-life look at what the work is like, how it is done, and potentially what it takes to do the job. Observation can be a useful method for grounding abstract concepts or theories

in practice, and can create opportunities for the observer to ask clarifying questions to facilitate understanding. Observing an assessment conducted via video conference (with the informed consent of the assessee) could also be an efficient way to "shadow" an assessor with little cost for either party.

- *on-the-job training*: Work experience grounds education and knowledge in practical experience. On-the-job training, or working as an apprentice alongside a more experienced assessor, can be quite an effective way to learn how to conduct assessments, provided one has the base level of competency to perform the job. This gives the trainee direct experience in the field and allows them to see how the work is done, and even participate in elements of the work under close supervision. In this way the trainee can gain direct work experience and expand and develop their skill set.
- *supervision/mentoring*: Supervision and mentoring are critical elements of the training and development of new and emerging executive assessors. Supervisors and mentors can not only provide direct advice and guidance on basic how-to level questions, but they can provide feedback to help the assessor examine blind spots or limitations, can provide insight into how to further develop the assessment skill set, and can help the assessor navigate complicated issues or ethical dilemmas that occur.

This list is not exhaustive but is intended to serve as a thought starter to those interested in continuing their training and development en route to becoming a competent executive assessor. To that end, another practical step consultants can take to improve assessment skills is to become very familiar with the assessment tools they are using (e.g., in-house tools at a consulting firm, Hogan Assessment Systems, Management Research Group, SHL). The best way to really learn the ins-and-outs of a given tool, after reading background materials (e.g., a technical manual) and any relevant research, is to assess a lot of people with that instrument and give a lot of feedback—in other words, gain as much experience in practice as possible. It can help to first do that in low-stakes environments if possible, for example, with other participants in a certification program such as those required by many test publishers, or under the supervision of a more experienced assessor who can assist as needed. Additionally, asking the assessee for feedback on the feedback process can be a good way to learn what descriptions resonate with clients and what ways of talking about traits and scales spark interest and insight. This type of practical application and repetition, paired with a deep understanding of the research, theory, and content of the tool, can help an assessor become more comfortable describing and interpreting results over time.

In the context of education and training, the issue of test certification bears some further consideration. Test publishers frequently require test users to complete a certification (e.g., Hogan Assessment Systems, Paradigm Personality Labs) before practitioners can access and use their instruments. Additionally, some test publishers (e.g., Pearson), and some governing bodies (e.g., British Psychological Society, n.d.) have qualifications for test use that limit the tests and measures users can purchase based on their level of education and/or membership in related professional associations (e.g., APA). These levels usually range from Level A tests, which require no specific qualifications to access, to Level B tests, which require a master's degree or an associated level of training or accreditation, and Level C tests, which require a doctoral level degree or licensure in a related field (Pearson, n.d.). Many firms, especially larger consultancies, however, have purchased or developed their own tools and methods that are used on a proprietary basis. For assessors within these groups, this may limit the flexibility they have to tailor the assessment method to any given situation. This certainly can eliminate a degree of complexity in determining what tools to use for a certain assessment context, although proprietary access should not be mistaken for reliability and validity by the informed practitioner. One still has an ethical and legal obligation to ensure the tools and methods one is using are job-related and fit to purpose.

In terms of specific training required to conduct executive assessments competently, assessors will benefit from applied training in interviewing, interpreting tools, writing reports, delivering feedback, and advising clients. Much of this training can likely be acquired on the job at firms that are organized to bring in junior level practitioners and bring them up to speed. It may also be possible to find individual practitioners who are interested in hiring a partner who can apprentice for a period of time before taking on more work as an independent assessor. Ideally, this type of training is structured so that new assessors can pick up pieces of the process and practice one at a time.

For example, an assessor may start by observing several assessments, then helping to assemble the assessment report with assistance from a more experienced assessor. After gaining some comfort with these elements of the process, the assessor may lead the feedback portion of the assessment and gain experience explaining results live, or perhaps conducting a portion of an assessment in the room with a more experienced assessor who can cover live and give feedback later. When I first began to participate actively in interviews, I would trade back and forth with the senior consultant. I would begin the interview and cover the executive's career history, then the senior consultant would take over more technical portions around specific competencies and technical work experience, and I would take back over toward the end for a portion of self-reflection in which the executive would describe their strengths and weaknesses and their career aspirations. I found this method helpful, because I was able to help conduct the interview but could participate in portions that felt more comfortable and less technical than interviewing for specific competencies, which was a skill I was still developing at the time.

Executive assessment is a specialty practice area within a technical domain of organizational consulting (i.e., individual assessment generally, and selection and development more broadly). Like most professions, it demands continuous learning and an ongoing commitment to personal training and development. Competence should be viewed as an aspiration rather than a destination, as even senior assessors will continue to adapt their practice to incorporate up to date research and evolve as business circumstances change (Lowman, 2012).

WHERE DO ASSESSORS WORK?

Assessors are employed in a wide variety of organizations and industries. Although they are frequently employed in independent consulting organizations or consulting organizations housed within larger firms, companies with more sophisticated HR practices may have assessors on staff, and other types of organizations (e.g., private equity firms) are starting to bring this capability in-house more and more (Gottfried & Cooper, 2018).

Leadership consulting firms such as RHR International, YSC Consulting, ghSmart, and DDI focus exclusively on leadership assessment, development, executive coaching, and other high-level, talent-centric consulting services. They tend to work with clients across a broad spectrum of industries on a wide range of management challenges.

Executive search firms such as Spencer Stuart, Egon Zehnder, Korn Ferry, Heidrick & Struggles, and Russell Reynolds Associates each provide executive assessment services to their clients, both as a part of the search process and in independent consulting engagements that tend to center on issues of leadership development, succession planning, and organizational culture change. Assessors within these firms may work within an independent group that partners with search consultants, or they may provide a blended service where search consultants are also trained in assessment services.

Large corporations with sophisticated HR groups employ psychologists and other professionals with leadership assessment and development skill sets. These types of jobs tend to be housed within talent management or talent development groups, and employees work on issues ranging from succession planning and leadership development to designing and delivering diversity and inclusion initiatives in senior leadership ranks (Beba & Church, 2020).

Private equity and venture capital firms are increasingly employing talent partners who can lead executive assessment and development initiatives across the portfolio (Executive Search Review, 2020; Ulrich & Allen, 2017). These positions tend to be held by experienced consultants, especially those with demonstrated expertise in executive search.

Finally, a large number of executive assessors work for small- to medium-sized boutique consulting firms or as solo practitioners. Though opportunities at such firms may be somewhat less structured or predictable, they may provide excellent opportunities for on-the-job training and direct mentorship.

THE ART AND SCIENCE OF EXECUTIVE ASSESSMENT

It is not uncommon, in the realm of executive assessment, to hear about the "art and science" of the practice; and frequently there is some disagreement about which is more important in conducting assessments effectively (Kuncel & Highhouse, 2011; Silzer & Jeanneret, 2011). In general, the "art and science" refers to the ways in which assessment information is collected and integrated in the formulation of recommendations.

Whereas the *art* tends to describe the assessor's understanding, judgment, and integration of assessment data in a holistic or clinical way, the *science* refers to the mathematical combination (also called mechanical combination) of assessment data using a formula or algorithm that dictates how the various parts of the assessment should be assimilated (Wunder et al., 2010). Research regarding data integration and the translation of individuals scores into actual recommendations is sparse in general and almost nonexistent in considering executive assessment in particular (Reynolds, McCauley, & Tsacoumis, 2018). Meta-analytic findings on individual assessment suggest that the mechanical combination of data significantly improves the validity of job performance predictions (Kuncel et al., 2013). Additionally, the decision-making biases and limits of human judgment in many circumstances (Kahneman, 2011), are almost certain to decrease the validity of inferences when relying solely on human judgment (Kuncel & Highhouse, 2011). However, even though mechanical combination may be an effective method for assimilating assessment data, assessors still need to involve organizational decision makers in order to best apply assessment results to decision making processes. As Wunder et al. (2010) noted, "do not put decision-makers in a position where they feel their judgment must compete with a formula. The formula will always eventually lose" (p. 395).

The highly specialized and individualized nature of senior level positions requires both consultative experience and intuition. The practitioner designs the assessment process based on what they have learned about the organizational needs, and in that process can integrate information that may be challenging (if not impossible) to represent as a quotient in an equation (Silzer & Jeanneret, 2011). Information, such as knowing how parts of an organization fit together, how the knowledge and experience represented on a team may inform an assessment decision, and how the organizational and industry history may inform perceptions of an executive's skills or experiences can be critical to using assessment results effectively in an applied setting. Assessors should always rely on sound evidence to support competent practice, proceeding with caution when evidence is sparse, and creating replicable data combination processes whenever possible. They should also bear in mind that the science must be delivered to organizational decision makers in a practical and actionable way in order to have its proper effect.

This is an area of research in which there is still much to be learned. Reynolds, McCauley, and Tsacoumis (2018) discussed similar issues with respect to traditional assessment centers, but their discussion is applicable to executive assessment as well:

> we need more research on integration and overall assessor decision making, including how to integrate individual scores into recommendations (e.g., the impact of adding ratings of dimensional importance) and how assessors might best bridge the gap between their conclusions and the development activities that best address weak competencies. Furthermore, additional work is needed to delineate the most critical role for human judgment in the assessment process and where mechanical aggregation is better suited to the task. (p. 647)

The practice of executive assessment goes beyond the gathering and combination of data and requires the contextualization and translation of that data into actionable insights and recommendations. In that way the assessor necessarily plays a prominent role in helping make the information gathered useful to organizational decision makers.

FUTURE DIRECTIONS IN EXECUTIVE ASSESSMENT

In my view, the future of executive assessment is bright. Organizations are focusing more and more on employee growth and the importance of developing and preparing internal candidates for leadership positions. They will continue to need systematic ways of understanding who is best qualified for these positions, and will continue to value data-driven support in making such decisions. Additionally, individual and executive assessment skills will continue to be valuable to organizations despite advancements in technology and algorithmic-based assessment. This information needs to be integrated into a coherent picture and communicated effectively to stakeholders to support decision making.

Software, the internet, and other technological advancements will likely continue to drive the most change in the assessment industry. Online-based assessments and technology will continue to make assessment tools easier to access and use. Additionally, the continued focus on quantifying and measuring talent in organizations will lead to certain types of assessments becoming more ubiquitous. Personality, values, and interest assessments, as well as cognitive ability tests are likely to all become more prominent as business leaders see the value in understanding what drives employees and what shapes how individuals lead; additionally more data will make it easier to connect the financial impact that strategic assessment protocols can have on business performance (Gottfried & Cooper, 2018).

I expect there will be a continued increase in positions within corporations for executive and senior leader assessment practitioners as the skill continues to grow in value. It may make more sense to have these types of professionals on staff for financial reasons, as well as to leverage internal institutional knowledge, and preserve confidentiality and data security in high-stakes development and succession decisions. Even still, consultants will remain valuable for their ability to bring unaffiliated external perspectives to the conversation.

More companies will hire those who can help develop new proprietary assessments for internal use at large organizations. To that end, tools will likely become more specialized and tailored to specific needs within organizations, and organizations will likely become more diligent about conducting validity studies at the local level (i.e., within the specific company). Of course, this type of development will more likely happen at large companies with employee counts that can support robust local research and that have funding for such projects.

With the proliferation of online storage systems and software that can house and organize massive amounts of data, assessment information is likely to increase in availability and persistence. The increased accessibility of this data may allow it to become ingrained into the way organizations think about assessment and development across the employee life cycle, and may allow organizations to become more systematic about providing tailored grow and development opportunities for leaders.

The accessibility and persistence of data will also make it easier to link assessment data to local performance data over time. Ongoing validity studies will become easier to conduct. Indeed, it is possible that the software platforms that host assessments will be able to plug into HR information systems and automatically analyze data, report patterns, norm groups, and recommendations based on machine learning algorithms. This may also ultimately increase potential for assembling large enough samples at senior and executive levels to conduct more robust research on executive populations, although this type of research will most likely occur within organizations that already have access to large senior leadership populations, such as multinational corporations and private equity firms with large portfolios.

It is important to note that even with more data available than ever, validity will be at more risk than ever, and it will become even more important for assessors to take a considered approach to using measures with robust evidence for valid and reliable inferences. Additionally, diversity, equity, and inclusion (DEI) will be at the forefront of every assessor's mind. DEI efforts within organizations "are perhaps more salient than ever" (Ferdman, 2020, p. 244), and assessors will play a key role in this work. From designing assessment systems that minimize adverse impact and differential treatment, to advising organizations on leadership decisions, assessors bear a responsibility to work toward a more equitable future in organizations. It will not be enough to simply know about it, they will need to play an active role.

As organizations grow and adapt to a dynamic and changing marketplace, their strategies and cultures will change. Companies will need to adapt to upstart competitors, disruptive technologies, and a changing global landscape (literally, in some ways), all of which will require them to reconsider what makes their organizations effective now, and what might make them effective in the future. Consider, for example, the 80-year-old investment management firm T. Rowe Price, which invested more than $100 million in 2017 and 2018 to build out a technology division so they could remain competitive in an industry that continues to undergo a digital transformation (Babcock, 2018).

Building out a new division staffed with people who bring new skill sets and new ways of thinking will begin to change the culture of the company. This type of change will need to be attended to on the talent assessment and development front, because what made leaders successful in the traditional company culture may no longer make them successful in the company as it evolves. Assessment is used as a sort of snapshot of an executive at a given time, and many organizations are currently changing so quickly that it will become necessary to reassess individuals as jobs, teams, and organizations change. Software platforms and algorithmic assessment methods may make this easier and more affordable to do, but there will be a continued need to help business leaders process and contextualize this information within specific organizational and decision-making contexts. The need for sound professional judgment will likely remain highly valuable. Organizations will continue to need advisors who are skilled at evaluating test and method quality, understanding how to design assessment protocols fit to purpose, and interpreting assessment results in an actionable way.

KEY TAKEAWAYS

- Develop a full understanding of the range of knowledge, skills, and competencies necessary to conduct executive assessments competently and effectively. Realistically evaluate your current level of development and where you would like to get to, and pursue education, training, and experience to close the gap.
- Take time to become familiar with the relevant literature on the types of assessments you are doing and commit to continuously keeping up

with new and emerging literature by reading relevant journals, attending conferences, and interacting with colleagues.

- When possible, engage a coach or counselor to help build self-awareness and a deeper understanding of personal biases, habits, and perceptions and how they may impact your work as an assessor.
- Don't go it alone—get supervision and mentorship to learn how to conduct executive assessments most effectively, and to strive for continuous improvement.
- Don't rely solely on either a mechanical or holistic combination of assessment data—the combination of both skills is what makes executive assessment work most impactful.

Glossary

360° FEEDBACK External perspectives on a leader's effectiveness and behavior gathered to provide a point of triangulation for test results and assessor observations; allows for a comparison between the assessee's self-perceptions and the perceptions of others (Gregory & Levy, 2015).

ADVERSE IMPACT Assessment procedures that tend to overselect members of the privileged group compared with underrepresented groups or protected classes (Sajjadiani et al., 2019).

ART AND SCIENCE (OF EXECUTIVE ASSESSMENT) The ways in which assessment information is collected and integrated in the formulation of recommendations: *art* refers to the assessor's understanding, judgement, and integration of assessment data in a holistic or clinical way; *science* refers to the use of a formula or algorithm to determine how the various parts of the assessment should be assimilated.

ARTIFICIAL INTELLIGENCE AND MACHINE LEARNING (AI/ML) Complex statistical methods that can allow a computer to mimic human-like intelligence (e.g., object recognition, problem solving, decision making; West, 2018).

COGNITIVE ABILITY An individual's ability to learn, understand, and process information; a commonly assessed trait because it is robust predictor of job performance across job types, contexts, and organizational levels (Finkelstein et al., 2018; Ryan & Ployhart, 2014).

COMPETENCY MODEL Frameworks of leadership competencies (see *leadership competencies*) that characterize the structure of the needs for a given job role.

COMPLEMENTARY FIT A circumstance in which an individuals' attributes (e.g., values, interests, personality traits) are different from the environment for which they are being evaluated (see *supplementary fit*).

CONFIDENCE INTERVAL The range within which a given value is expected to fall 95% of the time, with a *p* value of .05.

CONFIDENTIALITY Reasonable measures taken to protect confidential information; psychologists should discuss the limits of the confidentiality with their clients and obtain consent from clients before disclosing confidential information (APA, 2017a).

CONSTRUCT VALIDITY Evidence that a test measures what it intends to measure.

CONTENT VALIDITY Evidence that items included in a measure adequately represent the domain of knowledge or behavior that they are intended to measure.

CULTURAL RELATIVITY Avoiding judgment of different cultural values and assumptions and not viewing any cultural difference as inherently better or worse than another (Glover & Friedman, 2015).

CULTURE FIT The degree to which the behavioral preferences and *values* of an individual align with the behavioral norms that exist within an organization (Lu et al., 2019).

DERAILMENT When a formerly successful leader plateaus or fails below their expected level of achievement (Burrow et al., 2020; Inyang, 2013).

DEVELOPMENT ASSESSMENT Evaluation of an individual to understand their specific needs relative to their current job and to help them grow and improve as a leader.

DIGITAL TRANSFORMATION The incorporation of online and digital technology into business processes, products, and services.

EMOTIONAL INTELLIGENCE An individual's ability to perceive, understand, and regulate their own and others' emotions and feelings.

EVIDENCE-BASED PRACTICE Methodology based on research and that has been shown to make valid and reliable inferences.

EXECUTIVE An individual in the upper level of an organization who is responsible for managing and leading other people-leaders; see *senior leader.*

FACE VALIDITY The degree to an assessment's form indicates that it is measuring its intended content.

GAMIFICATION The incorporation of gaming elements (e.g., competition, badges, level advancement) into nongaming activities (Georgiou et al., 2019).

IMPRESSION MANAGEMENT An attempt by an individual to respond to items on a measure in a certain way to try to control how others perceive them (Peck & Levashina, 2017).

INFORMED CONSENT An individuals' ability to voluntarily decide to participate in an assessment with an understanding of the parameters, risks, and benefits of participation (Newman et al., 2002); should be obtained prior to beginning the assessment.

INTEGRATION (OF A MERGER OR ACQUISITION) The process by which one company incorporates another or two companies combine into one entity after a financial transaction.

INTERESTS Stable psychological characteristics of individuals that shape the type of activities they prefer; the alignment between interests and the characteristics of an individual's work environment are related to job performance and persistence (Nye et al., 2012, 2017).

INTERRATER RELIABILITY Evidence that a test conducted by different people would produce similar results.

IPSATIVE DATA Rank-ordered data—tends to be best at showing how traits occur within an individual (e.g., a rank-ordered list of values) rather than providing percentile comparisons with other individuals.

LEADER EFFECTIVENESS The extent to which an individual is successful in guiding and influencing a group to achieve a shared objective (Yukl, 2012).

LEADERSHIP COMPETENCIES Clusters of thought, skill, and behavior that relate to leadership effectiveness (Hogan et al., 2011, p. 10). One such example is *strategic agility*, which may be defined as how well a leader focuses on big picture issues, creates long-term plans, and develops and communicates a concept for the future of an organization.

LEADERSHIP EMERGENCE A common outcome variable of interest in organizational leadership research concerned with who is likely to become a leader within a given group.

LEADERSHIP STYLE Patterns of behavior leaders exhibit that shape how they interact with, direct, and motivate others.

LEARNING AGILITY The ability to observe, learn from experience, and apply new knowledge on an ongoing basis in new situations (De Meuse, 2019; De Meuse et al., 2010; Hoff & Burke, 2017).

MEASUREMENT EQUIVALENCE A statistical property that indicates that the same construct is being measured across assessment format (e.g., mobile vs. laptop/desktop computer vs. paper-and-pencil, or proctored vs. unproctored setting; Vandenberg & Lance, 2000).

MULTIPLE CORRELATION A type of regression equation in which several variables are included together as predictors of a given outcome.

MULTIPLE RELATIONSHIPS When a consultant is operating in more than one professional capacity with a client or is in potentially conflicting relationships with more than one client. Also called dual relationships, this situation is common in organizational consulting and can create a conflict of interest.

ONBOARDING The process of introducing new executives to an organization so they can begin to socialize and integrate with their team and other colleagues (Allen et al., 2017).

ORGANIZATIONAL CULTURE "The accumulated shared learning of a group as it solves its problems of external adaptation and internal integration" (Schein & Schein, 2017, p. 6). Also: "the way things are done around here."

PREDICTIVE VALIDITY Evidence that a measure can be used to make valid predictions; also called *criterion validity*.

PSYCHOMETRIC SOUNDNESS The reliability and validity of new assessment instruments.

RELIABILITY An estimation of the expected degree of consistency and inconsistency in replicated test scores to understand the sources of errors; includes *test–retest* and *interrater* dimensions.

SELECTION ASSESSMENT Gathering information about specific individuals that can be used to help advise organizational decision makers about whom to hire for a particular position.

SENIOR LEADER An individual in the upper level of an organization who is responsible for managing and leading other people-leaders (Reynolds, McCauley, & Tsacoumis, 2018); typically refers to those who oversee others, who themselves also have the responsibility of leadership.

SUCCESSION PLANNING A way of evaluating an organization's future leadership needs particular positions and assessing whether the existing talent within the organization can take on those leadership roles when transitions happen.

SUPPLEMENTARY FIT A circumstance in which an individual's attributes (e.g., values, interests, personality traits) are similar to the environment for which they are being evaluated (see *complementary fit*).

SYNTHETIC VALIDITY The construction of predictive equations based on personality facets and other relevant variables that can be used to design assessment protocols for specific situations (Hough & Johnson, 2012).

TEAM FIT The consideration of how compatible individual attributes, such as values or personality traits, are with the attributes of those on the team (Kristof-Brown et al., 2005; van Vianen, 2018; see *complementary fit* and *supplementary fit*).

TEST–RETEST RELIABILITY Evidence that a test is measuring the same construct each time it is taken.

TEST SECURITY Maintaining the integrity of test content and ensuring the test taker's identity; a particular concern with online testing.

TURNAROUND When new leadership is brought in to drive change and reenergize the workforce, usually with an intention to shift toward consolidation and realignment of the workforce toward a common goal or vision.

VALIDITY The compendium of evidence supporting different types of inferences made based on test scores (e.g., does a test measure something useful, and can the results be used to make a prediction about how an individual is likely to behave); includes dimensions such as construct, content, criterion.

VALIDITY GENERALIZATION Using previous validation research to inform the design of an assessment protocol to support valid and reliable inferences.

VALUES Standards or beliefs by which individuals determine the importance of different aspects of life; often examined in an assessment process to help understand culture and organizational fit.

VOCATIONAL ASSESSMENTS Process to identify and explore ideas for career exploration; usually requested by the individual being assessed.

WORK ANALYSIS The process by which an assessor builds an understanding of the knowledge, skills, abilities, and other traits (KSAOs) that would make an individual successful in a given job (Sackett et al., 2011).

References

Adler, S., Boyce, A. S., & Caputo, P. M. (2018). Employment testing. In J. C. Scott, D. Bartram, & D. H. Reynolds (Eds.), *Next generation technology-enhanced assessment: Global perspectives on occupational and workplace testing* (pp. 3–35). Cambridge University Press.

Allen, T. D., Eby, L. T., Chao, G. T., & Bauer, T. N. (2017). Taking stock of two relational aspects of organizational life: Tracing the history and shaping the future of socialization and mentoring research. *Journal of Applied Psychology, 102*(3), 324–337. https://doi.org/10.1037/apl0000086

American Bar Association. (2020). *Model rules of professional conduct.* https://www.americanbar.org/groups/professional_responsibility/publications/model_rules_of_professional_conduct/

American Educational Research Association, American Psychological Association, & National Council on Measurement in Education. (2014). *The standards for educational and psychological testing.* https://www.apa.org/science/programs/testing/standards

American Psychological Association. (2013). *Guidelines for the practice of telepsychology.* https://www.apa.org/practice/guidelines/telepsychology

American Psychological Association. (2017a). *Ethical principles of psychologists and code of conduct* (2002, Amended June 1, 2010, and January 1, 2017). http://www.apa.org/ethics/code/index.aspx

American Psychological Association. (2017b). *Guidelines for education and training at the doctoral and postdoctoral level in consulting psychology (CP)/organizational consulting psychology.* https://www.apa.org/about/policy/education-training.pdf

American Psychological Association. (2017c). *Multicultural guidelines: An ecological approach to context, identity, and intersectionality.* http://www.apa.org/about/policy/multicultural-guidelines.pdf

Anderson, M. (2015, April 30). Racial and ethnic differences in how people use mobile technology. *FactTank: News in the numbers* [Blog post]. Pew Research Center. https://www.pewresearch.org/fact-tank/2015/04/30/racial-and-ethnic-differences-in-how-people-use-mobile-technology/

Anderson, M. (2019, June 13). Mobile technology and home broadband 2019. *Internet & Technology.* Pew Research Center. https://www.pewresearch.org/internet/2019/06/13/mobile-technology-and-home-broadband-2019/

Anthony, S. D. (2016, July 15). Kodak's downfall wasn't about technology. *Harvard Business Review.* https://hbr.org/2016/07/kodaks-downfall-wasnt-about-technology?registration=success

Antonakis, J., House, R. J., & Simonton, D. K. (2017). Can super smart leaders suffer from too much of a good thing? The curvilinear effect of intelligence on perceived leadership behavior. *Journal of Applied Psychology, 102*(7), 1003–1021. https://doi.org/10.1037/apl0000221

Armstrong, M. B., & Landers, R. N. (2018). Gamification of employee training and development. *International Journal of Training and Development, 22*(2), 162–169. https://doi.org/10.1111/ijtd.12124

Arthur, W., Jr., Day, E., McNelly, T., & Edens, P. (2003). A meta-analysis of the criterion-related validity of assessment center dimensions. *Personnel Psychology, 56*(1), 125–155. https://doi.org/10.1111/j.1744-6570.2003.tb00146.x

Ash, L. (2012, July 6). Personality tests: Can they identify the real you? *BBC News.* https://www.bbc.com/news/magazine-18723950#:~:text=In the US alone%2C there, military agencies around the world.

Asplund, J., Agrawal, S., Hodges, T., Harter, J., & Lopez, S. J. (2014). *The Clifton Strengthsfinder® 2.0 technical report—2014 update.* https://www.strengthsquest.com/193766/clifton-strengthsfinder-technical-report-2014-update.aspx

Babcock, S. (2018, January 30). T. Rowe Price is pumping big money into its tech team. *Technical.ly.* https://technical.ly/baltimore/2018/01/30/t-rowe-price-tech-investments/

Bar-On, R. (1997). *Bar-On Emotional Quotient Inventory: Technical manual.* Multihealth Systems.

Barrick, M. R., & Mount, M. K. (1991). The big five personality dimensions and job performance: A meta-analysis. *Personnel Psychology, 44*(1), 1–26. https://doi.org/10.1111/j.1744-6570.1991.tb00688.x

Barrick, M. R., Mount, M. K., & Judge, T. A. (2001). Personality and performance at the beginning of the new millennium: What do we know and where do we go next? *International Journal of Selection and Assessment*, *9*(1–2), 9–30. https://doi.org/10.1111/1468-2389.00160

Barrick, M. R., & Parks-Leduc, L. (2019). Selection for fit. *Annual review of organizational psychology and organizational behavior*, *6*(1), 171–193. https://doi.org/10.1146/annurev-orgpsych-012218-015028

Beba, U., & Church, A. H. (2020). Changing the game for women leaders at PepsiCo: From local action to enterprise accountability. *Consulting Psychology Journal*, *72*(4), 288–302. https://doi.org/10.1037/cpb0000169

Berkelaar, B. L. (2014). Cybervetting, online information, and personnel selection: New transparency expectations and the emergence of a digital social contract. *Management Communication Quarterly*, *28* (4), 479–506. https://doi.org/10.1177/0893318914541966

Bertrand, M., & Mullainathan, S. (2004). Are Emily and Greg more employable than Lakisha and Jamal? *American Economic Review*, *94*(4), 991–1013. https://doi.org/10.1257/0002828042002561

Bleidorn, W., Hopwood, C. J., & Wright, A. G. (2017). Using big data to advance personality theory. *Current Opinion in Behavioral Sciences*, *18*, 79–82. https://doi.org/10.1016/j.cobeha.2017.08.004

Blickle, G., Meurs, J., Wihler, A., Ewen, C., Plies, A., & Günther, S. (2013). The interactive effects of conscientiousness, openness to experience, and political skill on job performance in complex jobs: The importance of context. *Journal of Organizational Behavior*, *34*(8), 1145–1164. https://doi.org/10.1002/job.1843

Bourton, S., Lavoie, J., & Vogel, T. (2018, March 29). Leading with inner agility. *The McKinsey Quarterly*. https://www.mckinsey.com/business-functions/organization/our-insights/leading-with-inner-agility

Boyatzis, R. E. (2008). Competencies in the 21st century. *Journal of Management Development*, *27*(1), 5–12. https://doi.org/10.1108/02621710810840730

Boyatzis, R. E. (2018). The behavioral level of emotional intelligence and its measurement. *Frontiers in Psychology*, *9*, 1438. https://doi.org/10.3389/fpsyg.2018.01438

Bracken, D. W., Rose, D. S., & Church, A. H. (2016). The evolution and devolution of 360° feedback. *Industrial and Organizational Psychology*, *9*(4), 761–794. https://doi.org/10.1017/iop.2016.93

Brannick, M. T., Pearlman, K., & Sanchez, J. I. (2017). Work analysis. In J. L. Farr & N. T. Tippins (Eds.), *Handbook of employee selection* (2nd ed., pp. 134–162). Routledge.

British Psychological Society. (n.d.) *The BPS Qualifications in test use*. https://ptc.bps.org.uk/bps-qualifications-test-use

British Psychological Society. (2017). *BPS practice guidelines (2017)*. https://www.bps.org.uk/news-and-policy/practice-guidelines

Brown, F. W., & Reilly, M. D. (2009). The Myers-Briggs type indicator and transformational leadership. *Journal of Management Development, 28*(10), 916–932. https://doi.org/10.1108/02621710911000677

Brynjolfsson, E., Horton, J. J., Ozimek, A., Rock, D., Sharma, G., & TuYe, H.-Y. (2020). *COVID-19 and remote work: An early look at US data* (National Bureau of Economic Research Working Paper No. 27344). https://doi.org/10.3386/w27344

Burrow, A. L., Hill, P. L., Ratner, K., & Fuller-Rowell, T. E. (2020). Derailment: Conceptualization, measurement, and adjustment correlates of perceived change in self and direction. *Journal of Personality and Social Psychology, 118*(3), 584–601. https://doi.org/10.1037/pspp0000209

Cable, D. M., & Judge, T. A. (1997). Interviewers' perceptions of persons–organization fit and organizational selection decisions. *Journal of Applied Psychology, 82*(4), 546–561. https://doi.org/10.1037/0021-9010.82.4.546

Cadwalladr, C., & Graham-Harrison, E. (2018, March 17). Revealed: 50 million Facebook profiles harvested for Cambridge Analytica in major data breach. *The Guardian*. https://www.theguardian.com/news/2018/mar/17/cambridge-analytica-facebook-influence-us-election

Cameron, K. S., & Quinn, R. E. (2011). *Diagnosing and changing organizational culture: Based on the Competing Values Framework* (3rd ed.). Jossey-Bass.

Canadian Psychological Association. (2017). *Canadian code of ethics for psychologists* (4th ed.). https://cpa.ca/docs/File/Ethics/CPA_Code_2017_4thEd.pdf

Cao, M., & Drasgow, F. (2019). Does forcing reduce faking? A meta-analytic review of forced-choice personality measures in high-stakes situations. *Journal of Applied Psychology, 104*(11), 1347–1368. https://doi.org/10.1037/apl0000414

Carnevale, J. B., & Hatak, I. (2020). Employee adjustment and well-being in the era of COVID-19: Implications for human resource management. *Journal of Business Research, 116*, 183–187. https://doi.org/10.1016/j.jbusres.2020.05.037

Chamorro-Premuzic, T., Akhtar, R., Winsborough, D., & Sherman, R. A. (2017). The datafication of talent: How technology is advancing the science of human potential at work. *Current Opinion in Behavioral Sciences, 18*, 13–16. https://doi.org/10.1016/j.cobeha.2017.04.007

Chamorro-Premuzic, T., Winsborough, D., Sherman, R. A., & Hogan, R. (2016). New talent signals: Shiny new objects or a brave new world? *Industrial and Organizational Psychology, 9*(3), 621–640. https://doi.org/10.1017/iop.2016.6

Chan, D. (2017). Values, styles, and motivational constructs. In J. L. Farr & N. T. Tippins (Eds.), *Handbook of employee selection* (2nd ed., pp. 326–341). Routledge. https://doi.org/10.4324/9781315690193-14

Chan, D. (2019). Team-level constructs. *Annual Review of Organizational Psychology and Organizational Behavior, 6*(1), 325–348. https://doi.org/10.1146/annurev-orgpsych-012218-015117

Chao, J., Kaetzler, B., Lalani, N., & Lynch, L. (2020). *Talent retention and selection in M&A*. McKinsey & Co. https://www.mckinsey.com/business-functions/m-and-a/our-insights/talent-retention-and-selection-in-m-and-a

Chen, A. (2018, October 10). How accurate are personality tests? *Scientific American*. https://www.scientificamerican.com/article/how-accurate-are-personality-tests/

Christian, M. S., Edwards, B. D., & Bradley, J. C. (2010). Situational judgment tests: Constructs assessed and a meta-analysis of their criterion-related validities. *Personnel Psychology*, *63*(1), 83–117. https://doi.org/10.1111/j.1744-6570.2009.01163.x

Church, A. H., Rotolo, C. T., Ginther, N. M., & Levine, R. (2015). How are top companies designing and managing their high-potential programs? A follow-up talent management benchmark study. *Consulting Psychology Journal: Practice and Research*, *67*(1), 17–47. https://doi.org/10.1037/cpb0000030

Conger, J. A., & Fulmer, R. M. (2003, December). Developing your leadership pipeline. *Harvard Business Review*, *81*(12), 76–84, 125. https://hbr.org/2003/12/developing-your-leadership-pipeline

Cook, R., Jones-Chick, R., Roulin, N., & O'Rourke, K. (2020). Job seekers' attitudes toward cybervetting: Scale development, validation, and platform comparison. *International Journal of Selection and Assessment*, *28*(4), 383–398. https://doi.org/10.1111/ijsa.12300

Coyne, I., & Bartram, D. (2018). Standards and best practices for technology-enhanced assessments. In J. C. Scott, D. Bartram, & D. H. Reynolds (Eds.), *Next generation technology-enhanced assessment: Global perspectives on occupational and workplace testing* (pp. 317–349). Cambridge University Press.

Criteria Corp. (n.d.). *Cognify* [Cognitive aptitude assessment]. https://www.criteriacorp.com/assessments/cognitive-aptitude/cognify

Dabke, D. (2016). Impact of leader's emotional intelligence and transformational behavior on perceived leadership effectiveness: A multiple source view. *Business Perspectives and Research*, *4*(1), 27–40. https://doi.org/10.1177/2278533715605433

Daniel, D. (1990). Validity of a standardized reference checklist. *Applied H.R.M. Research*, *1*(2), 51–66. http://applyhrm.asp.radford.edu/1990/Daniel.pdf

Davies, J. (2019, June 25). Think you're sending too many surveys? How to avoid survey fatigue. *Qualtrics*. https://www.qualtrics.com/blog/avoiding-survey-fatigue/

Day, D. V., & Dragoni, L. (2015). Leadership development: An outcome-oriented review based on time and levels of analyses. *Annual Review of Organizational*

Psychology and Organizational Behavior, 2(1), 133–156. https://doi.org/10.1146/annurev-orgpsych-032414-111328

de Kock, F. S., & Hauptfleisch, D. B. (2018). Reducing racial similarity bias in interviews by increasing structure: A quasi-experiment using multilevel analysis. *International Perspectives in Psychology, 7*(3), 137–154. https://doi.org/10.1037/ipp0000091

de la Merced, M. J. (2012, January 19). Eastman Kodak files for bankruptcy. *The New York Times*. https://dealbook.nytimes.com/2012/01/19/eastman-kodak-files-for-bankruptcy/

De Meuse, K. P. (2019). A meta-analysis of the relationship between learning agility and leader success. *Journal of Organizational Psychology, 19*(1), 25–34. https://doi.org/10.33423/jop.v19i1.1088

De Meuse, K. P., Dai, G., & Hallenbeck, G. S. (2010). Learning agility: A construct whose time has come. *Consulting Psychology Journal: Practice and Research, 62*(2), 119–130. https://doi.org/10.1037/a0019988

de Vries, R. E., Bakker-Pieper, A., & Oostenveld, W. (2010). Leadership = communication? The relations of leaders' communication styles with leadership styles, knowledge sharing and leadership outcomes. *Journal of Business and Psychology, 25*, 367–380. https://doi.org/10.1007/s10869-009-9140-2

Denison, D. R., & Ko, I. (2016). Cultural due diligence in mergers and acquisitions. In S. Finkelstein & C. L. Cooper (Eds.), *Advances in mergers and acquisitions* (Vol. 15, pp. 53–72). Emerald Group Publishing. https://doi.org/10.1108/S1479-361X20160000015004

Digman, J. M. (1990). Personality structure: Emergence of the five-factor model. *Annual Review of Psychology, 41*, 417–440. https://doi.org/10.1146/annurev.ps.41.020190.002221

Dilchert, S. (2018). Cognitive ability. In D. S. Ones, N. Anderson, C. Viswesvaran, & H. K. Sinangil (Eds.), T*he SAGE handbook of industrial, work and organizational psychology: Personnel psychology and employee performance* (pp. 248–276). SAGE. https://doi.org/10.4135/9781473914940.n10

Donnellan, M. B., & Lucas, R. E. (2008). Age differences in the big five across the life span: Evidence from two national samples. *Psychology and Aging, 23*(3), 558–566. https://doi.org/10.1037/a0012897

Drasgow, F., & Olson-Buchanan, J. B. (2018). Technology-drive developments in psychometrics. In J. C. Scott, D. Bartram, & D. H. Reynolds (Eds.), *Next generation technology-enhanced assessment: Global perspectives on occupational and workplace testing* (pp. 239–264). Cambridge University Press.

Dwight, S. A., & Donovan, J. J. (2003). Do warnings not to fake reduce faking? *Human Performance, 16*(1), 1–23. https://doi.org/10.1207/S15327043HUP1601_1

Eagly, A. H., & Karau, S. J. (2002). Role congruity theory of prejudice toward female leaders. *Psychological Review, 109*(3), 573–598. https://doi.org/10.1037/0033-295X.109.3.573

The Economist. (2018, September 22). *The high costs of staff turnover.* https://www.economist.com/business/2018/09/20/the-high-costs-of-staff-turnover

Edelman, P., & van Knippenberg, D. (2018). Emotional intelligence, management of subordinate's emotions, and leadership effectiveness. *Leadership and Organization Development Journal, 39*(5), 592–607. https://doi.org/10.1108/LODJ-04-2018-0154

European Federation of Psychologists' Associations. (2015). *Model code of ethics.* http://ethics.efpa.eu/metaand-model-code/model-code/

Executive Search Review. (2020). *Fundamental shift underway in private equity talent acquisition strategies.* https://huntscanlon.com/wp-content/uploads/2020/09/2020-Private-Equity-Special-Issue-5.pdf

Farr, J. L., & Tippins, N. T. (Eds.). (2017). *Handbook of employee selection* (2nd ed.). Routledge. https://doi.org/10.4324/9781315690193

Ferdman, B. M. (2020). The state of progress in diversity and inclusion initiatives: Perspectives for consulting psychology. *Consulting Psychology Journal: Practice and Research, 72*(4), 243–246. https://doi.org/10.1037/cpb0000191

Ferris, G. R., Harris, J. N., Russell, Z. A., & Maher, L. P. (2018). Politics in organizations. In D. S. Ones, N. Anderson, C. Viswesvaran, & H. K. Sinangil (Eds.), *The SAGE handbook of industrial, work and organizational psychology: Organizational psychology* (p. 469–486). SAGE. https://doi.org/10.4135/9781473914957.n21

Finkelstein, L. M., Costanza, D. P., & Goodwin, G. F. (2018). Do your high potentials have potential? The impact of individual differences and designation on leader success. *Personnel Psychology, 71*(1), 3–22. https://doi.org/10.1111/peps.12225

Fuqua, D. R., Newman, J. L., Simpson, D. B., & Choi, N. (2012). Who is the client in organizational consultation? *Consulting Psychology Journal: Practice and Research, 64*(2), 108–118. https://doi.org/10.1037/a0027722

Furnham, A., & Boo, H. C. (2011). A literature review of the anchoring effect. *Journal of Socio-Economics, 40*(1), 35–42. https://doi.org/10.1016/j.socec.2010.10.008

Furnham, A., & Crump, J. (2015). The Myers-Briggs Type Indicator (MBTI) and promotion at work. *Psychology, 6*(12), 1510–1515. https://doi.org/10.4236/psych.2015.612147

Garman, A. N., & Glawe, J. (2004). Succession planning. *Consulting Psychology Journal, 56*(2), 119–128. https://doi.org/10.1037/1061-4087.56.2.119

General Data Protection Regulation (GDPR). (2016). Regulation (EU) 2016/679 of the European Parliament and of the Council of 27 April 2016 on the protection of natural persons with regard to the processing of personal data and on the free movement of such data, and repealing Directive 95/46. *Official Journal of the European Union, 59*, 1–88. https://eur-lex.europa.eu/eli/reg/2016/679/oj

Georgiou, K., Gouras, A., & Nikolaou, I. (2019). Gamification in employee selection: The development of a gamified assessment. *International Journal of Selection and Assessment, 27*(2), 91–103. https://doi.org/10.1111/ijsa.12240

Ghisletta, P., Rabbitt, P., Lunn, M., & Lindenberger, U. (2012). Two thirds of the age-based changes in fluid and crystallized intelligence, perceptual speed, and memory in adulthood are shared. *Intelligence, 40*(3), 260–268. https://doi.org/10.1016/j.intell.2012.02.008

Gibby, R., Ahmed, F., & Neale, M. (2019, October 25–26). AI x AI: Let's talk assessment innovation and artificial intelligence [Workshop]. SIOP Leading Edge Consortium 2019: Advancing the Edge: Assessment for the 2020s, Atlanta, GA, United States. https://www.siop.org/Leading-Edge-Consortium/Workshops

Glover, J., & Friedman, H. L. (2015). *Transcultural competence: Navigating cultural differences in the global community*. American Psychological Association.

Goldberg, E. (2019, September 17). Personality tests are the astrology of the office. *The New York Times*. https://www.nytimes.com/2019/09/17/style/personality-tests-office.html

Gonzalez, A. M., Steele, J. R., Chan, E. F., Lim, S. A., & Baron, A. S. (2021). Developmental differences in the malleability of implicit racial bias following exposure to counterstereotypical exemplars. *Developmental Psychology, 57*(1), 102–113. https://doi.org/10.1037/dev0001128

Gonzalez, M., Capman, J. F., Oswald, F. L., Theys, E. R., & Tomczak, D. L. (2019). "Where's the I-O?" Artificial intelligence and machine learning in talent management systems. *Personnel Assessment and Decisions, 5*(3), 33–44. https://doi.org/10.25035/pad.2019.03.005

Gottfried, M., & Cooper, L. (2018, July 9). Billionaire's secret buyout formula: 110 instructions and an intelligence test. *The Wall Street Journal*. https://www.wsj.com/articles/billionaires-secret-buyout-formula-110-instructions-and-an-intelligence-test-1531151197

Graham, E. K., Weston, S. J., Gerstorf, D., Yoneda, T. B., Booth, T., Beam, C. R., Petkus, A. J., Drewelies, J., Hall, A. N., Bastarache, E. D., Estabrook, R., Katz, M. J., Turiano, N. A., Lindenberger, U., Smith, J., Wagner, G. G., Pedersen, N. L., Allemand, M., Spiro, A., III, . . . Mroczek, D. K. (2020). Trajectories of Big Five personality traits: A coordinated analysis of 16 longitudinal samples.

European Journal of Personality, *34*(3), 301–321. https://doi.org/10.1002/per.2259

Gregory, J. B., & Levy, P. E. (2015). *Using feedback in organizational consulting*. American Psychological Association. https://doi.org/10.1037/14619-000

Greiner, L. E. (1998, July–August). Evolution and revolution as organizations grow [Updated]. *Harvard Business Review*. https://hbr.org/1998/05/evolution-and-revolution-as-organizations-grow (Original work published 1972)

Groysberg, B., Lee, J., Price, J., & Cheng, J. Y.-J. (2018, January–February). The culture factor. *Harvard Business Review*, 43–57.

Guchait, P., Ruetzler, T., Taylor, J., & Toldi, N. (2014). Video interviewing: A potential selection tool for hospitality managers—A study to understand applicant perspective. *International Journal of Hospitality Management*, *36*, 90–100. https://doi.org/10.1016/j.ijhm.2013.08.004

Guion, R. M. (2010). Employee selection: Musings about its past, present, and future. In J. L. Farr & N. T. Tippins (Eds.), *Handbook of employee selection* (pp. 943–957). Routledge.

Gupta, A., Nadkarni, S., & Mariam, M. (2019). Dispositional sources of managerial discretion: CEO ideology, CEO personality, and firm strategies. *Administrative Science Quarterly*, *64*(4), 855–893. https://doi.org/10.1177/0001839218793128

Gupta, N., & Beehr, T. A. (2014). Industrial-organizational psychologists moving to business schools: Potholes in the road to migration? *Industrial and Organizational Psychology*, *7*(3), 320–324. https://doi.org/10.1111/iops.12155

Guzzo, R. A., Fink, A. A., King, E., Tonidandel, S., & Landis, R. S. (2015). Big data recommendations for industrial-organizational psychology. *Industrial and Organizational Psychology*, *8*(4), 491–508. https://doi.org/10.1017/iop.2015.40

Harrell, E. (2016, December). Succession planning: What the research says. *Harvard Business Review*. https://hbr.org/2016/12/succession-planning-what-the-research-says

Harris, N. (2018, May 16). A practical guide to the European Union's GDPR for American businesses. *Vox*. https://www.vox.com/2018/5/16/17360944/gdpr-us-business-eu-european-union-data-protection-privacy

Hartnell, C. A., Kinicki, A. J., Lambert, L. S., Fugate, M., & Doyle Corner, P. (2016). Do similarities or differences between CEO leadership and organizational culture have a more positive effect on firm performance? A test of competing predictions. *Journal of Applied Psychology*, *101*(6), 846–861. https://doi.org/10.1037/apl0000083

Harwell, D. (2019, November 6). A face-scanning algorithm increasingly decides whether you deserve the job. *The Washington Post*. https://www.washingtonpost.com/technology/2019/10/22/ai-hiring-face-scanning-algorithm-increasingly-decides-whether-you-deserve-job/

Hawkes, B., Cek, I., & Handler, C. (2018). The gamification of employee selection tools: An exploration of viability, utility, and future directions. In J. C. Scott, D. Bartram, & D. H. Reynolds (Eds.), *Next generation technology-enhanced assessment: Global perspectives on occupational and workplace testing* (pp. 288–313). Cambridge University Press.

Heilman, M. E., Wallen, A. S., Fuchs, D., & Tamkins, M. M. (2004). Penalties for success: Reactions to women who succeed at male gender-typed tasks. *Journal of Applied Psychology, 89*(3), 416–427. https://doi.org/10.1037/0021-9010.89.3.416

Heimann, A. L., Ingold, P. V., & Kleinmann, M. (2020). Tell us about your leadership style: A structured interview approach for assessing leadership behavior constructs. *The Leadership Quarterly, 31*(4), 101364. https://doi.org/10.1016/j.leaqua.2019.101364

Hermelin, E., Lievens, F., & Robertson, I. T. (2007). The validity of assessment centres for the prediction of supervisory performance ratings: A meta-analysis. *International Journal of Selection and Assessment, 15*(4), 405–411. https://doi.org/10.1111/j.1468-2389.2007.00399.x

Highhouse, S. (2002). Assessing the candidate as a whole: A historical and critical analysis of individual psychological assessment for personnel decision making. *Personnel Psychology, 55*(2), 363–396. https://doi.org/10.1111/j.1744-6570.2002.tb00114.x

Hoff, D. F., & Burke, W. W. (2017). *Learning agility: The key to leadership potential.* Hogan Press.

Hoffman, C. C., & Thornton, G. C., III. (1997). Examining selection utility where competing predictors differ in adverse impact. *Personnel Psychology, 50*(2), 455–470. https://doi.org/10.1111/j.1744-6570.1997.tb00916.x

Hogan, J., Hogan, R., & Kaiser, R. B. (2011). Management derailment. In S. Zedeck (Ed.), *APA handbook of industrial and organizational psychology: Vol. 3. Maintaining, expanding, and contracting the organization* (pp. 555–575). American Psychological Association. https://doi.org/10.1037/12171-005

Hogan, R. (2005). In defense of personality measurement: New wine for old whiners. *Human Performance, 18*(4), 331–341. https://doi.org/10.1207/s15327043hup1804_1

Hogan, R., & Hogan, J. (2010). *Motives, values, preferences inventory manual.* Hogan Assessment Systems.

Hogan, R., & Judge, T. A. (2012). Personality and leadership. In M. G. Rumsey (Ed.), *The Oxford handbook of leadership* (pp. 37–46). https://doi.org/10.1093/oxfordhb/9780195398793.013.0003

Holland, J. L. (1959). A theory of vocational choice. *Journal of Counseling Psychology, 6*(1), 35–45. https://doi.org/10.1037/h0040767

Holusha, J. (1989, December 9). Click: Up, down and out at Kodak. *The New York Times*. https://www.nytimes.com/1989/12/09/business/click-up-down-and-out-at-kodak.html

Hooijberg, R., Hunt, J. G., & Dodge, G. E. (1997). Leadership complexity and development of the leaderplex model. *Journal of Management, 23*(3), 375–408. https://doi.org/10.1177/014920639702300305

Hough, L. M., & Dilchert, S. (2017). Personality: Its measurement and validity for employee selection. In J. L. Farr & N. T. Tippins (Eds.), *Handbook of employee selection* (2nd ed., pp. 298–325). Routledge. https://doi.org/10.4324/9781315690193-13

Hough, L. M., & Johnson, J. W. (2012). Use and importance of personality variables in work settings. In I. B. Weiner (Ed.), *Handbook of psychology: Industrial and organizational psychology* (2nd ed., pp. 211–243). John Wiley & Sons.

Howard, A., & Thomas, J. N. (2010). Executive and managerial assessment. In J. C. Scott & D. H. Reynolds (Eds.), *Handbook of workplace assessment* (pp. 395–437). Jossey-Bass.

Hu, J., & Judge, T. A. (2017). Leader-team complementarity: Exploring the interactive effects of leader personality traits and team power distance values on team processes and performance. *Journal of Applied Psychology, 102*(6), 935–955. https://doi.org/10.1037/apl0000203

Hu, J., Zhang, Z., Jiang, K., & Chen, W. (2019). Getting ahead, getting along, and getting prosocial: Examining extraversion facets, peer reactions, and leadership emergence. *Journal of Applied Psychology, 104*(11), 1369–1386. https://doi.org/10.1037/apl0000413

Huffcutt, A. I., Conway, J. M., Roth, P. L., & Klehe, U. C. (2004). The impact of job complexity and study design on situational and behavior description interview validity. *International Journal of Selection and Assessment, 12*(3), 262–273. https://doi.org/10.1111/j.0965-075X.2004.280_1.x

Inyang, B. J. (2013). Exploring the concept of leadership derailment: Defining new research agenda. *International Journal of Business and Management, 8*(16), 78–85. https://doi.org/10.5539/ijbm.v8n16p78

Jaques, E. (1986). The development of intellectual capability: A discussion of stratified systems theory. *The Journal of Applied Behavioral Science, 22*(4), 361–383. https://doi.org/10.1177/002188638602200402

Jeanneret, P. R., & Zedeck, S. (2017). Professional guidelines/standards. In J. L. Farr & N. T. Tippins (Eds.), *Handbook of employee selection* (2nd ed., pp. 599–630). Routledge. https://doi.org/10.4324/9781315690193-27

Jeanneret, R. (1998). Ethical, legal, and professional issues for individual assessment. In R. Jeanneret & R. Silzer (Eds.), *Individual psychological assessment* (pp. 88–131). Jossey-Bass.

Jeanneret, R., & Silzer, R. (2011). Individual psychological assessment: A core competency for industrial-organizational psychology. *Industrial and Organizational Psychology*, *4*(3), 342–351. https://doi.org/10.1111/j.1754-9434.2011.01352.x

Joseph, D. L., & Newman, D. A. (2010). Emotional intelligence: An integrative meta-analysis and cascading model. *Journal of Applied Psychology*, *95*(1), 54–78. https://doi.org/10.1037/a0017286

Jost, J. T., Rudman, L. A., Blair, I. V., Carney, D. R., Dasgupta, N., Glaser, J., & Hardin, C. D. (2009). The existence of implicit bias is beyond reasonable doubt: A refutation of ideological and methodological objections and executive summary of ten studies that no manager should ignore. *Research in Organizational Behavior*, *29*, 39–69. https://doi.org/10.1016/j.riob.2009.10.001

Judge, T. A., Bono, J. E., Ilies, R., & Gerhardt, M. W. (2002). Personality and leadership: A qualitative and quantitative review. *Journal of Applied Psychology*, *87*(4), 765–780. https://doi.org/10.1037/0021-9010.87.4.765

Kahneman, D. (2011). *Thinking, fast and slow*. Farrar, Straus and Giroux.

Kaiser, R. B., LeBreton, J. M., & Hogan, J. (2013). The dark side of personality and extreme leader behavior. *Applied Psychology*, *64*(1), 55–92. https://doi.org/10.1111/apps.12024

Kaiser, R. B., & Overfield, D. V. (2011). Strengths, strengths overused, and lopsided leadership. *Consulting Psychology Journal*, *63*(2), 89–109. https://doi.org/10.1037/a0024470

Kehoe, J. F., & Murphy, K. R. (2010). Current concepts of validity, validation, and generalizability. In J. L. Farr & N. T. Tippins (Eds.), *Handbook of employee selection* (pp. 56–92). Routledge.

Kerr, R., Garvin, J., Heaton, N., & Boyle, E. (2006). Emotional intelligence and leadership effectiveness. *Leadership and Organization Development Journal*, *27*(4), 265–279. https://doi.org/10.1108/01437730610666028

Kim, H., & Kim, T. (2017). Emotional intelligence and transformational leadership: A review of empirical studies. *Human Resource Development Review*, *16*(4), 377–393. https://doi.org/10.1177/1534484317729262

Knapp, S., Gottlieb, M. C., & Handelsman, M. M. (2017). Enhancing professionalism through self-reflection. *Professional Psychology: Research and Practice*, *48*(3), 167–174. https://doi.org/10.1037/pro0000135

Krajewski, H. T., Goffin, R. D., McCarthy, J. M., Rothstein, M. G., & Johnston, N. (2006). Comparing the validity of structured interviews for managerial-level employees: Should we look to the past or focus on the future? *Journal of Occupational and Organizational Psychology*, *79*(3), 411–432. https://doi.org/10.1348/096317905X68790

Krishnamurthy, R., VandeCreek, L., Kaslow, N. J., Tazeau, Y. N., Miville, M. L., Kerns, R., Stegman, R., Suzuki, L., & Benton, S. A. (2004). Achieving competency in psychological assessment: Directions for education and training. *Journal of Clinical Psychology, 60*(7), 725–739. https://doi.org/10.1002/jclp.20010

Kristof, A. L. (1996). Person-organization fit: An integrative review of its conceptualizations, measurement, and implication. *Personnel Psychology, 49*(1), 1–49. https://doi.org/10.1111/j.1744-6570.1996.tb01790.x

Kristof-Brown, A., Barrick, M. R., & Stevens, C. K. (2005). When opposites attract: A multi-sample demonstration of complementary person–team fit on extraversion. *Journal of Personality, 73*(4), 935–958. https://doi.org/10.1111/j.1467-6494.2005.00334.x

Kuncel, N. R., & Highhouse, S. (2011). Complex predictions and assessor mystique. *Industrial and Organizational Psychology, 4*(3), 302–306. https://doi.org/10.1111/j.1754-9434.2011.01343.x

Kuncel, N. R., Klieger, D. M., Connelly, B. S., & Ones, D. S. (2013). Mechanical versus clinical data combination in selection and admissions decisions: A meta-analysis. *Journal of Applied Psychology, 98*(6), 1060–1072. https://doi.org/10.1037/a0034156

Kurpius, S. E. R., Fuqua, D. R., Gibson, G., Kurpius, D. J., & Froehle, T. C. (1995). An occupational analysis of consulting psychology: Results of a national survey. *Consulting Psychology Journal: Practice and Research, 47*(2), 75–88. https://doi.org/10.1037/1061-4087.47.2.75

Landy, F. L., Gutman, A., & Outtz, J. L. (2010). A sampler of legal principles in employment selection. In J. L. Farr & N. T. Tippins (Eds.), *Handbook of employee selection* (pp. 627–650). Routledge.

Langer, M., König, C. J., & Krause, K. (2017). Examining digital interviews for personnel selection: Applicant reactions and interviewer ratings. *International Journal of Selection and Assessment, 25*(4), 371–382. https://doi.org/10.1111/ijsa.12191

Larcker, D. F., & Tayan, B. (2020). Diversity in the C-suite: The dismal state of diversity among fortune 100 senior executives. *Rock Center for Corporate Governance at Stanford University closer look series: Topics, issues and controversies in corporate governance* No. CGRP-82. https://ssrn.com/abstract=3587498

Le Corff, Y., Gingras, V., & Busque-Carrier, M. (2017). Equivalence of unproctored internet testing and proctored paper-and-pencil testing of the Big Five. *International Journal of Selection and Assessment, 25*(2), 154–160. https://doi.org/10.1111/ijsa.12168

Lefkowitz, J., & Lowman, R. L. (2017). Ethics of employee selection. In J. L. Farr & N. T. Tippins (Eds.), *Handbook of employee selection* (2nd ed., pp. 575–598). Routledge. https://doi.org/10.4324/9781315690193-26

Levashina, J., Hartwell, C. J., Morgeson, F. P., & Campion, M. A. (2014). The structured employment interview: Narrative and quantitative review of the research literature. *Personnel Psychology, 67*(1), 241–293. https://doi.org/10.1111/peps.12052

Li, W. D., Li, S., Feng, J. J., Wang, M., Zhang, H., Frese, M., & Wu, C. H. (2020). Can becoming a leader change your personality? An investigation with two longitudinal studies from a role-based perspective. *Journal of Applied Psychology*. Advance online publication. https://doi.org/10.1037/apl0000808

London, M., & McFarland, L. A. (2017). Assessment feedback. In J. L. Farr & N. T. Tippins (Eds.), *Handbook of employee selection* (2nd ed., pp. 406–426). Routledge. https://doi.org/10.4324/9781315690193-19

Lopez, F. J., Hou, N., & Fan, J. (2019). Reducing faking on personality tests: Testing a new faking-mitigation procedure in a U.S. job applicant sample. *International Journal of Selection and Assessment, 27*(4), 371–380. https://doi.org/10.1111/ijsa.12265

Lowman, R. L. (1991). *The clinical practice of career assessment: Abilities, interests, and personality*. American Psychological Association. https://doi.org/10.1037/10091-000

Lowman, R. L. (Ed.) (2006). *The ethical practice of psychology in organizations* (2nd ed.). American Psychological Association. https://doi.org/10.1037/11386-000

Lowman, R. L. (2010). Interests. In I. B. Weiner & W. E. Craighead (Eds.), *The Corsini encyclopedia of psychology* (4th ed.). John Wiley & Sons. https://doi.org/10.1002/9780470479216.corpsy0453

Lowman, R. L. (2012). The scientist-practitioner consulting psychologist [Editorial]. *Consulting Psychology Journal: Practice and Research, 64*(3), 151–156. https://doi.org/10.1037/a0030365

Lowman, R. L. (2016). *An introduction to consulting psychology: Working with individuals, groups and organizations*. American Psychological Association.

Lowman, R. L. (2018). Ethical issues and standards in research and applications of industrial, work, and organizational psychology. In D. S. Ones, N. Anderson, H. K. Singagil (Eds.), *SAGE handbook of industrial, work and organizational psychology: Personnel psychology and employee performance* (pp. 39–51). SAGE. https://doi.org/10.4135/9781473914940.n3

Lowman, R. L., & Cooper, S. E. (2018). *The ethical practice of consulting psychology*. American Psychological Association. https://doi.org/10.1037/0000058-000

Lu, R., Chatman, J. A., Goldberg, A., & Srivastava, S. B. (2019). *Situated cultural fit: Value congruence, perceptual accuracy, and the interpersonal transmission of culture* (Working Paper No. 3603). https://www.gsb.stanford.edu/faculty-research/working-papers/situated-cultural-fit-value-congruence-perceptual-accuracy

Macan, T. H., Avedon, M. J., Paese, M., & Smith, D. E. (1994). The effects of applicants' reactions to cognitive ability tests and an assessment center. *Personnel Psychology, 47*(4), 715–738. https://doi.org/10.1111/j.1744-6570.1994.tb01573.x

Mannix, E., & Neale, M. A. (2005). What differences make a difference? The promise and reality of diverse teams in organizations. *Psychological Science in the Public Interest, 6*(2), 31–55. https://doi.org/10.1111/j.1529-1006.2005.00022.x

Matz, S. C., & Harari, G. M. (2020). Personality-place transactions: Mapping the relationships between big five personality traits, states, and daily places. *Journal of Personality and Social Psychology*. Advance online publication. https://doi.org/10.1037/pspp0000297

Mayer, J. D., Roberts, R. D., & Barsade, S. G. (2008). Human abilities: Emotional intelligence. *Annual Review of Psychology, 59*, 507–536. https://doi.org/10.1146/annurev.psych.59.103006.093646

Mayer, J. D., Salovey, P., Caruso, D. R., & Cherkasskiy, L. (2011). Emotional intelligence. In R. J. Sternberg & S. B. Kaufman (Eds.), *The Cambridge handbook of intelligence* (pp. 528–549). Cambridge University Press. https://doi.org/10.1017/CBO9780511977244.027

McCaulley, M. H. (2000). Myers-Briggs Type Indicator: A bridge between counseling and consulting. *Consulting Psychology Journal: Practice and Research, 52*(2), 117–132. https://doi.org/10.1037/1061-4087.52.2.117

McColl, R., & Michelotti, M. (2019). Sorry, could you repeat the question? Exploring video interview recruitment practice in HRM. *Human Resource Management Journal, 29*(4), 637–656. https://doi.org/10.1111/1748-8583.12249

McDaniel, M. A., Hartman, N. S., Whetzel, D. L., Grubb, W. L. III, (2007). Situational judgment tests, response instructions, and validity: A meta-analysis. *Personnel Psychology, 60*(1), 63–91. https://doi.org/10.1111/j.1744-6570.2007.00065.x

McDaniel, M. A., Whetzel, D. L., Schmidt, F. L., & Maurer, S. D. (1994). The validity of employment interviews: A comprehensive review and meta-analysis. *Journal of Applied Psychology, 79*(4), 599–616. https://doi.org/10.1037/0021-9010.79.4.599

Menand, L. (2018, September 3). What personality tests really deliver. *The New Yorker*. https://www.newyorker.com/magazine/2018/09/10/what-personality-tests-really-deliver

Menkes, J. (2006). *Executive intelligence: What all great leaders have*. Harper Collins.

Meriac, J. P., Hoffman, B. J., Woehr, D. J., & Fleisher, M. S. (2008). Further evidence for the validity of assessment center dimensions: A meta-analysis of the incremental criterion-related validity of dimension ratings. *Journal of Applied Psychology*, *93*(5), 1042–1052. https://doi.org/10.1037/0021-9010.93.5.1042

Michael, J. (2003). Using the Myers-Briggs Type Indicator as a tool for leadership development? Apply with caution. *Journal of Leadership & Organizational Studies*, *10*(1), 68–81. https://doi.org/10.1177/107179190301000106

Mollick, E. (n.d.). *The Startup Game*. The Alfred West Jr. Learning Lab, The Wharton School, University of Pennsylvania. https://simulations.wharton.upenn.edu/startup-game/

Morelli, N. A., Mahan, R. P., & Illingworth, A. J. (2014). Establishing the measurement equivalence of online selection assessments delivered on mobile versus nonmobile devices. *International Journal of Selection and Assessment*, *22*(2), 124–138. https://doi.org/10.1111/ijsa.12063

Morgan, W. G. (2002). Origin and history of the earliest Thematic Apperception Test pictures. *Journal of Personality Assessment*, *79*(3), 422–445. https://doi.org/10.1207/S15327752JPA7903_03

Mueller-Hanson, R., Heggestad, E. D., & Thornton, G. C., III. (2003). Faking and selection: Considering the use of personality from select-in and select-out perspectives. *Journal of Applied Psychology*, *88*(2), 348–355. https://doi.org/10.1037/0021-9010.88.2.348

Mui, C. (2012, January 18). How Kodak failed. *Forbes*. https://www.forbes.com/sites/chunkamui/2012/01/18/how-kodak-failed/?sh=7806e20e6f27

Myers-Briggs. (2020). The Myers-Briggs Type Indicator (MBTI). https://www.themyersbriggs.com/en-US/Products-and-Services/Myers-Briggs

Newman, J. L., Robinson-Kurpius, S. E., & Fuqua, D. R. (2002). Issues in the ethical practice of consulting psychology. In R. L. Lowman (Ed.), *The California School of Organizational Studies handbook of organizational consulting psychology* (pp. 733–758). Jossey-Bass. http://lib.stikes-mw.id/wp-content/uploads/2020/06/Jossey-Bass-Handbook-of-Organizational-Consulting-Psycholo.pdf

Nye, C. D., Su, R., Rounds, J., & Drasgow, F. (2012). Vocational interests and performance: A quantitative summary of over 60 years of research. *Perspectives on Psychological Science*, *7*(4), 384–403. https://doi.org/10.1177/1745691612449021

Nye, C. D., Su, R., Rounds, J., & Drasgow, F. (2017). Interest congruence and performance: Revisiting recent meta-analytic findings. *Journal of Vocational Behavior*, *98*, 138–151. https://doi.org/10.1016/j.jvb.2016.11.002

O'Boyle, E. H., Jr., Humphrey, R. H., Pollack, J. M., Hawver, T. H., & Story, P. A. (2011). The relation between emotional intelligence and job performance: A meta-analysis. *Journal of Organizational Behavior, 32*(5), 788–818. https://doi.org/10.1002/job.714

Ones, D. S. (2005). Personality at work: Raising awareness and correcting misconceptions. *Human Performance, 18*(4), 389–404. https://doi.org/10.1207/s15327043hup1804_5

Ones, D. S., Dilchert, S., Viswesvaran, C., & Judge, T. (2007). In support of personality assessment in organizational settings. *Personnel Psychology, 60*(4), 995–1027. https://doi.org/10.1111/j.1744-6570.2007.00099.x

Ones, D. S., Dilchert, S., Viswesvaran, C., & Salgado, J. F. (2017). Cognitive abilities: Measurement and validity for employee selection. In J. L. Farr & N. T. Tippins (Eds.), *Handbook of employee selection* (2nd ed., pp. 251–276). Routledge. https://doi.org/10.4324/9781315690193-11

Ones, D. S., Viswesvaran, C., & Dilchert, S. (2005). Cognitive ability in selection decisions. In O. Wilhelm & R. W. Engle (Eds.), *Handbook of understanding and measuring intelligence* (pp. 431–468). SAGE. https://doi.org/10.4135/9781452233529.n24

O'Reilly, C. A., III, Caldwell, D. F., Chatman, J. A., & Doerr, B. (2014). The promise and problems of organizational culture. *Group & Organization Management, 39*(6), 595–625. https://doi.org/10.1177/1059601114550713

O'Reilly, C. A., III, Chatman, J., & Caldwell, D. F. (1991). People and organizational culture: A profile comparison approach to assessing person-organization fit. *Academy of Management Journal, 34*(3), 487–516. https://doi.org/10.5465/256404

Partnoy, F. (2018, June). An SAT for CEOs. *The Atlantic*. https://www.theatlantic.com/magazine/archive/2018/06/vista-ceo-testing/559148/

Pearlman, K., & Sanchez, J. I. (2010). Work analysis. In J. L. Farr & N. T. Tippins (Eds.), *Handbook of employee selection* (pp. 73–94). Routledge.

Pearson. (n.d.). Qualifications policy. https://www.pearsonassessments.com/professional-assessments/ordering/how-to-order/qualifications/qualifications-policy.html

Peck, J. A., & Levashina, J. (2017). Impression management and interview and job performance ratings: A meta-analysis of research design with tactics in mind. *Frontiers in Psychology, 8*, 201. https://doi.org/10.3389/fpsyg.2017.00201

Pekaar, K. A., van der Linden, D., Bakker, A. B., & Born, M. P. (2017). Emotional intelligence and job performance: The role of enactment and focus on others' emotions. *Human Performance, 30*(2–3), 135–153. https://doi.org/10.1080/08959285.2017.1332630

Perrin, A., & Kumar, M. (2019, July 25). About three-in-ten U.S. adults say they are 'almost constantly' online. *FactTank: News in the numbers* [Blog post]. Pew Research Center. https://www.pewresearch.org/fact-tank/2019/07/25/americans-going-online-almost-constantly/

Perrin, A., & Turner, E. (2019, August 20). Smartphones help blacks, Hispanics bridge some—but not all—digital gaps with whites. *FactTank: News in the Numbers* [Blog post]. Pew Research Center. https://www.pewresearch.org/fact-tank/2019/08/20/smartphones-help-blacks-hispanics-bridge-some-but-not-all-digital-gaps-with-whites/

Pittenger, D. J. (2005). Cautionary comments regarding the Myers-Briggs Type Indicator. *Consulting Psychology Journal: Practice and Research, 57*(3), 210–221. https://doi.org/10.1037/1065-9293.57.3.210

Putka, D. J., & Sackett, P. R. (2010). Reliability and validity. In J. L. Farr & N. T. Tippins (Eds.), *Handbook of employee selection* (pp. 9–50). Routledge.

Rabier, M. R. (2017). Acquisition motives and the distribution of acquisition performance. *Strategic Management Journal, 38*(13), 2666–2681. Advance online publication. https://doi.org/10.1002/smj.2686

Raddant, M., & Kenett, D. Y. (2021). Interconnectedness in the global financial market. *Journal of International Money and Finance, 110*, Article 102280. https://doi.org/10.1016/j.jimonfin.2020.102280

Reynolds, D. H., McCauley, C. D., & Tsacoumis, S. (2018). A critical evaluation of the state of assessment and development for senior leaders. *Industrial and Organizational Psychology, 11*(4), 630–652. https://doi.org/10.1017/iop.2018.84

Reynolds, D. H., Scott, J. C., & Bartram, D. (2018). Recurring themes in the application of technology-enhanced assessments. In J. C. Scott, D. Bartram, & D. H. Reynolds (Eds.), *Next generation technology-enhanced assessment: Global perspectives on occupational and workplace testing* (pp. 375–394). Cambridge University Press.

Riggio, R. E. (2008). Leadership development: The current state and future expectations. *Consulting Psychology Journal: Practice and Research, 60*(4), 383–392. https://doi.org/10.1037/1065-9293.60.4.383

Rudman, L. A., Ashmore, R. D., & Gary, M. L. (2001). "Unlearning" automatic biases: The malleability of implicit prejudice and stereotypes. *Journal of Personality and Social Psychology, 81*(5), 856–868. https://doi.org/10.1037/0022-3514.81.5.856

Rudman, L. A., & Glick, P. (2001). Prescriptive gender stereotypes and backlash toward agentic women. *Journal of Social Issues, 57*(4), 743–762. https://doi.org/10.1111/0022-4537.00239

Ryan, A. M., Greguras, G. J., & Ployhart, R. E. (1996). Perceived job relatedness of physical ability testing for firefighters: Exploring variations in reactions. *Human Performance, 9*(3), 219–240. https://doi.org/10.1207/s15327043hup0903_3

Ryan, A. M., & Ployhart, R. E. (2014). A century of selection. *Annual Review of Psychology, 65*(1), 693–717. https://doi.org/10.1146/annurev-psych-010213-115134

Sackett, P. R., Shen, W., Myors, B., & Associates. (2010). Perspectives from twenty-two countries on the legal environment for selection. In J. L. Farr & N. T. Tippins (Eds.), *Handbook of employee selection* (pp. 651–676). Routledge.

Sackett, P. R., Walmsley, P. T., & Laczo, R. M. (2011). Job and work analysis. In I. Weiner, N. W. Schmitt, & S. Highhouse (Eds.), *Handbook of psychology* (2nd ed., Vol. 12, pp. 48–87). John Wiley & Sons. https://doi.org/10.1002/9781118133880.hop212004

Sadri, G. (2012). Emotional intelligence and leadership development. *Public Personnel Management, 41*(3), 535–548. https://doi.org/10.1177/009102601204100308

Sajjadiani, S., Sojourner, A. J., Kammeyer-Mueller, J. D., & Mykerezi, E. (2019). Using machine learning to translate applicant work history into predictors of performance and turnover. *Journal of Applied Psychology, 104*(10), 1207–1225. https://doi.org/10.1037/apl0000405

Salgado, J. F., & Bastida, M. (2017). Predicting expatriate effectiveness: The role of personality, cross-cultural adjustment, and organizational support. *International Journal of Selection and Assessment, 25*(3), 267–275. https://doi.org/10.1111/ijsa.12178

Salgado, J. F., & Moscoso, S. (2002). Comprehensive meta-analysis of the construct validity of the employment interview. *European Journal of Work and Organizational Psychology, 11*(3), 299–324. https://doi.org/10.1080/13594320244000184

Salovey, P., & Mayer, J. D. (1990). Emotional intelligence. *Imagination, Cognition and Personality, 9*(3), 185–211 https://doi.org/10.2190/DUGG-P24E-52WK-6CDG

Sanchez, J. I., & Levine, E. L. (2012). The rise and fall of job analysis and the future of work analysis. *Annual Review of Psychology, 63*(1), 397–425. https://doi.org/10.1146/annurev-psych-120710-100401

Schein, E. H., & Schein, P. (2017). *Organizational culture and leadership* (5th ed.). John Wiley & Sons.

Schepker, D. J., Nyberg, A. J., Ulrich, M. D., & Wright, P. M. (2018). Planning for future leadership: Procedural rationality, formalized succession processes, and CEO influence in chief executive officer succession planning. *Academy of Management Journal, 61*(2), 523–552. https://doi.org/10.5465/amj.2016.0071

Schmidt, F. L., & Hunter, J. (2004). General mental ability in the world of work: Occupational attainment and job performance. *Journal of Personality and Social Psychology, 86*(1), 162–173. https://doi.org/10.1037/0022-3514.86.1.162

Schmidt, F. L., & Hunter, J. E. (1977). Development of a general solution to the problem of validity generalization. *Journal of Applied Psychology, 62*(5), 529–540. https://doi.org/10.1037/0021-9010.62.5.529

Schmidt, F. L., & Hunter, J. E. (1998). The validity and utility of selection methods in personnel psychology: Practical and theoretical implications of 85 years of research findings. *Psychological Bulletin, 124*(2), 262–274. https://doi.org/10.1037/0033-2909.124.2.262

Schmitt, N. (2014). Personality and cognitive ability as predictors of effective performance at work. *Annual Review of Organizational Psychology and Organizational Behavior, 1*(1), 45–65. https://doi.org/10.1146/annurev-orgpsych-031413-091255

Schultz, D. P., & Schultz, S. E. (2012). *A history of modern psychology* (10th ed.). Wadsworth Cengage.

Schwartz, S. H. (1994). Are there universal aspects in the structure and contents of human values? *The Journal of Social Issues, 50*(4), 19–45. https://doi.org/10.1111/j.1540-4560.1994.tb01196.x

Schwartz, S. H. (2012). An overview of the Schwartz theory of basic values. *Online Readings in Psychology and Culture, 2*(1), 1–20. https://doi.org/10.9707/2307-0919.1116

SHL. (2019). *OPQ32r TM reimagined technical manual supplement.* https://support.shl.com/servlet/fileField?retURL=%2Fapex%2FViewArticle%3Fid%3DkA0D00000000Cph%26kb_gp%3Dclient%26l%3Den_US%26lva%3D000010877&entityId=ka04G0000004g76QAA&field=Attachment2__Body__s

Silzer, R., & Jeanneret, R. (2011). Individual psychological assessment: A practice and science in search of common ground. *Industrial and Organizational Psychology, 4*(3), 270–296. https://doi.org/10.1111/j.1754-9434.2011.01341.x

Sinar, E. (2018). Leading with data-driven decisions: The culture and skills driving higher returns on data. *Global leadership forecast 2018: 25 Research insights to fuel your people strategy.* 16–17. Development Dimensions International, The Conference Board, EYGM. https://media.ddiworld.com/research/global-leadership-forecast-2018_au-nz-report_ddi_tr.pdf

Society for Industrial and Organizational Psychology. (2016). *Guidelines for education and training in industrial-organizational psychology.* https://www.siop.org/Events-Education/Graduate-Training-Program/Guidelines-for-Education-and-Training

Society for Industrial and Organizational Psychology. (2018). Principles for the validation and use of personnel selection procedures. *Industrial and Organizational Psychology, 11*(S1), 1–97. https://doi.org/10.1017/iop.2018.195

Somech, A. (2006). The effects of leadership style and team process on performance and innovation in functionally heterogeneous teams. *Journal of Management*, 32(1), 132–157. https://doi.org/10.1177/0149206305277799

Smith, M., & Robertson, I. T. (1993). *The theory and practice of systematic personnel selection*. Palgrave Macmillan. https://doi.org/10.1007/978-1-349-22754-9_14

Stamoulis, D. (2009). *Senior executive assessment: A key to responsible corporate governance*. Wiley-Blackwell. https://doi.org/10.1002/9781444310276

Stasielowicz, L. (2020). How important is cognitive ability when adapting to changes? A meta-analysis of the performance adaptation literature. *Personality and Individual Differences, 166*, 110178. https://doi.org/10.1016/j.paid.2020.110178

Sterman, J. (n.d.). *Platform wars: Simulating the battle for video game supremacy*. [Teaching resource]. MIT Sloan School of Management. https://mitsloan.mit.edu/teaching-resources-library/platform-wars-simulating-battle-video-game-supremacy

Strauss, I. E. (2015, September 16). Soul searching through the Myers-Briggs Test. *The Atlantic*. https://www.theatlantic.com/health/archive/2015/09/people-love-the-myers-briggs-personality-test/404737/

Su, R. (2018). The three faces of interests: An integrative review of interest research in vocational, organizational, and educational psychology. *Journal of Vocational Behavior, 116B*(103240). https://doi.org/10.1016/j.jvb.2018.10.016

Super, D. E. (1949). Review of Assessment of men: Selection of personnel for the office of strategic services [Review of the book *Assessment of men: Selection of personnel for the office of strategic services*, by T. O. A. Staff]. *Journal of Applied Psychology, 33*(5), 511–515. https://doi.org/10.1037/h0049651

Taylor, P. J., Pajo, K., Cheung, G. W., & Stringfield, P. (2004). Dimensionality and validity of a structured telephone reference check procedure. *Personnel Psychology, 57*(3), 745–772. https://doi.org/10.1111/j.1744-6570.2004.00006.x

Taylor, P. J., & Small, B. (2002). Asking applicants what they would do versus what they did do: A meta-analytic comparison of situational and past behaviour employment interview questions. *Journal of Occupational and Organizational Psychology, 75*(3), 277–294. https://doi.org/10.1348/096317902320369712

Tett, R. P., Hundley, N. A., & Christiansen, N. D. (2017). Meta-analysis and the myth of generalizability. *Industrial and Organizational Psychology, 10*(3), 421–456. https://doi.org/10.1017/iop.2017.26

Thomas, J. C. (2010). *Specialty competencies in organizational and business consulting psychology*. Oxford University Press.

Thornton, G. C., III, Johnson, S. K., & Church, A. H. (2017). Selecting leaders: Executives and high potentials. In J. L. Farr & N. T. Tippins (Ed.), *Handbook of employee selection* (2nd ed., pp. 833–852). Routledge. https://doi.org/10.4324/9781315690193-38

Thorsteinson, T. J. (2018). A meta-analysis of interview length on reliability and validity. *Journal of Occupational and Organizational Psychology, 91*(1), 1–32. https://doi.org/10.1111/joop.12186

Uhl-Bien, M., & Arena, M. (2018). Leadership for organizational adaptability: A theoretical synthesis and integrative framework. *The Leadership Quarterly, 29*(1), 89–104. https://doi.org/10.1016/j.leaqua.2017.12.009

Ulrich, D., & Allen, J. (2017, August 11). New role: Leadership capital partner. *Harvard Business Review*. https://hbr.org/2017/08/pe-firms-are-creating-a-new-role-leadership-capital-partner

UNCTAD. (n.d.). *Data protection and privacy legislation worldwide*. United Nations Conference on Trade and Development. https://unctad.org/page/data-protection-and-privacy-legislation-worldwide

Vandenberg, R. J., & Lance, C. E. (2000). A review and synthesis of the measurement invariance literature: Suggestions, practices, and recommendations for organizational research. *Organizational Research Methods, 3*(1), 4–70. https://doi.org/10.1177/109442810031002

Van Iddekinge, C. H., Aguinis, H., Mackey, J. D., & DeOrtentiis, P. S. (2018). A meta-analysis of the interactive, additive, and relative effects of cognitive ability and motivation on performance. *Journal of Management, 44*(1), 249–279. https://doi.org/10.1177/0149206317702220

van Vianen, A. E. M. (2018). Person–environment fit: A review of its basic tenets. *Annual Review of Organizational Psychology and Organizational Behavior, 5*(1), 75–101. https://doi.org/10.1146/annurev-orgpsych-032117-104702

Vergauwe, J., Kaiser, R. B., Wille, B., De Fruyt, F., & Hofmans, J. (2018). A method for capturing context in the assessment of leaders: The too little/too much rating scale. *Industrial and Organizational Psychology, 11*(4), 657–662. https://doi.org/10.1017/iop.2018.127

Volmer, J., Koch, I. K., & Göritz, A. S. (2016). The bright and dark sides of leaders' dark triad traits: Effects on subordinates' career success and well-being. *Personality and Individual Differences, 101*, 413–418. https://doi.org/10.1016/j.paid.2016.06.046

Vuletich, H. A., & Payne, B. K. (2019). Stability and change in implicit bias. *Psychological Science, 30*(6), 854–862. https://doi.org/10.1177/0956797619844270

Wang, M., & Wanberg, C. R. (2017). 100 years of applied psychology research on individual careers: From career management to retirement. *Journal of Applied Psychology, 102*(3), 546–563. https://doi.org/10.1037/apl0000143

Wasylyshyn, K. M. (2019). The trusted leadership advisor: Defined, unpacked, encouraged. *Consulting Psychology Journal: Practice and Research, 71*(1), 1–15. https://doi.org/10.1037/cpb0000126

Weiner, I. B., & Greene, R. L. (2017). *Handbook of personality assessment* (2nd ed.). John Wiley & Sons.

West, D. M. (2018, October 4). *What is artificial intelligence?* Brookings. https://www.brookings.edu/research/what-is-artificial-intelligence/

Williams, D. K., & Scott, M. M. (2012, May 31). Seven "non-negotiables" to prevent a bad hire. *Harvard Business Review.* https://hbr.org/2012/05/7-non-negotiables-to-prevent-a

Winsborough, D., & Chamorro-Premuzic, T. (2013). Consulting psychology in the digital era: Current trends and future directions. *Consulting Psychology Journal: Practice and Research, 65*(4), 319–324. https://doi.org/10.1037/a0035698

Woehr, D. J., & Arthur, W., Jr. (2003). The construct-related validity of assessment center ratings: A review and meta-analysis of the role of methodological factors. *Journal of Management, 29*(2), 231–258. https://doi.org/10.1177/014920630302900206

Woods, S. A., Ahmed, S., Nikolaou, I., Costa, A. C., & Anderson, N. R. (2020). Personnel selection in the digital age: A review of validity and applicant reactions, and future research challenges. *European Journal of Work and Organizational Psychology, 29*(1), 64–77. https://doi.org/10.1080/1359432X.2019.1681401

Wunder, R. S., Thomas, L. L., & Luo, Z. (2010). Administering assessments and decision-making. In J. L. Farr & N. T. Tippins (Eds.), *Handbook of employee selection* (pp. 377–398). Routledge.

Xu, H., Zhang, N., & Zhou, L. (2019). Validity concerns in research using organic data. *Journal of Management, 46*(7), 1257–1274. https://doi.org/10.1177/0149206319862027

Yukl, G. (2012). Effective leadership behavior: What we know and what questions need more attention. *The Academy of Management Perspectives, 26*(4), 66–85. https://doi.org/10.5465/amp.2012.0088

Yukl, G., Mahsud, R., Prussia, G., & Hassan, S. (2019). Effectiveness of broad and specific leadership behaviors. *Personnel Review, 48*(3), 774–783. https://doi.org/10.1108/PR-03-2018-0100

Zaccaro, S. J., Green, J. P., Dubrow, S., & Kolze, M. J. (2018). Leader individual differences, situational parameters, and leadership outcomes: A comprehensive review and integration. *The Leadership Quarterly*, *29*(1), 2–43. https://doi.org/10.1016/j.leaqua.2017.10.003

Zickar, M. J. (2018). Using social media for assessment. In J. C. Scott, D. Bartram, & D. H. Reynolds (Eds.), *Next generation technology-enhanced assessment: Global perspectives on occupational and workplace testing* (pp. 217–238). Cambridge University Press.

Zickar, M. J., Cortina, J. M., & Carter, N. T. (2017). Evaluation of measures: Sources of error, sufficiency, and contamination. In J. L. Farr & N. T. Tippins (Eds.), *Handbook of employee selection* (2nd ed., pp. 397–405). Routledge.

Index

About the Author

J. Ross Blankenship, PhD, is a consulting psychologist and entrepreneur in Atlanta, Georgia. Dr. Blankenship is the cofounder and CEO of Leadhr (pronounced "leader"), a leadership advisory firm that partners with organizations on leadership assessment and development, executive coaching, team effectiveness, and organizational culture assessment and change. He also serves as a lecturer in the McIntire School of Commerce at the University of Virginia. Previously, he worked in the leadership advisory group of a leading multinational executive search firm, where he consulted with clients across industries on initiatives related to executive assessment and development, top team effectiveness, and organizational culture assessment and transformation. Prior to that, Dr. Blankenship founded and led the leadership assessment and development practice of an executive search firm in San Diego, California, where he worked with private-equity backed software companies to build and develop high performing senior leadership teams. He also served as adjunct faculty at the Center for Creative Leadership (CCL), where he delivered leadership development programs, conducted research, and completed an executive coaching practicum. He is coauthor of "Coaching the Derailing Leader" in the *CCL Handbook of Coaching in Organizations*, and his research and writing have been published in *The Leadership Quarterly*, *Psychology Today*, and *Forbes*. He completed his PhD in consulting psychology at the California School of Professional Psychology at Alliant International University, and his BA in English Language and Literature at the University of Virginia. Dr. Blankenship is a member of the Society for Consulting Psychology and the Society for Industrial and Organizational Psychology.